SQL Server 7 Administration

Andy Ruth
Anil Desai

New Riders

201 West 103rd Street, Indianapolis, Indiana 46290

MCSE Fast Track: SQL Server 7 Administration

Copyright © 1999 by New Riders Publishing

All rights reserved. No part of this book shall be reproduced, stored in a retrieval system, or transmitted by any means, electronic, mechanical, photocopying, recording, or otherwise, without written permission from the publisher. No patent liability is assumed with respect to the use of the information contained herein. Although every precaution has been taken in the preparation of this book, the publisher and author(s) assume no responsibility for errors or omissions. Neither is any liability assumed for damages resulting from the use of the information contained herein.

International Standard Book Number: 0-7357-0041-9

Library of Congress Catalog Card Number: 98-89437

Printed in the United States of America

First Printing: April, 1999

03 02 01 00 99   7 6 5 4 3 2 1

Interpretation of the printing code: The rightmost double-digit number is the year of the book's printing; the rightmost single-digit number is the number of the book's printing. For example, the printing code 99-1 shows that the first printing of the book occurred in 1999.

Trademarks

All terms mentioned in this book that are known to be trademarks or service marks have been appropriately capitalized. New Riders cannot attest to the accuracy of this information. Use of a term in this book should not be regarded as affecting the validity of any trademark or service mark.

SQL Server 7 is a registered trademark of Microsoft Corporation.

Warning and Disclaimer

Every effort has been made to make this book as complete and as accurate as possible, but no warranty or fitness is implied. The information provided is on an "as is" basis. The authors and the publisher shall have neither liability nor responsibility to any person or entity with respect to any loss or damages arising from the information contained in this book.

Executive Editor
Mary Foote

Acquisitions Editors
Stacey Beheler
Steve Weiss

Development Editor
Howard A. Jones

Managing Editor
Sarah Kearns

Project Editor
Caroline Wise

Copy Editor
Gayle Johnson

Indexer
Cheryl Landis

Technical Editors
Gerry High
Jim Cooper

Proofreader
Debra Neel

Layout Technician
Liz Johnston

Contents at a Glance

INTRODUCTION

PART I WHAT THE SQL SERVER 7.0 ADMINISTRATION EXAM (70-028) COVERS
   1 Planning   15
   2 Installing and Configuring SQL Server 7   47
   3 Configuring and Managing Security   69
   4 Managing and Maintaining Data   93
   5 Monitoring and Optimization   127
   6 Troubleshooting   153
   Objective Review Notes   173

PART II INSIDE THE SQL SERVER 7.0 ADMINISTRATION EXAM (70-028)
   7 Fast Facts Review   193
   8 Insider's Spin on Exam 70-028   205
   9 Hotlist of Exam-Critical Concepts   219
   10 Sample Test Questions   229
   11 Did You Know?   245

INDEX   251

TABLE OF CONTENTS

Part I: What's Important to Know About Exam 70-028

1 Planning 15

Product Overview 17
Client/Server Relationship 17
SQL Server Components and Integration 18
Tools and Online Help 20
Communications 21
Roles 22
Databases 23
Objects 25
System Tables 26
SQL Application Design 28

Security 30
NT or SQL Authentication 31
Using NT Groups to Control Rights 31
Defining Server Roles 32
Mapping Groups 32
Selecting NT Accounts for SQL Services 33
Planning an Application's Security Strategy 33
Security Requirements for Linked Databases 34

Capacity Planning 34
Physical File Placement 34
Using Filegroups 35
Growth 35
Hardware 36
Communications 37

Data Availability Solutions 38
Standby Server 40
SQL Server Failover Support 40

Migration Plan 40
Upgrading from a Previous Version 41
Migrating from Other Data Sources 41

Replication Strategy 42
Replication Models 42
Single Publisher/Multiple Subscriber 42
Multiple Publisher/Single Subscriber 43

MCSE Fast Track: SQL Server 7 Administration

      Multiple Publisher/Multiple Subscriber   43
      Remote Distributor Server   43
    Replication Types   43
      Snapshot   44
      Transactional   44
      Merge   44

What Is Important to Know   45

2 Installing and Configuring SQL Server 7   47

Installing SQL Server 7   49
    Choosing the Character Set   52
    Choosing the Appropriate Sort Order   52
    Choosing the Unicode Collation Sequence   54
    Installing Network Libraries and Protocols   54
    Installing Services   56
    Installing and Configuring the SQL Server Client   59
    Performing an Unattended Setup   60

Upgrading from SQL Server 6.x   60

Configuring SQL Server 7   62

Configuring SQL Mail   62
    Configuring Default ANSI Settings   62

Installing and Configuring the Full-Text Search Service   63
    Installing the Full-Text Search Service   64
    Customizing Full-Text Search   64
    Creating and Managing the Full-Text Search Indexes   65

Notes   66

What Is Important to Know   67

3 Configuring and Managing Security   69

An Overview of SQL Server Security   70

Managing SQL Server Logins   71
    Creating SQL Server Logins   72
    Mapping Windows NT Accounts   73

Adding Users to Databases   75

Managing Roles   77
    Server Roles   78
    Application Roles   80
    Database Roles   80
    Creating User-Defined Database Roles   81
    Adding Users to Roles   82

Managing SQL Server Permissions 83
  Assigning Object Permissions 83
Auditing Database Activity 86
  SQL Server Profiler 89
What Is Important to Know 92

4 Managing and Maintaining Data 93

Creating and Managing Data 95
  Creating Files, Logs, and Filegroups 95
  Growing Your Database 98
Loading Data 99
  The INSERT Statement 100
  The SELECT Statement 100
  BCP 101
  DTS 101
  The BULK INSERT Statement 104
Backups and Restorations 104
  Planning a Backup Strategy 106
  Full Backups 109
  Transaction Log Backups 111
  Differential Backups 111
  Filegroup Backups 111
  Backup Strategy 112
Managing Replication 113
  Configuring Servers 117
  Creating Publications 117
  Subscriptions 118
Automating Administrative Tasks 118
  Defining Jobs 119
  Defining Alerts 119
  Defining Operators 120
Remote Data Access 122
  Linked Server Configuration 122
  Linked Database Security 123
What Is Important to Know 124

5 Monitoring and Optimization 127

Performance Monitoring Basics 128
Monitoring SQL Server Performance 128

Using Performance Monitor   129
Using SQL Profiler   133
Using SQL Query Analyzer   135
Summary of Performance Monitoring Tools   137

Tuning and Optimizing SQL Server   138
Processor and Memory Settings   138
Setting SQL Server Configuration Settings   140
Tuning Windows NT Memory Settings   142

Improving Query Performance   143
Using Stored Procedures   143
Setting the Query Governor Cost Limit   144

Other Ways to Optimize Performance   145
Scheduling Jobs   145
Setting Alerts with SQL Server Agent   147
Hardware Upgrades   148

What Is Important to Know   150

6 Troubleshooting   153

Before You Begin   154

Diagnosing and Resolving Problems with Upgrading from SQL Server 6.x   155
Disk Space   155
Other Common Problems   156

Diagnosing Backup and Restoration Problems   157

Diagnosing and Resolving Replication Problems   159

Diagnosing and Resolving Job or Alert Failures   160

Diagnosing and Resolving Distributed Query Problems   162

Diagnosing and Resolving Client Connectivity Problems   164

Diagnosing and Resolving Access Problems   167

What Is Important to Know   170

Objective Review Notes   173
Planning   175
Installation and Configuration   177
Configuring and Managing Security   178
Managing and Maintaining Data   181
Monitoring and Optimization   184
Troubleshooting   186

Part II: Inside Exam 70-028

7 Fast Facts Review 193

What to Study 194
   Planning 194
   Installing and Configuring SQL Server 7 196
   Configuring and Managing Security 198
   Managing and Maintaining Data 199
   Monitoring and Optimization 201
   Troubleshooting 202

8 Insider's Spin on Exam 70-028 205

Get into Microsoft's Mindset 208
Understand the Exam's Time Frame 209
Get Used to Answering Questions Quickly 210
Taking the Test 212
Where the Questions Come From 214
Different Flavors of Questions 215
In the Future 217

9 Hotlist of Exam-Critical Concepts 219

10 Sample Test Questions 229

Questions 230
Answers and Explanations 240

11 Did You Know? 245

Choosing a Database Server 246
   Evaluating SQL Server 246
Web Database Publishing 247
Multitier Client/Server Architecture 248
Distributed Management 249
On-Line Analytical Processing (OLAP) 249
Moving Forward 250

Index 251

About the Authors

Andy Ruth has been in the computer industry since the late 1970s, when he joined the U.S. Navy and provided systems support on flight simulators. In the corporate environment, he has provided systems support for computers ranging from large mainframes to small PC networked environments. He holds the Microsoft MCSE+I and MCT certifications, as well as others. Ruth is currently Vice President of Hudlogic, where he teaches technology classes, is a consultant to local clients, and is a guest speaker at technology seminars.

Anil Desai, MCSE, Oracle DBA, is currently a technical analyst with Sprint Paranet, Inc., a leading integrator of hardware, software, networks, and people. Desai specializes in Windows NT implementation, integration, and management. Much of his database administration experience is drawn from consulting experiences gained from working in multiple heterogeneous environments. He is also the author of *Windows NT Network Management: Reducing Total Cost of Ownership* (New Riders Publishing, 1999). He has spoken at many national professional conferences, and he regularly writes technical articles for IT staffs and managers. When he's not working with computers, Desai enjoys playing the electric guitar, playing computer games, and cycling in and around Austin, Texas.

Dedication

This book is dedicated to Jaylene, my love, my life, who makes all things possible.   Andy Ruth

Acknowledgments

Thanks to New Riders team leader Steve Weiss for giving me the opportunity to work on this series of books, which are great study aids for the MCSE candidate. Also, thanks to the technical editors, Gerry High and Jim Cooper, who not only make sure we give correct information, but also make sure the information we give is to the point and provides a good explanation without getting too windy.

Thanks to Howard Jones, the development editor and a good guy, for making Anil and me sound better than we would have without his help and guidance. Also, thanks to the large crew of people who provide the rest of the support needed to put out a book worth reading.

Last, in the place of honor, thanks to my internal support staff, who boost me up and keep me young, though they might disagree. In no specific order, thanks to Stephanie Denis, Joshua Liedka, Dan Denis, Justin Ruth, Jacob Liedka, Ryan Register, Jessica Liedka, Dylan Crow, Shawn Evans, Dakota Crow, and Lauryn Crow.

—Andy Ruth

Tell Us What You Think!

As the reader of this book, *you* are our most important critic and commentator. We value your opinion and want to know what we're doing right, what we could do better, what areas you'd like to see us publish in, and any other words of wisdom you're willing to pass our way.

As the Executive Editor for the Certification team at New Riders Publishing, I welcome your comments. You can fax, e-mail, or write me directly to let me know what you did or didn't like about this book—as well as what we can do to make our books stronger.

Please note that I can't help you with technical problems related to this book, and that due to the high volume of mail I receive, I might not be able to reply to every message.

When you write, please be sure to include this book's title and author, as well as your name and phone or fax number. I will carefully review your comments and share them with the author and editors who worked on the book.

Fax: 317-581-4663

E-mail: certification@mcp.com

Mail: Mary Foote
Executive Editor
Certification
New Riders Publishing
201 West 103rd Street
Indianapolis, IN 46290 USA

Introduction

The *MCSE Fast Track* series is written as a study aid for people preparing for Microsoft Certification Exams. The series is intended to help reinforce and clarify information that you're already familiar with. This series is not intended to be a single source of student preparation, but rather a review of information and a set of practice tests to help increase your likelihood of success when taking the actual exam.

WHY WE DID THIS BOOK: A WORD FROM THE PUBLISHER

Again, New Riders *MCSE Fast Tracks* are not intended to be single sources of exam preparation. These books have been uniquely written and developed to work as supplements to your existing knowledge base.

But exactly what makes them different?

1. **Brevity.** Many other exam training materials seek Microsoft approval (you've probably seen the official Microsoft Approved Study Guide logo on other books, for example), meaning that they must include 50 percent tutorial material and cover every objective for every exam in exactly the same manner and to the same degree. MCSE Fast Tracks break out of that mold by focusing on what you really need to know to pass the exam.

2. **Focus.** *MCSE Fast Tracks* are targeted primarily at those who know the technology but who don't yet have the certification. No superfluous information is included. *MCSE Fast Tracks* feature only what the more-experienced candidate needs to know to pass the exam. *MCSE Fast Tracks* are affordable study material for the experienced professional.

3. **Concentrated value and learning power.** Frankly, we wouldn't be surprised if *MCSE Fast Tracks* prove to appeal to a wider audience than just advanced-level candidates. We've tried to pack as much

distilled exam knowledge as possible into *MCSE Fast Tracks,* creating a digest of exam-critical information. No matter what level you're at, you may well see this digest on certification training as a logical starting point for exam study.

4. **Classroom tested, instructor proven.** With tens of thousands of new certification candidates entering the training routine each year, trainers on the forefront of the certification education lines are finding themselves in front of classes comprised of increased numbers of candidates who have a measurable understanding of the technology and a desire for efficient, "just-the-facts" training.

It became evident that no books truly existed that adequately filled the need to provide an easy way to review the key elements of each certification technology without being bogged down with elementary-level information, and to present this information from an insider's perspective.

Think of *MCSE Fast Tracks* as the set of instructor's notes you always wished you could get your hands on. These notes only truly help you if you already know the material and are ready to take the exam. It's then that this book is designed to help you shine. Good luck, and may your hard work pay off.

What This Book Covers

This book is specifically intended to help you prepare for Microsoft's Administering Microsoft SQL Server 7.0 (70-028) exam—one of the electives available in the MCSE program.

How This Book Helps You

This book is designed to help you make the most of your study time by presenting concise summaries of information that you need to understand to succeed on the exam.

How to Use This Book

When you feel prepared for the exam, use this book as a test of your knowledge.

After you have taken the practice test and feel confident in the material on which you were tested, you're ready to schedule your exam. Use this book for a final quick review just before taking the test to make sure that all the important concepts are set in your mind.

Part I: What the SQL Server 7.0 Administration Exam (70-028) Covers

The Administering SQL Server 7.0 certification exam measures your ability to administer a Microsoft SQL Server 7 database. The exam focuses on determining your abilities in six major categories:

- Planning
- Installing and Configuring SQL Server 7
- Configuring and Managing Security
- Managing and Maintaining Data
- Monitoring and Optimization
- Troubleshooting

The Administering Microsoft SQL Server 7.0 certification exam uses these categories to measure your abilities. Before taking this exam, you should be proficient in the job skills discussed in the following sections.

Planning

The Planning section is designed to make sure that you understand the issues involved in planning a security strategy, capacity planning, providing data availability, migrating other databases to SQL Server 7, and configuring a replication structure. This portion of the test will verify your overall knowledge of SQL Server 7. The knowledge needed here also requires understanding of general NT network administration concepts.

Objectives for Planning

- Develop a security strategy:
  - Assess whether to use NT or SQL user accounts.
  - Determine if the NT group structure should be used.
  - Plan SQL Server roles, including fixed server, fixed database, and user-defined database.
  - Assess whether to map NT groups to a database or a role.
  - Assess which NT accounts will be used to run SQL Server services.
  - Plan an *n*-tier application security strategy.
  - Plan the security requirements for linked databases.
- Develop a SQL Server capacity plan:
  - Plan the physical placement of files, including data and log files.
  - Plan the use of filegroups.
  - Plan for growth over time.
  - Plan the physical hardware system.
  - Assess the communication requirements.
- Develop a data availability solution:
  - Choose the appropriate backup and restoration strategy.
  - Assess whether to use a standby server.
  - Assess whether to use clustering.
- Develop a migration plan:
  - Plan an upgrade from the previous version of SQL Server.
  - Plan the migration of data from other data sources.

- Develop a replication strategy:
  - Given a scenario, design the appropriate replication model.
  - Choose the replication type, including snapshot, transactional, and merge.

INSTALLING AND CONFIGURING SQL SERVER 7

The Installation and Configuration part of the Administering SQL Server 7.0 exam tests your knowledge of the selections available when installing and configuring SQL Server 7.

Objectives for Installing and Configuring SQL Server 7

- Install SQL Server 7:
  - Choose the character set.
  - Choose the Unicode collation sequence.
  - Choose the appropriate sort order.
  - Install network libraries and protocols.
  - Install services.
  - Install and configure the SQL Server client.
  - Perform an unattended setup.
  - Upgrade from the SQL Server 6.x database.
- Configure SQL Server:
  - Configure SQL Mail.
  - Configure default ANSI settings.
  - Install and configure the Full-Text Search Service.

Configuring and Managing Security

The Configuring and Managing Security component of the Administering Microsoft SQL Server 7.0 certification exam concentrates on configuring security. SQL Server 7 provides a user-friendly interface. Other than planning, configuring and managing security issues is one of the key concerns of using the product. Therefore, expect this topic to be covered heavily on the test.

Objectives for Configuring and Managing Security

- Assign SQL Server access to Windows NT accounts, SQL Server login accounts, and built-in administrator accounts.
- Assign database access to Windows NT accounts, SQL Server login accounts, the Guest user account, and the DBO user account.
- Create and assign SQL Server roles, including fixed server, fixed database, public, user-defined database, and application.
- Grant to database users and roles the appropriate permissions to database objects and statements.
- Audit server and database activity by using the SQL Server Profiler.

Managing and Maintaining Data

The Managing and Maintaining Data component of the Administering Microsoft SQL Server 7.0 certification exam covers the creation and management of databases, care and maintenance of those databases, and defining the administrative tasks concerned with data management.

Objectives for Managing and Maintaining Data

- Create and manage databases. Create data files, filegroups, and transaction logs, and specify growth characteristics.

- Load data using various methods, including the INSERT, SELECT INTO, and BULK INSERT statements, BCP, DTS, HDR, and Transfer Manager.
- Back up and restore system and user databases by performing a full backup, a transaction log backup, a differential backup, and a filegroup backup.
- Manage replication:
  - Configure servers, including distribution, publisher, and subscriber servers.
  - Create publications.
  - Set up and manage subscriptions.
- Automate administrative tasks:
  - Define jobs.
  - Define alerts.
  - Define operators.
  - Set up SQL Server Agent Mail for job notification and alerts.
- Enable access to remote data:
  - Set up linked servers.
  - Set up security for linked databases.

MONITORING AND OPTIMIZATION

The Monitoring and Optimization component of the Administering Microsoft SQL Server 7.0 certification exam tests your knowledge of monitoring and optimization techniques employed when maintaining SQL Server 7.

Objectives for Monitoring and Optimization

- Monitor SQL Server performance by using Performance Monitor and Profiler.

- Tune and optimize SQL Server memory and CPU usage.
- Limit queries' resource use by using the Query Governor.

TROUBLESHOOTING

The Troubleshooting component of the Administering Microsoft SQL Server 7.0 certification exam challenges your troubleshooting skills. You will use all the knowledge you gained in the previous chapters to create a logical troubleshooting technique.

Objectives for Troubleshooting

- Diagnose and resolve problems with upgrading from SQL Server 6.x.
- Diagnose and resolve problems with backup and restore operations.
- Diagnose and resolve replication problems.
- Diagnose and resolve job or alert failures.
- Diagnose and resolve distributed query problems.
- Use the Client Configuration Utility to diagnose and resolve client connectivity problems.
- Diagnose and resolve problems with access to SQL Server, databases, and database objects.

OBJECTIVE REVIEW NOTES

The Objective Review Notes chapter of the *Fast Track* series lists each subobjective covered in the book. Each subobjective is listed under the main exam objective category—just where you'd expect to find it. I strongly suggest that you review each subobjective, make note of your knowledge level, and then return to the Objective Review Notes chapter repeatedly and document your progress. Your ultimate goal should be to review this section by itself and determine if you are ready for the exam.

Here is how I suggest you use the Objective Review Notes:

1. Read the objective. Refer to the part of the book where it's covered. Then ask yourself the following questions:

   - Do you already know this material? Then check "Got it" and make a note of the date.

   - Do you need to brush up on the objective area? Check "Review it" and make a note of the date. While you're at it, write down the page numbers you checked, because you'll need to return to that section.

   - Is this material something you're largely unfamiliar with? Check the "Help!" box and write down the date. Now you can get to work.

2. You get the idea. Keep working through the material in this book and in any other study materials you have. The more you understand the material, the quicker you can update and upgrade each Objective Review Notes section from "Help!" to "Review it" to "Got it."

3. Cross-reference using all your exam preparation materials. Most people who take certification exams use more than one resource. Write down where this material is covered in other books, software programs, and videotapes you're using.

Think of this as your personal study diary—your documentation of how you'll beat this exam.

HARDWARE AND SOFTWARE RECOMMENDED FOR PREPARATION

This book is meant to help you review concepts with which you already have training and hands-on experience. To make the most of the review, you need to have as much background and experience as possible. The best way to do this is to combine studying and working with the Microsoft SQL Server 7 product. This section describes the minimum computer requirements you will need in order to build a solid practice environment.

Computers

The minimum computer requirements to ensure that you can study everything on which you'll be tested are one or more workstations running Windows 95 or Windows NT Workstation, and two or more servers running Windows NT Server, all connected by a network.

Workstations: Windows 95 and Windows NT

- Computer on the Microsoft Hardware Compatibility List
- 486DX 66MHz
- 16MB of RAM
- 200MB hard disk
- 3½-inch 1.44MB floppy drive
- VGA video adapter
- VGA monitor
- Mouse or equivalent pointing device
- Two-speed CD-ROM drive
- Network Interface Card (NIC)
- Presence on an existing network, or use of a hub to create a test network
- Microsoft Windows 95 or Windows NT Workstation 4.0

Servers: Windows NT Server

- Two computers on the Microsoft Hardware Compatibility List
- 486DX2 66MHz
- 32MB of RAM
- 540MB hard disk
- 3½-inch 1.44MB floppy drive
- VGA video adapter
- VGA monitor
- Mouse or equivalent pointing device

- Two-speed CD-ROM drive
- Network Interface Card (NIC)
- Presence on an existing network, or use of a hub to create a test network
- Microsoft Windows NT Server 4.0

PART II: INSIDE THE SQL SERVER 7.0 ADMINISTRATION EXAM (70-028)

Part II of this book is designed to round out your exam preparation by providing you with the following chapters:

- Fast Facts Review is a digest of all the "What Is Important to Know" sections from all Part I chapters. Read this chapter right before you take the exam: It's all here, in an easy-to-review format.

- Insider's Spin on Exam 70-028 grounds you in the particulars of preparing mentally for this exam and for Microsoft testing in general.

- Hotlist of Exam-Critical Concepts is your resource for cross-checking technical terms. Although you're probably up to speed on most of this material already, double-check yourself anytime you run across an item you're not 100 percent certain about; it could make a difference at exam time.

- Sample Test Questions provides a full-length practice exam that tests you on the material covered in Part I. If you mastered the material there, you should be able to pass with flying colors here.

- Did You Know? is the last-day-of-class bonus chapter. It briefly touches on peripheral information. It's designed to be helpful and of interest to anyone using this technology to the point that they want to be certified in its mastery.

PART I
WHAT'S IMPORTANT TO KNOW ABOUT EXAM 70-028

MCSE Fast Track: SQL Server 7 Administration is written as a study aid for people preparing for Microsoft Certification Exam 70-028. The book is intended to help reinforce and clarify information with which the student is already familiar. This series is not intended to be a single source for exam preparation, but rather a review of information and set of practice materials to help increase the likelihood of success when taking the actual exam.

Part I of this book is designed to help you make the most of your study time by presenting concise summaries of information that you need to understand to succeed on the exam. Each chapter covers a specific exam objective area as outlined by Microsoft:

1 **Planning**

2 **Installing and Configuring SQL Server 7**

3 **Configuring and Managing Security**

4 **Managing and Maintaining Data**

5 **Monitoring and Optimization**

6 **Troubleshooting**

About the Exam

Exam Number:	70-028
Minutes:	90
Questions:	TBD*
Passing Score:	TBD*
Single Answer Questions:	Yes
Multiple Answer with Correct Number Given	Yes
Multiple Answer without Correct Number Given	Yes
Ranking Order	No
Choices of A-D	Yes
Choices of A-E	Yes
Objective Categories	6

At the time of publication, this information was unavailable.

OBJECTIVES

A good plan is necessary for a successful upgrade or deployment of any product, and it's critical when the product is supporting an enterprise-wide database. The planning component of the Microsoft SQL Server 7.0 Administration certification test will test your knowledge of planning a deployment in five different areas. Several topics are covered under each area.

This chapter provides a brief product overview and then covers these certification test objectives:

▶ Develop a security strategy:
- Assess whether to use Microsoft Windows NT or Microsoft SQL Server accounts.
- Assess whether to leverage the Windows NT group structure.
- Plan the use and structure of SQL Server roles to include fixed server, fixed database, and user-defined database.
- Assess whether to map Windows NT groups directly into a database or to map them into a role.
- Assess which Windows NT accounts will be used to run SQL Server services.

▶ continues...

CHAPTER 1

Planning

OBJECTIVES continued

- Plan an *n*-tier application security strategy, determining whether to use application roles or other mid-tier security mechanisms such as Microsoft Transaction Server.
- Plan the security requirements for linked databases.

▶ Develop a SQL Server capacity plan:
- Plan the physical placement of data and log files.
- Plan the use of filegroups.
- Plan for growth over time.
- Plan the physical hardware system.
- Assess the communication requirements.

▶ Develop a data availability solution:
- Choose the appropriate backup and restore strategy to include full backup, full and transaction log backup, differential backup with full backup and transaction log backup, and database files or transaction log backup.
- Assess whether to use a standby server.
- Assess whether to use clustering.

▶ Develop a migration plan:
- Plan an upgrade from a previous version of SQL Server.
- Plan the migration of data from other data sources.

▶ Develop a replication strategy:
- Given a scenario, design the proper replication model, including single-publisher/multi-subscriber, multi-publisher/single-subscriber, multi-publisher/multi-subscriber, and remote distribution server.
- Choose the replication type, including snapshot, transactional, and merge.

Product Overview

Microsoft SQL Server 7 is a powerful, robust relational database that has been operationally tested with a 1 terabyte database that has more than 150 million rows. This database can be found at http://terraserver.microsoft.com.

Client/Server Relationship

SQL Server 7 is a client/server relational database management system (RDBMS) that uses Transact-SQL, an implementation of the ANSI SQL-92 standard.

The client software, shown in Figure 1.1, is responsible for the following:

- Forming the request for the data
- Presenting the requested data to the user

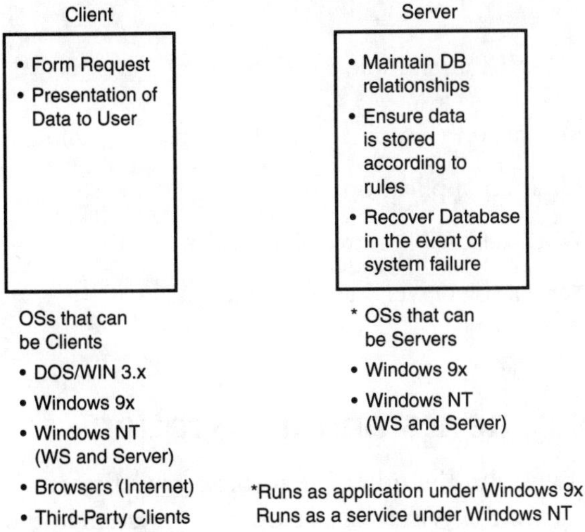

Client	Server
• Form Request • Presentation of Data to User	• Maintain DB relationships • Ensure data is stored according to rules • Recover Database in the event of system failure
OSs that can be Clients • DOS/WIN 3.x • Windows 9x • Windows NT (WS and Server) • Browsers (Internet) • Third-Party Clients	*OSs that can be Servers • Windows 9x • Windows NT (WS and Server) *Runs as application under Windows 9x Runs as a service under Windows NT

FIGURE 1.1
Client/server structure and responsibilities.

The server receives the request for data, verifies that the client has the proper permissions to make the request, performs the query on the database, and then sends the response to the client. If the client doesn't have proper authority to make the request, an error message is generated and returned to the client. The server is responsible for the following:

- Maintaining the relationships between the data in the database
- Ensuring that the data is stored according to the rules that define the database relationship
- Recovering data to a known point in the event of system failure

Supported SQL Server clients include the following:

- Windows NT 4.0 (Workstation and Server) and newer
- Windows 95 and 98
- Windows 3.x
- DOS
- Internet browsers
- Third-party, such as UNIX and Apple Macintosh

SQL Server can run as a server on the following platforms:

- Windows 95 and 98, as an application
- Windows NT 4.0 Workstation (or newer), as a service
- Windows NT 4.0 Server (or newer), as a service

SQL Server Components and Integration

SQL Server 7 integrates fully with the other Microsoft BackOffice products and can take advantage of the Windows NT operating system in the following ways:

- **Security.** SQL Server 7 integrates with the Windows NT security system, allowing a client to provide one user name and password for domain authentication as well as SQL server access.
- **Event Viewer.** SQL 7 writes events into Windows NT's application, security, and system event logs.

- **Windows NT Services.** On Windows NT systems, SQL Server 7 runs as a service, making it easy to stop and start remotely.

- **Performance Monitor.** SQL Server 7 provides counters specific to SQL Server 7 for monitoring and tuning performance.

- **Multiprocessor support.** SQL Server 7 is a symmetric multiprocessing-capable application that automatically takes advantage of any installed processor chips.

- **Index Server.** SQL Server 7 can use Index Server, which is a full-text indexing and search engine that can be used by some of the Microsoft BackOffice products.

Although the SQL Server code is essentially the same when run on all platforms, Windows 95 doesn't provide all of the functionality just listed. SQL Server 7 is implemented as an application rather than a series of services. Windows 95 doesn't provide the security or robust set of tools available with the Windows NT operating system.

The three services (applications on Windows 95 and 98 systems) used with Microsoft SQL Server 7 are as follows:

- **MSSQLServer.** This service provides data management, transaction and query processing, and data integrity. It is responsible for allocating system resources among concurrent users, for preventing logical problems, such as when two updates to an item come in at the same time, and for ensuring data consistency and integrity.

- **SQL Server Agent.** This service is responsible for creating, scheduling, and managing local or multi-server jobs, alerts, and operators. The duties performed by the SQL Server Agent include the following:

  - **Alert management.** Provides information about the status of a process and monitors the Windows NT application Event log.

  - **Notification.** Can send an e-mail message, page an operator, or spawn another application when an alert occurs.

  - **Job execution.** Responsible for the execution of jobs that are created and scheduled using the SQL Server job creation and scheduling engine.

  - **Replication management.** Responsible for synchronizing data between servers, monitoring the data, and replicating the information to other servers.

- **MS DTC.** The Microsoft Distributed Transaction Coordinator service (MS DTC) is the transaction manager that allows a client to use several different data sources for one transaction. MS DTC ensures that each transaction is complete and made permanent, or canceled, in the event of an error. MS DTC is a component of Microsoft Transaction Server.

Tools and Online Help

Several graphical tools that come with SQL Server 7 are used to design and create databases, query data, administer the server, or view help files. These tools use SQL Distributed Management Objects (SQL-DMO), which can also be used to write administrative scripts for SQL Server. These tools include the following:

- **SQL Server Client Configuration.** Used to manage the client configuration and communication components of SQL Server 7.
- **SQL Server Performance Monitor.** Used to start Windows NT Performance Monitor and view data pertinent to SQL Server.
- **SQL Server Profiler.** Used to capture and store a record of SQL Server activity and provide an audit trail.
- **SQL Server Query Analyzer.** Used to manage multiple queries simultaneously, view statistics information, and analyze query structures.
- **SQL Server Service Manager.** Used to start, stop, and pause SQL Server 7 services.
- **SQL Server Setup.** Used to install or reconfigure SQL Server 7.
- **SQL Server Wizards.** Used to perform difficult SQL Server 7 configuration tasks in a question/answer format.

Several command-line utilities are available for creating and starting scripts and entering Transact-SQL statements. Here are two of the most useful of these utilities:

- **BCP.** This batch utility is used to import and export data to and from the SQL Server. It can also copy data to or from a data file in a user-specified format, such as comma-delimited text.

- **OSQL.** This utility uses ODBC to communicate with the SQL Server. It's typically used to execute batch files that contain one or more SQL statements.

As is the case with most of the Microsoft products, extensive help is available with the product. This help is broken into three different groupings:

- **SQL Server documentation.** This is the SQL Server 7 Books Online. It provides information pertinent to the SQL Server and is accessed from the Start button.
- **Transact-SQL Help.** When you're using the SQL Server Query Analyzer, you access this tool by pressing Shift+F1. It provides information on the query analyzer tool.
- **Application Help.** This is the help tool for use with SQL Server Enterprise Manager and SQL Server Profiler. It also offers general information for the SQL Server Query Analyzer tool.

Communications

As shown in Figure 1.2, SQL Server 7 uses a layered communications architecture that allows you to perform application development without any understanding of the underlying network. On the client side is the application, the database interface, and the network library. On the server side is the SQL Server application and support services, the Open Data services, and a network library.

The client and server are connected through the use of a Tabular Data Stream (TDS), which provides a secure application-level communications link across a transport protocol, such as TCP/IP. A brief description of each component follows:

- **Application.** On the client, the application is developed using a database API to provide the user with an interface application for requesting SQL data. The native API support provided with SQL Server 7 is OLE DB and ODBC support. The Data Object Interface support provided is ActiveX Data Objects (ADO) and Remote Data Objects (RDO).
- **Database Interface.** On the client, this component provides the actual capability of making requests to a SQL Server.

```
  Server                    *Client
┌─────────────────┐     ┌──────────────────┐
│   SQL Server    │     │   Application    │
├─────────────────┤     ├──────────────────┤
│   Open Data     │     │    Database      │
│   Services      │     │    Interface     │
├─────────────────┤     ├──────────────────┤
│ Network Library │     │ Network Library  │
├─────────────────┤     ├──────────────────┤
│                 │ Tabular Data│         │
│                 │    TDS      │         │
│                 │   Stream    │         │
└─────────────────┘     └──────────────────┘
```

*Data Object Interface
support provided
includes
• ADO
• RDO

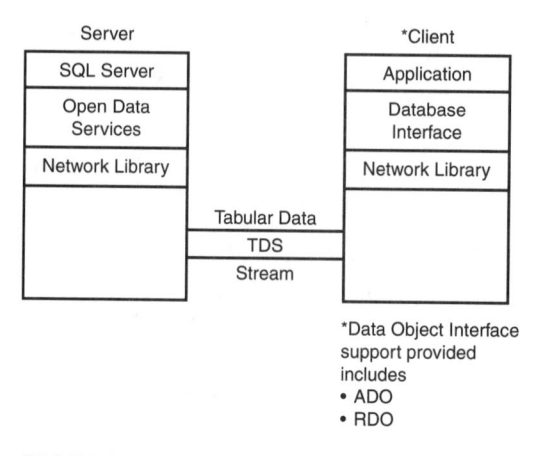

FIGURE 1.2
SQL Server components and communications.

- **Network Library.** On both the client and the server, this is the communications software that packages the database requests from the client and server results for transfer across the network. This is the lower-layer communications component.

- **Tabular Data Stream (TDS).** This is the application layer protocol used for communication between the client and the server.

- **Open Data Services.** This is the SQL Server component responsible for handling network connections and passing client requests to the SQL Server. The Open Data Services "listen" to all server Network Libraries installed on the server.

- **SQL Server.** On the SQL Server, this is the actual SQL Server software, including all services and support applications.

Roles

Roles are used to give users or groups of users permission to perform certain tasks on a server or database. There are fixed roles for the server as well as fixed roles for the database. Custom user-defined roles can be created for databases. Table 1.1 details the fixed server and database roles for SQL Server 7.

TABLE 1.1

FIXED SERVER AND DATABASE ROLES

Fixed Server Role	Description
dbcreator	Creates and alters databases.
diskadmin	Manages disk files.
processadmin	Manages SQL Server processes.
securityadmin	Manages and audits SQL Server logins.
serveradmin	Configures server-wide settings.
setupadmin	Installs replication.
sysadmin	Performs any activity.
Fixed Database Role	**Description**
db_accessadmin	Adds and removes database users, groups, and roles.
db_backupoperator	Backs up and restores databases.
db_datareader	Reads data from any table.
db_datawriter	Adds, deletes, and modifies data from any table.
db_ddladmin	Adds, changes, and drops database objects.
db_denydatareader	Prevents data in any table from being read.
db_denydatawriter	Prevents data in any table from being changed.
db_owner	Performs any database role activity.
db_securityadmin	Assigns statement and object permissions.
public	Maintains all default permissions for users in a database.

Databases

Four system databases and two user databases are installed when Microsoft SQL Server 7 is installed. Table 1.2 lists the installed databases and gives a brief description of each.

TABLE 1.2

INSTALLED DATABASES

System Database	Description
master	Keeps track of user accounts, configurable environment variables, and system errors, thereby providing control over the user databases and the operation of SQL Server.
Model	Used as a template for new databases.
Tempdb	Provides a storage area for temporary tables and other working storage needs. Similar to the temp directory used in DOS and Windows.
Distribution	Stores the history and transaction data used with replication.
Msdb	This system database is used with the SQL Server Agent and provides a storage area for scheduling information and job history. This database can be deleted, but that reduces the SQL Server functionality.

User Databases	Description
northwind	A sample database that can be used as a learning tool.
Pubs	Another sample database that can be used as a learning tool.
user-created databases	All new databases created by the user fall into this group.

In relational databases, a database is a collection of data, tables, and other objects. A *schema* is created when a database is created. It defines the database's structure. Here are some of the terms and definitions used to describe Microsoft SQL Server 7 database objects:

- **Constraint.** The standard tool used to define or limit the type of data allowed in a table column.
- **Data type.** Defines what form the data can take for a given column or variable. Examples include date, bitmap, and numerical data.
- **Default.** The value stored in a column if no other data is specified.
- **Index.** A structure that provides fast data retrieval. An index can also enforce data integrity in the same manner as a constraint. Two types of indexes are used:
  - **Clustered index.** The logical and physical order of rows are the same.
  - **Non-clustered index.** The logical and physical order of rows do not necessarily match.

- **View.** Helps define valid entries for a column or data type, such as a valid date or percentage amount.

- **Stored procedure.** A named group of Transact-SQL statements that execute together, much like a batch or script file.

- **Table.** A collection of rows and associated columns.

- **Trigger.** A stored procedure that is executed automatically when table data is modified.

- **View.** Provides a way to look at data from various tables or views in a database.

Objects

When you're naming SQL Server objects, the fully qualified name has four identifiers: the server name, the database name, the owner name, and the object name, each separated by a period. Fully qualified names are written in the following format:

servername.databasename.ownername.objectname

Each object created must have a unique name. When you reference an object, you don't have to provide the complete fully qualified name, but the periods must be present if an intermediate identifier is not used. The following can be used when referencing this object:

server1.db1.owner1.object1

- *server1.db1.owner1.object1*
- *server1..owner1.object1*
- *server1.db1..object1*
- *server1...object1*
- *db1.owner1.object1*
- *db1..object1*
- *owner1.object1*
- *object1*

Here are some examples of incorrect names:

- `object1.owner1.db1.server1`
- `server1.db1.owner1..`
- `server1.owner1.object1`
- `server1.object1`

When you're creating a new object, you can specify a certain owner if you have the proper permissions. It is recommended that the db operator account be made the owner of new objects in the database. Most object references don't specify the server, unless a distributed query or remote procedure is being performed. The following defaults are applied if no data is given:

- The server defaults to the local server
- The database defaults to the current database
- The owner defaults to the database username associated with the current connection's login ID

System Tables

System tables store *metadata,* which is information about the system and objects. Each database has a collection of system tables that store metadata about that database. This collection of tables is the *database catalog.* The master database also has a unique set of tables that make up the *system catalog.* The system catalog is a group of tables that store metadata about the entire system and all databases. All system catalog tables have a *sys* prefix. Here are some of the frequently used tables:

- **sysdatabases.** Has one row for each database on a SQL Server.
- **syslogins.** Has one row for each login account that can connect to SQL Server.
- **sysmessages.** Has one row for each system error or warning that SQL Server can return.

- **sysobjects.** Has one row for each object in a database.
- **sysusers.** Has one row for each Windows NT user, Windows NT group, SQL Server user, and SQL server role in a database.

When you're writing applications to retrieve metadata from system tables, system stored procedures, system functions, or system-supplied information, you should use schema views. System tables can be viewed and modified in the same manner as other database tables, but if you're not careful, you could undermine the integrity and recoverability of SQL Server. Some of the more common system stored procedures, system functions, and information schema views are listed in Table 1.3.

TABLE 1.3

COMMON SYSTEM STORED PROCEDURES, SYSTEM FUNCTIONS, AND INFORMATION SCHEMA VIEWS

System Stored Procedure	Description
sp_help *objectname*	Provides information on the named database object.
sp_helpdb *databasename*	Provides information on the named database.
sp_helpindex *tablename*	Provides information on the indexes in the named table.

System Function	Description
COL_LENGTH *column*	Returns the column's width.
DATALENGTH *data type*	Returns the length of an expression of any data type.
DB_ID *name*	Returns the database ID.
STATS_DATE *index*	Returns the date when the statistics for the named index were last updated.
USER_NAME ID	Returns the user's name.

Information Schema View	Description
information_schema.columns	Provides information on the columns defined in the database.
information_schema.tables	Provides a list of tables in the database.
information_schema.tables_privileges	Provides security information for tables in the database.

SQL Application Design

When you're designing a client/server application, it's often beneficial to divide the application into layers, as shown in Figure 1.3. This lets you move portions of the application to different servers, provides greater flexibility, and provides more management choices.

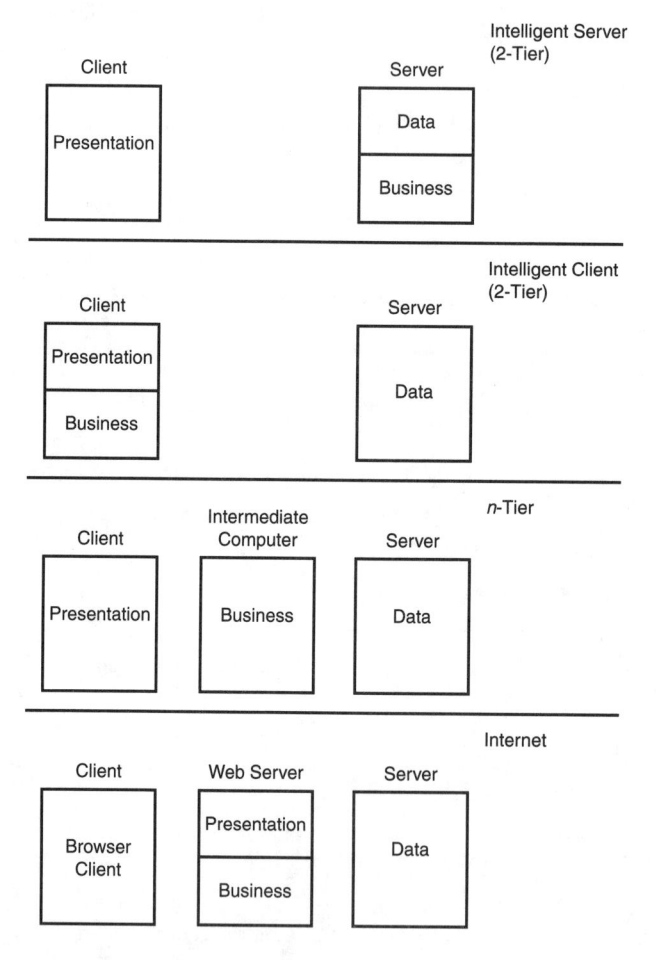

FIGURE 1.3
SQL Server application design and implementation.

Here are the three logical layers a SQL application can be divided into:

- **Data.** These are the procedures that are closely related to the data, such as database definition, data integrity logic, and stored procedures. SQL Server plays a key role in this layer.
- **Business.** This includes the application logic and business rules. SQL Server can, but doesn't have to, be involved with this layer.
- **Presentation.** This layer forms client requests and presents the data to the client. This layer almost always resides on the client computer.

If the database application is to be layered, the different logical components can be distributed across several computers, each responsible for its layer of functionality. The following are some of the typical application configurations that can be used:

- **Intelligent server (2-tier).** With the intelligent server, most of the processing occurs on the server, which handles the data and presentation layers. The client is then only responsible for the presentation layer. This allows the client computers to be less powerful. It can also cause a bottleneck at the server because the server is responsible for supporting two layers of the application. Many times, large, corporate databases implement this design.
- **Intelligent client (2-tier).** With the intelligent client, most of the processing is performed on the client's computer. For this type of structure, the client computers must be more powerful, but the server is less likely to be the cause of a bottleneck, and heavier network traffic is generated. Many times, small companies implement this design.
- *n*-tier. With an *n*-tier design, the data layer is located on one server, the business layer is on another server, and the presentation layer is on the client. This minimizes the chance of a bottleneck at the server and makes expansion easier. However, the design is more complex and requires the SQL administrators to have a higher level of knowledge. Many times, enterprise-wide applications are best suited for this design.

- **Internet.** When accessing a Web site, many of the Web servers access SQL databases. In this case, the client uses a Web browser to request information from the Web server. The Web server has the presentation and business layers, and the SQL Server supports the data layer. This design works well with large Web sites.

Implementing a SQL Server database involves several steps. After the database is designed and implemented, ongoing support is required. Here are some of the typical steps involved in implementing a database:

- Design a database that is efficient and expandable, provides solid application logic, defines data types properly, and properly specifies the relationship between columns and tables.
- Design a functional disaster recovery program.
- Create the database, including tables, data access and entry objects, data integrity mechanisms, indexes, and proper levels of security.
- Test and tune for proper operation and peak performance. After deploying the database, analyze the workload and indexing to ensure peak performance.
- Administer the application after deployment. This includes the following:
  - Install and configure SQL Server and verify network security.
  - Build databases, transfer data into the database, set security, allocate disk space for the data and logs, automate tasks, configure replication, and publish.
  - Manage ongoing tasks, back up and restore data, and test and implement a viable disaster recovery program.

SECURITY

A security plan is needed before you install SQL Server 7. The networking structure and access capabilities play an important part. The planning considerations are broken into several general areas.

NT or SQL Authentication

SQL Server 7 users can be authenticated and given permission to access a database through the Windows NT user names and groups or through the SQL Server authentication component. The choice of which to use comes down to tighter security versus more account flexibility and end-user ease of use. Generally, planning these differences will determine which accounts you use with SQL Server 7:

- **Windows NT authentication.** Advantages include ease of use for the end-user (because he needs to remember only one user account and password) and the ability to better control the user account. Windows NT provides the capability to disable an account after a certain date, lock the account if the password is mistyped too many times in a given period, set a minimum password length, and enable Windows NT auditing to provide greater capabilities than are available with the SQL Server accounts.

- **Mixed mode.** With mixed mode, the NT user can log on with a Windows NT user account and password and then provide a SQL Server user account for access to the SQL Server. This provides an additional layer of security that the user must pass in order to gain access to the SQL Server. By using mixed mode, non-Windows NT clients and Internet clients as well as Windows NT clients can have a SQL Server authentication path without having a Windows NT user account. In mixed mode, non-Windows NT clients only need to log on to the SQL Server.

Using NT Groups to Control Rights

You can provide permissions to users by using the Windows NT group structure. To provide users with different capabilities, you can simply add the user to a Windows NT group that provides the abilities the user needs.

If the user changes positions and needs to lose or gain greater access capabilities, the Windows NT administrator can provide or deny the right by adding the user to or removing the user from a group without the need for SQL Server modifications.

This eases the SQL Server administrator's job but requires the Windows NT administrator to configure groups to support the SQL Server deployment.

Defining Server Roles

Server roles provide a way to easily provide users with the capabilities they need to perform tasks on the SQL Server computer or to a SQL database.

The fixed server roles and fixed database roles provide basic SQL Server capabilities, much like built-in local and global groups provide Windows NT users with basic capabilities. Like the built-in Windows NT group accounts, fixed server and fixed database roles can't be added, modified, or removed. A big difference is that any user account assigned to a role can add other login accounts to the role.

Users should be provided the minimum capabilities they need to perform their designated tasks. Sysadmin capabilities should be limited to as few users as possible. The sysadmin role is equivalent to the sa login, which is the SQL Server built-in administrator login. When SQL Server is installed, the sa login id is not assigned a password.

The fixed roles should be used when possible, but SQL Server 7 does provide the ability to create custom user-defined database roles. User-defined roles can be used when the SQL Server administrator doesn't have the ability to manage Windows NT user accounts, or when a group of people need to be able to access a specific set of activities but no Windows NT group is defined.

You should plan which login accounts will be added to which fixed server, fixed database, and user-defined database roles before the actual installation and implementation of SQL Server 7 and its associated databases.

Mapping Groups

Windows NT users and groups can be assigned to a role or directly into a database. If the Windows NT groups are assigned to a role and the role is assigned to a database, database administration is made easier. The user or group is assigned to a role that provides the capability the user needs.

The administrators who maintain the different databases need not assign capabilities on a user-by-user basis, but they can assign the various roles the capability.

By assigning Windows NT users and groups to a role, the database administrator is given an easy-to-use tool for assigning capabilities, but control is blurred because users and groups are not given the capabilities —the roles are.

Selecting NT Accounts for SQL Services

When you're configuring SQL Server, a domain user account or a Local System account can be used to start the SQL services.

If the system is standalone, the Local System account can be used. If the SQL Server computer is working in a domain or multi-domain environment, a domain user account should be used to start the SQL Server services. The user account should be added to the Administrators local group and set for the password to never expire. Using a domain user account provides the following advantages:

- The SQL Server computer can replicate data to other servers in the same domain or a different domain.
- Notifications can be sent through e-mail.
- You can communicate with other BackOffice products on a domain.

Planning an Application's Security Strategy

Application roles are special roles that allow security to be enforced on a specific application, and that can restrict users from gaining access to data, except through the specified application.

Users cannot be assigned to an application role. Instead, they have to have a password to activate the application role. The application role has no members, and its rights override the user's other permissions in a given database.

When you're planning, application roles can be used to allow a user to access data through a specific interface but otherwise lock the user out of a database. Users are not added to application roles, and application roles are not always active.

Application roles are created specifically for accessing a database with a specific application. When a user accesses a database through an application with a defined application role, the application role provides the database authentication by using the sp_setapprole stored procedure for authentication.

All user rights are refused, and the application role's rights are the only rights the connection will have. Generally, this is the best way to allow database access, because it provides the most control over database access and rights no matter what rights the individual user has.

Security Requirements for Linked Databases

When databases are linked across multiple SQL Servers, the accounts used for managing the databases have to have rights on each machine the databases will reside on.

If the SQL servers are standalone, the user accounts used to start the services or provide the rights to access the various databases must have rights on each of the servers accessed. If the servers are standalone, the names and passwords that are used must be the same. If the servers are each members of the same domain, a common domain user account can be used. If the servers are in multiple domains, the proper trust relationships must be in place to allow the account rights on the system the access is being performed on.

Capacity Planning

One of the most difficult parts of planning is designing a deployment that will optimize the use of hardware and provide adequate overall performance.

Physical File Placement

The physical placement of the data and log files will greatly affect performance and reliability. If possible, put the data files and log files on different physical drives. This will provide better performance and offer some level of fault tolerance. Also, using a RAID fault tolerance implementation provides additional reliability and recoverability from a single point of failure.

Using Filegroups

When a SQL Server has multiple physical drives, specific objects and files can be placed on different drives. When this is done, a filegroup must be created. A *filegroup* is a named collection of files that makes that group of files one unit for administrative and management purposes. There are two types of filegroups: default and user-defined.

By default, the default filegroup will be used, but you can specify a user-defined filegroup using the ALTER TABLE statement. Creating and using filegroups is an advanced database design technique that can increase performance and backup capabilities by spreading data access over multiple drives. It is important that the size of the default filegroup be large enough to hold all system tables and other tables not assigned to user-defined filegroups.

Here are some basic rules when using filegroups:

- A file can belong to only one filegroup.
- A filegroup can be used by only one database.
- Log files are never part of a filegroup.

Growth

Typically, databases grow rather than shrink. SQL Server 7 lets you either increase or shrink the database size automatically. When you increase the size of a database, both the data and log file size must be increased. You can:

- Set the database and log files to increase automatically, in specified increments.
- Manually increase the current or maximum size of existing files.
- Manually add secondary database and log files.

When estimating the size of a database, you need to consider the size of the model database, data stored in tables, indexes, transaction log, and system tables. When you're planning, a rule of thumb is to estimate 20 percent of the database size to the transaction log. By default, the transaction log is 25 percent of the size of the data files.

To help determine the amount of storage space needed for a database, use the following figures:

- Data is stored in 8KB pages with SQL 7, which means that 128 pages fit in 1MB of storage space. With SQL 6.5, the size of a page was 2KB. Rows can't span pages, so the maximum size of a row is 8KB.

- Extents are used to store tables and indexes. An extent is eight contiguous 8KB pages, so an extent is 64KB, and 16 extents will fit in 1MB of storage space.

- The number of pages in a table will determine the amount of storage space needed for that table. To estimate the number of pages in a table, determine how many bytes are in a row. Find the number of rows in a data page by dividing 8,092 by the number of bytes in a row. Divide the number of rows in a table by the number of rows in one data page. This is an estimate and will be dependent on the average size of variable-length columns, but it will give you a number you can use when estimating the amount of storage needed for a given database with a given amount of growth.

Hardware

Hardware must always be sized to support the OS, services, and applications on each server. SQL Server is memory- and CPU-intensive, so the number of processors and the amount of installed RAM are critical to optimum performance.

Here are the minimum requirements for installing Microsoft SQL Server 7:

- Intel or DEC Alpha system
- 32MB of RAM
- 70MB of hard disk space for a minimal installation, 160MB of hard disk space for a typical installation
- FAT or NTFS file system (NTFS is preferred)

- Windows 95, Windows NT Workstation 4.0, or Windows NT Server 4.0 with Service Pack 3 applied; newer versions of each of these products are also supported
- Microsoft Internet Explorer 4.01 (or newer)

Note that these are minimum requirements for installing SQL Server 7. That actual amount of hardware needed for your installation will depend on the network layout, types of databases, methods of accessing those databases, and the number of simultaneous user connections to the SQL Server.

Each user connection requires about 40KB of resource overhead, so when planning the hardware needs, one must take into account the number of user connections expected, as well as the types of database queries that will be performed. Also, the configuration of the resources will play an important role in overall system performance. These topics are covered in Chapter 5, "Monitoring and Optimization."

Communications

Sufficient network bandwidth must be available to support the SQL implementation, along with the other traffic generated on the network.

Replication can be configured to help diminish the amount of client/server traffic across a WAN by making the data available on a server located on the client's segment, but this will increase the server/server traffic generated to update the data. To minimize the traffic generated for subscriber updates, you can schedule them for off-peak hours. Therefore, the performance when most clients are accessing the data is increased.

When you're planning, the use of replication and the design of the application architecture will have a significant effect on traffic. You should test in a nonproduction environment to help determine the overall bandwidth needs of your SQL deployment.

The physical placement of servers must take the following into account:

- Where most of the client traffic is being generated
- What type of queries are being performed

- Whether the majority of data being accessed is somewhat stable or constantly changing
- How important it is to get the updated data to the client

A good rule of thumb is to place a subscriber server on the same physical segment where most of the client traffic is generated. If the data is somewhat stable, schedule replication for off-peak hours. If the data is constantly changing and the clients need the most current data, the updates must occur during peak hours. If the update traffic is greater than the client query traffic, replication might not be the best choice.

The connection between a client and server is accomplished through TDS, which is then encapsulated for transport across the network with a transport protocol, such as TCP/IP or NWLink. The TDS packet size for most clients is typically 4KB, but you can adjust this size to better fit the physical network by adjusting the SQL Server packet size. However, the 4KB size has been found to be optimal for most configurations.

Data Availability Solutions

The current industry standard is to have all network functionality available 24 hours a day, seven days a week. To minimize downtime in the event of catastrophic events or failure, malicious or accidental data destruction, or theft, you must plan for proper physical security, hardware fault tolerance, and a proper backup strategy.

SQL Server allows backups to occur while users work with a database. The amount of processor time devoted to the backup task can be limited so the impact to the SQL Server clients is minimized. The backup captures the database activities that occur during the backup. The following items are backed up:

- The schema and file structure
- Data
- The portion of the transaction log that is available when the backup starts

Here are the types of backups that can be performed:

- **Full backup.** A full backup provides a baseline copy of your databases, including all original files, objects, and data. SQL Server backs up the activity that took place during the backup and any uncommitted transactions in the transaction log. A full backup may be the only type of backup needed if the database is small, or if the database is read-only or is rarely modified.

- **Differential backup.** Backs up the changes to the database since the last full backup and the transactions that took place during the backup, but does not back up the transaction logs. This can be used to minimize restoration time, but it should be performed only if a known, good full backup exists. Restoration time is minimized because a series of transaction logs doesn't need to be installed during recovery.

- **Transaction log backup.** The transaction log can be backed up separately. It provides a backup of any database changes since the last full, differential, or transaction log backup. This type of backup requires a full database backup to restore. Combining a full, differential, and transaction log backup can provide the fastest means of recovery with the least amount of data loss.

It is recommended that during the planning of a SQL Server deployment you devise a backup strategy using the full and differential backup, making sure to back up system databases after they have been modified. One backup strategy that could be used would be to perform a full backup once a week, differential backups nightly, then transaction log backup hourly (during business hours). In the event of disaster, restore the full backup, the latest differential backup, then any transaction log backups since the differential backup.

Backup should be scheduled during off hours to minimize the effect on system performance and create a set of permanent backups to help automate backups. If you're backing up large databases, employ filegroups to save time.

The backup procedure is configured to run only when the CPU utilization is below 10 percent, so the performance of transaction log backups during normal network operations should have minimal impact on users. Transaction log backups can be scheduled to occur during the day at regular intervals. Then, in the event of failure, the latest full backup can be restored. To restore the most current data, restore each transaction log backup in order from oldest to most recent. This will reduce the amount of data lost.

Standby Server

A warm standby SQL Server can be configured. This server would be configured to contain the databases in use on one or more production servers, which are updated at regular intervals. In the event of the failure of one of the production servers, users can be switched to the standby server. This doesn't happen automatically; it's instigated by an administrator. This provides quick recovery time, but not non-stop client support.

SQL Server Failover Support

SQL Server 7 provides support for a virtual SQL server that is backed by two physical servers. The servers have shared disk drives. If one server fails, the other server automatically picks up the processing being done by the failed server. This provides server-level fault tolerance. This doesn't provide load balancing between the two servers. Instead, it provides a secondary system that will take over operations in the event of a failure.

To configure a failover server, you must use Microsoft Cluster Server (product name Wolfpack). The communication available for Wolfpack requires shared hard disks, and it communicates using named pipes. This is a one-to-one relationship, so a failover server would need to be configured for each SQL Server. Conversely, a standby server can be configured to provide backup for several SQL Servers and can use all forms of communication available with SQL Server.

MIGRATION PLAN

Migration can be broken into two major areas: migration from a previous version of SQL Server, and migration from data sources other than SQL Server.

Upgrading from a Previous Version

An upgrade path is available for upgrading from SQL Server 6.x to 7. There is not a direct upgrade path from SQL Server 4.x to SQL Server 7. Instead, the SQL Server 4.x system must be upgraded to SQL Server 6.x, and then up to SQL Server 7.x.

SQL Server 7 provides a SQL Server Upgrade Wizard that will upgrade any or all databases and transfer all catalog data, objects, and user data. It can also be used to transfer replication settings, SQL Executive settings, and most of the SQL Server 6.x configuration options. This upgrade can be performed using named pipes or a tape backup.

Migrating from Other Data Sources

Upgrade wizards are not available to upgrade from other database products to SQL Server 7, but several tools are available to import the data from almost any database to SQL Server 7.

There are several Data Transformation Services (DTS) tools available for importing data from heterogeneous sources. The DTS Import and DTS Export wizards provide an interactive tool for simple data transfers between different data sources.

If the data needs to be manipulated, or run through complex workflows during the import or exports of data, the DTS Package Designer provides a more robust set of tools to accommodate these needs.

The DTS Transfer Manager can be used to move data, objects, and schema between SQL servers running on different processor platforms, such as an Intel-based server to a DEC Alpha-based server.

The bcp command-line utility can also be used to transfer data. You can also use Transact-SQL statements such as SELECT INTO, INSERT SELECT, and BULK INSERT. Backups and restores can be used to transfer data from one SQL Server to another. Alternatively, sp_attach_db can be used to move and attach a single database from one SQL Server to another.

Replication Strategy

Replication allows a SQL server to store data that can be modified and distributed to other SQL servers. This way, data can be distributed to several SQL servers for load balancing and optimal network performance, without having to re-create the information on each server manually.

To implement replication, you must first decide what data to publish, determine what SQL servers will receive the data, and decide how often the data will be synchronized. This will have a significant impact on network traffic, so bandwidth capacity must be considered. Here are the three components to consider:

- **Publisher.** Maintains the source database, publishes the data, and then sends the published data to a distributor. The publisher SQL Server can also be the distributor.
- **Distributor.** Receives and stores changes, and then forwards the changes to a subscriber SQL Server.
- **Subscriber.** Receives and holds a copy of the published data, then clients access the data from the subscriber SQL Server.

When planning replication, you must determine what is an acceptable timeframe for data updates, what type of replication should be used (snapshot, transactional, or merge), and whether or not to allow updates to the replicated data. Last, the physical model must be designed to match your needs and network.

Replication Models

A replication model is the physical implementation of replication. The replication type determines how the data will be distributed. Any replication type can be used with any replication model.

Single Publisher/Multiple Subscriber

With this model, one Publisher/Distributor server distributes data to any number of Subscriber servers. The Publisher and Distributor functions can be on the same server or separated to increase performance. In this case, the Publisher is the primary owner or source of the data, and the subscribers should mark their copies of the data as read-only. This model should be used if the data needs to be published (modified) from a central location.

Multiple Publisher/Single Subscriber

With this model, one Subscriber server receives updates from several Publisher/Distributor servers to provide a centralized repository for data retrieval. With this model, it is important to mark all data with a unique local owner so that the various Publisher/Distributor servers don't overwrite each other's data. This model should be used when the data needs to be stored and retrieved by clients from a central location.

Multiple Publisher/Multiple Subscriber

This is the most flexible yet most complex structure to design. In this case, servers can perform the role of Publisher, Distributor, and Subscriber, being the source for some data and the destination for other data. You should use this model if the data is to be published and stored across an entire network.

Remote Distributor Server

A remote Distributor server can be configured to receive updates from a Publisher server across a high-speed connection and then distribute filtered data sets to Subscriber servers across slower links. This can be used by a Publisher server to place all published data at a central Distributor and then forward only data that is pertinent to an individual Subscriber server.

Replication Types

There are three different replication types: snapshot, transactional, and merge.

Snapshot

With snapshot replication, new snapshots of the data on a Publisher are periodically transferred to the Distributor server. This is the easiest replication to use, but the data should be marked as read-only, and data latency can be a problem, because updates occur periodically. This form of replication can be used if data updates aren't critical.

Transactional

With transactional replication, incremental changes are replicated out, so latency is minimized. The data should be marked as read-only. This form of replication should be used if data updates need to occur with minimal latency.

Merge

With merge replication, all Subscriber servers are allowed to make changes to the data, and then the updates are merged by the Publisher server. The merging can be performed periodically or on demand. This form of replication is susceptible to data conflict, which requires a resolution design based on predefined priorities. This form of replication is best when the data needs to be partitioned by business needs and then merged and redistributed.

What Is Important to Know

The following bullets summarize the chapter and accentuate the key concepts to memorize for the exam:

- Planning can be broken into five areas: security, capacity, data availability, migration, and replication.

- With security planning, you have to decide whether to use Windows NT accounts, SQL Server accounts, or a combination of the two. If all users are Windows clients, use Windows NT accounts. If some of the users are non-Windows clients, use a mixture of Windows NT accounts and SQL Server accounts.

- When configuring security and permissions, use fixed server and fixed database roles to provide users with capabilities.

- For capacity planning, realize that SQL Server is an SMB application that can take full advantage of multiple processors. It's also CPU- and RAM-intensive. Replication and the application model selected will have a significant effect on network bandwidth utilization, so communications plays a big role in planning an efficient design.

- A migration wizard is available for upgrading from SQL Server 6.x to SQL Server 7. It upgrades database and transaction logs, as well as most configuration settings. No migration wizards are available for other database programs, but several import utilities are available for converting data from most database types.

- Replication planning is key, because it is used to distribute data to locations where the clients can access it. When configuring replication, the three models used are single publisher/multiple subscriber, multiple publisher/single subscriber, and multiple publisher/multiple subscriber.

OBJECTIVES

In the last chapter, we looked at several important issues you should address when planning a SQL Server installation. In this chapter, we'll look at what's needed to put that plan into action. SQL Server 7 provides a setup routine that has been simplified from that of earlier versions. The majority of users will choose the defaults for most options and won't need to specify any changes. However, it's important to understand what the options are, since many of them will affect your database and the applications that use it.

This chapter discusses the following test objectives:

▶ Install SQL 7:
- Choose a character set
- Choose the appropriate sort order
- Choose the Unicode collation sequence
- Install the network libraries and protocols
- Install services
- Install and configure a SQL Server client
- Perform an unattended setup
- Upgrade from a SQL Server 6.x database

▶ continues...

CHAPTER 2

Installing and Configuring SQL Server 7

OBJECTIVES continued

- Configure SQL Server:
  - Configure SQL Mail
  - Configure default ANSI settings
- Install and configure the Full-Text Search service:
  - Install the Full-Text Search service
  - Enable Full-Text Search for specific columns and tables
  - Create and manage indexes to support Full-Text Search

INSTALLING SQL SERVER 7

Although the SQL Server 7 installation process has been greatly simplified, it's important to know how to do the following for the exam:

- Choose the character set.
- Choose the appropriate sort order.
- Choose the Unicode collation sequence.
- Install network libraries and protocols.
- Install services.
- Install and configure the SQL Server client.
- Perform an unattended setup.
- Upgrade from the SQL Server 6.x database.

In this section, we'll take a look at the various options available when installing SQL Server 7. Several of the choices made during setup can't easily be changed afterward. Therefore, you should understand them in detail.

Before starting the installation process, you need to log on to the machine as a member of the Administrators group. First, you need to determine which version of SQL Server you want to install:

- **Enterprise Edition.** Includes all features of the standard database server, plus support for high-volume database applications that require clustering support. This option is available only if you purchased the Enterprise Edition. This option is designed for installation on Windows NT Server, Enterprise Edition.

- **Database Server: Standard Edition.** The full version of the SQL Server 7 database server, designed for installation on Windows NT Server.

- **Database Server: Desktop Edition.** For stand-alone development or installation on Windows 95/Windows NT Workstation computers.

Table 2.1 lists the minimum system requirements for installing SQL Server 7. In addition, you'll need a CD-ROM drive or access to a network in order to install the software itself.

TABLE 2.1
SQL Server 7 Minimum System Requirements

Configuration	Requirements
Processor	DEC Alpha and compatible systems; Intel® or compatible (Pentium-166 or higher)
Memory	Enterprise: 64MB minimum
	Other Editions: 32MB minimum
Hard disk space	65MB (minimum)
	170MB (typical)
	180MB (full)
Operating System	Windows NT Server/Enterprise Server or Workstation 4.0 with Service Pack 4; Windows 95/98 with latest Service Packs

After starting SQL Server Setup, you're prompted to choose whether you want to install the product on the local machine or on a remote machine. To perform a remote installation, you must have Administrator access on that computer. This section assumes you'll be doing a local installation. Next, you are prompted to enter your name, your company's name, and a serial number. You also need to choose an installation type (see Table 2.2). If you choose the Typical or Minimal option during configuration, you'll be prompted only for information about the SQL Server Service logon accounts (described later in this chapter).

TABLE 2.2
Setup Types

Installation Type	Components Included	Comments
Typical	Server, documentation, sample files	This setting is valid for most users.
Minimal	Server and required components only	Used if disk space is limited or if only required files are necessary.
Custom	Specified by user	Allows the selection of character sets, sort order, network libraries, and so on.

A Typical installation includes the SQL Server Management tools and online docs, but not the Full-Text Search option (described later in this chapter), sample files, or development tools. To add these to the setup, you must choose the Custom option. Figure 2.1 shows the Custom installation options box. If you change your mind later, you can easily add or remove any of these components by rerunning SQL Server Setup.

Next, you need to specify the path used by SQL Server to store its own files. Setup uses three different directories for copying programs and data. Table 2.3 lists the default installation paths and the types of files that are stored within them.

TABLE 2.3

SQL SERVER 7 DIRECTORIES

Directory	Default	Types of Files Used	Notes
Program Files	c:\mssql7	Static binary files used by SQL Server	Size will remain constant.
Data Files	c:\mssql7	Database devices, log files, system databases, and sample databases	Size will increase with database size. Databases include master, model, tempdb, msdb, northwind, and pubs.
System Files	Subdirectories of %windir%	Shared program files and DLLs	Size will remain constant. Path cannot be changed.

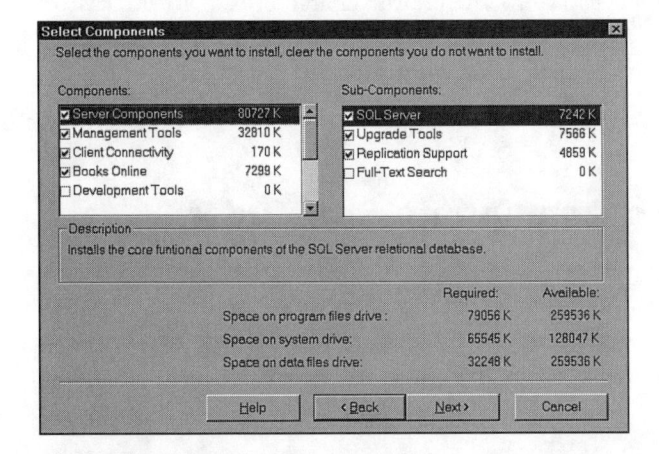

FIGURE 2.1
The Custom setup options dialog box.

Choosing the Character Set

If you choose the Custom setup option during installation, you will be prompted to specify options for a character set, sort order, and Unicode collation. Figure 2.2 shows the options screen that you will see. These settings affect all databases on this SQL Server installation and govern which types of characters can be stored in text datatypes (such as VARCHAR and TEXT). It is important to choose appropriate values during installation, because the only way to change these values is to rerun Setup and rebuild all your databases. If you're planning to upgrade previous SQL Server databases, it's a good idea to keep the collation sequence, character set, and sort order consistent. If you don't, applications might not perform as expected, and you may experience incompatibilities in queries and result sets.

A character set (also known as a *code page*) specifies a set of 256 characters that may be used by SQL Server text data-types (such as CHAR, VARCHAR, and TEXT). All character sets contain the same first 128 characters (based on uppercase and lowercase letters, numbers, and specific symbols). The remaining 128 characters are different in each set and may represent international characters and symbols. Figure 2.3 shows the characters available in a character set using the character map utility. If you'll be using foreign-language applications on this SQL Server, consider changing the default. Otherwise, don't change this option. For most applications, the default ISO character set will be fine. If you have special requirements such as supporting databases in multiple languages, however, it may be necessary to change the character set. In the case of databases in multiple languages, the servers may require different character sets and you will need to handle any differences through your application and data transfer processes.

Choosing the Appropriate Sort Order

Databases must be able to compare values in order to sort in queries, indexes, and other operations. Although this is generally a secondary concern, the sort order you choose can also affect performance (case-insensitive sorts are faster than case-sensitive). To make sure that

Installing SQL Server 7   53

you and SQL Server are thinking about this in the same way, you'll need to choose a specific option. The default setting is Dictionary order, case-insensitive. This specifies that, for example, the word "Andy" will be sorted before "ANil," regardless of capitalization. In most database applications, this will be appropriate. However, other choices include case-sensitive and foreign-language rules. If you are unsure of what to choose, the best bet is to select the default. Figure 2.4 shows the available sort order options. Although the two settings are largely independent, the UNICODE collation sequence and sort order must be compatible, because changing one option might automatically change the other.

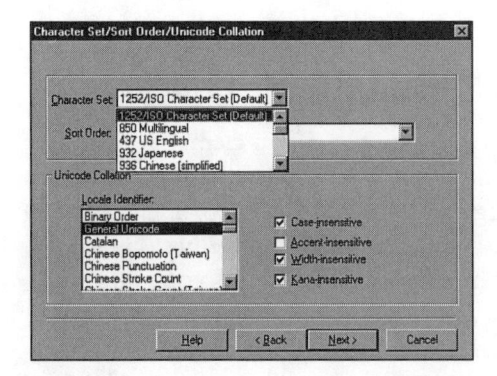

FIGURE 2.2
Choosing the character set during setup.

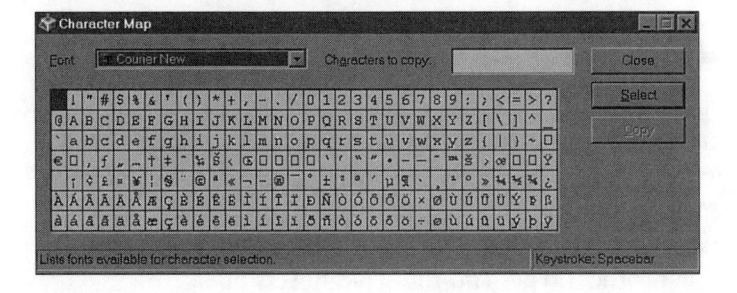

FIGURE 2.3
Characters within a code page.

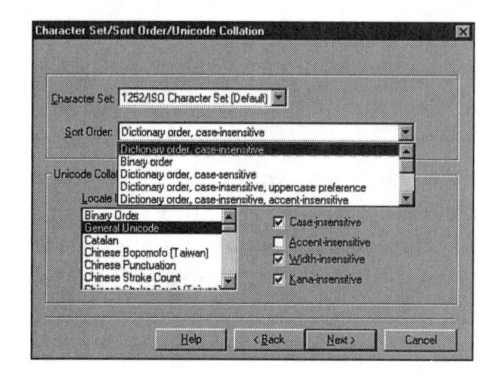

54 CHAPTER 2 Installing and Configuring SQL Server 7

FIGURE 2.4
Choosing a sort order during setup.

Choosing the Unicode Collation Sequence

The Unicode character set can contain up to 65,536 elements. It incorporates a large subset of all the characters used in all the languages of the world. Unicode collation settings are completely independent of sort order settings. The default option is General. This is the best choice for most languages, including North American English. If you want SQL Server to use other rules for sorting, highlight the appropriate option. For any language choice, you can choose from four character-sensitivity options. These rules will specify how sorting will occur for Unicode characters. For most U.S. users, the defaults will be fine.

Installing Network Libraries and Protocols

In order for clients and the database server to communicate, a common method of data transfer must be determined. The default selections for Network Libraries (shown in Figure 2.5) will be appropriate for most TCP/IP-based environments. SQL Server can use any number of Network Libraries to communicate, but each must be enabled. Table 2.4 lists the available protocol types and the typical users of each.

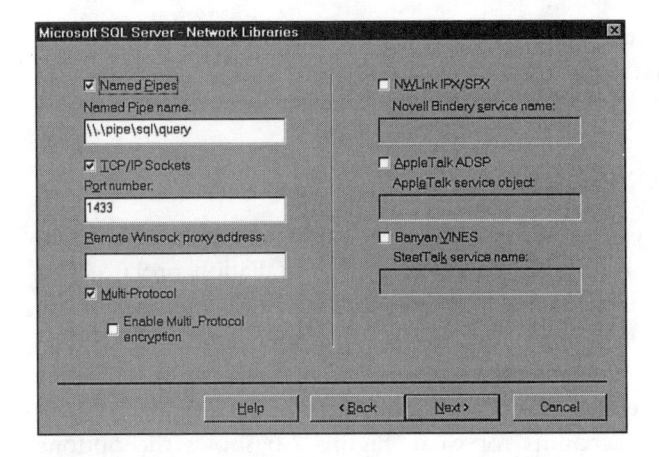

FIGURE 2.5
Default Network Libraries options.

TABLE 2.4
NETWORK LIBRARIES

Protocol Type	Suggested Client Types	Notes
Named Pipes	Windows 95/98/NT only	Works on TCP/IP NetBEUI or IPX/SPX networks.
TCP/IP Sockets	All TCP/IP clients	Uses TCP Port 1433 by default. Also supports Microsoft Proxy Server.
Multi-Protocol	All	Uses any protocol type. Data and authentication encryption are possible.
NWLink IPX/SPX	Novell NetWare clients and servers	Can connect to NetWare Bindery.
AppleTalk ADSP	Macintosh clients	Uses local AppleTalk zone for communications.
Banyan VINES	VINES clients	Supports SPP communications. Available only on the Intel platform.
Shared Memory	Windows 95/98 only	Used for connecting to a server on the same machine.

You can modify these options after server installation by using the Server Network Configuration program.

Installing Services

The services used by SQL Server must have a user account under which these processes can run. Prior to starting the installation process, you should create a special account. This account must be a member of the Administrators group. The account also requires specific user rights, but SQL Server Setup will grant these automatically. Both the SQL Server and SQL Agent services may use the same logon (the default), or you may assign separate accounts for each. Figure 2.6 shows the options available. Enter the domain name for this user account or the name of the server if the machine isn't participating in a domain. Finally, you'll need to specify whether you want the services to start automatically on startup or be set to manual (the default).

Alternatively, you can choose to use the Local System Account. However, this restricts the operations that can be performed by SQL Server to only the local machine. In a stand-alone environment, this setting is appropriate. However, using a Windows NT account will allow the services to handle distributed transactions across remote servers, perform replication, and manage network backups. Also, the SQL Mail component might require a unique account based on your e-mail system. If you have multiple SQL Servers in a single domain, they might all use the same domain account. Table 2.5 lists the services installed with SQL Server 7.

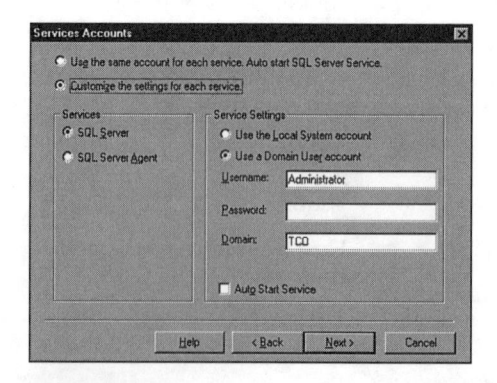

FIGURE 2.6
Assigning service accounts during SQL Server setup.

Installing SQL Server 7   57

TABLE 2.5

SQL SERVER 7 SERVICES

Service Name	Executable	Function
SQL Server 7 (MSSQL Server)	sqlservr.exe	Database server.
SQL Server Agent (SQLServer Agent)	sqlagent.exe	Schedules SQL Server 7 batch jobs. See Chapter 5, "Monitoring and Optimization," for more information.
MS Distributed Transaction Coordinator (MSDTC)	msdtc.exe	Allows real-time transactions involving multiple servers.
Full-Text Search (Microsoft Search)	mssearch.exe	Allows the user to search for text information within database objects.

Table 2.6 lists the various services used by SQL Server, along with their functions. After installation, you can start, stop, and pause these services using the SQL Server Service Control Manager in the SQL Server program group. Alternatively, you can select Control Panel | Services or use the NET command from a command prompt. Finally, the fourth (and easiest) way to control the SQL Server services is to use the stoplight system tray icon.

TABLE 2.6

METHODS OF CONTROLLING THE SQL SERVER SERVICES

Method	Location	Notes
Service Manager	System tray	Must be loaded at startup or run from a SQL Server program group.
Services Configuration	Control Panel	Also allows modification of service accounts.
Enterprise Manager	SQL Server 7 program group	Can be used to control local and remote SQL Servers.
NET START *servicename*	Command prompt	Requires the name of the service.

All services can be stopped or started. The MSSQL Server service can also be paused. Table 2.7 shows the meaning of these states.

TABLE 2.7

MSSQL SERVER SERVICE STATES

Option	Effect
Start	Allows users to connect to the database server.
Stop	Disconnects all users and stops the service.
Pause	Prevents new database connections, but current users will be able to continue using the server.

SQL Server can also be run as an application from the command line for special situations. The command `sqlservr` can be followed by an `-m` switch to start the database in single-user mode, or an `-f` switch to start with a minimum fail-safe configuration. Both options can be helpful in database maintenance and/or troubleshooting.

> **NOTE** You can't start, stop, or pause the MSSQL Server using the Services options if you started it from the command line since this process isn't running as a service.

In the Control Panel Services applet, the Startup value determines whether or not SQL Server will start when the system boots. Automatic indicates that it will, while Manual means you must start the server before using it.

The final option you'll need to choose is the Licensing mode. You will need to specify whether you want to use Per Server mode (which allows a specific number of concurrent connections) or Per Seat (which requires each client accessing the server to have a separate access license). The number of licenses you can install will be specified on the product package.

Once you've made all of these selections, SQL Server will begin copying files to your system. At the end of the setup routine, the SQL Server services will be started.

Installing and Configuring the SQL Server Client

After installing SQL Server 7 on a computer, you'll find the SQL Server Client Configuration option in the Control Panel and the Client Network Utility in the Microsoft SQL Server 7 program group. Either can be used to specify which network libraries are available for client connections. Figure 2.7 shows the options available. The selected protocols specify how the client will communicate with the server. In order for connections to be made, the client must be configured to use at least one of the protocols supported on the server.

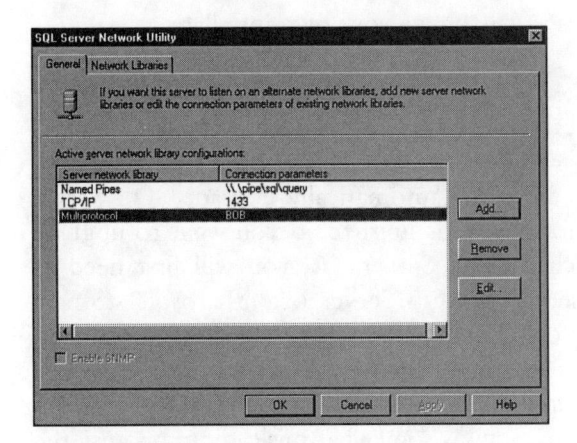

FIGURE 2.7
The SQL Server Client Configuration utility.

Performing an Unattended Setup

In most cases, you'll perform a local installation of a SQL Server—that is, you'll manually select options. If you're rolling out several SQL Servers or you want to schedule the upgrade process, you can perform an unattended installation using the command line. To do this, you use the SetupSQL command as follows:

```
Start d:\x86\setup\setupsql.exe -f1c:\mydirectory\SQL7Install.iss -s
```

- The -f1 switch specifies the location of an automated setup file (the pathname is arbitrary). This text file includes answers to all the setup prompts and can be edited using any standard editor.

- The -s switch suppresses any output from the command.

When the command is run, Setup copies all the needed files and starts the SQL Server service automatically. Microsoft has included sample *.iss files in the root directory of the SQL Server 7 CD-ROM. You can use these files as templates to customize your own installation.

UPGRADING FROM SQL SERVER 6.X

SQL Server 7 offers the ability to automatically upgrade SQL Server 6.0 or later databases before Setup is finished. If you want to upgrade from earlier versions, such as SQL Server 4.2, you will first need to upgrade your database server to SQL Server 6.x. Microsoft strongly recommends that you perform a complete backup of your previous database before performing an upgrade. Figure 2.8 shows the dialog box option you're given if Setup detects a previous version of SQL Server on your system. The term "upgrade" is somewhat misleading, because the wizard actually imports information from a previous version of SQL Server. All original information is left intact, so you can choose to import only certain databases and then rerun the wizard for others. The upgrade can transfer data and server settings (such as replication and alert settings) to your new installation from the local machine or from a SQL Server installation on a remote computer. It uses the Named Pipes protocol to transfer data, so it's important to have this enabled on the server and the client. If you check the box, the SQL Server Upgrade Wizard will be started immediately after SQL Server is installed.

Upgrading from SQL Server 6.x   61

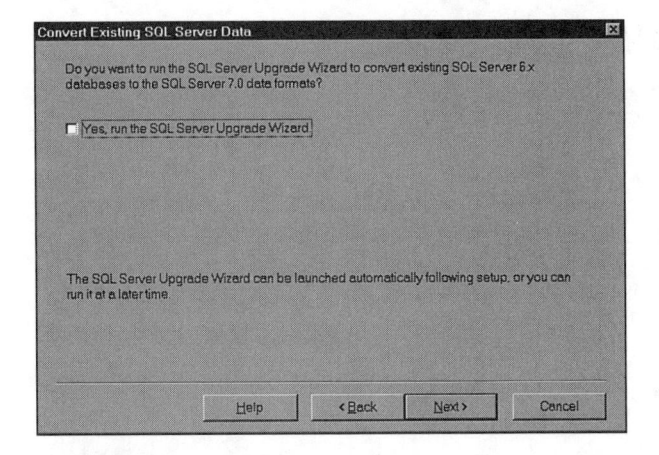

FIGURE 2.8
The SQL Server Upgrade Wizard prompt.

> **TIP**
> Although you may have two versions of SQL Server installed on the same machine, only one can be running at a time. To switch between the versions, click the Microsoft SQL Server | Switch icon in the Microsoft SQL Server | Switch program group.

To perform a SQL Server 6.x upgrade after SQL Server 7 is installed, select Start | Programs | MS SQL Server | Switch | SQL Server Upgrade Wizard. Figure 2.9 shows a few of the options available in this wizard.

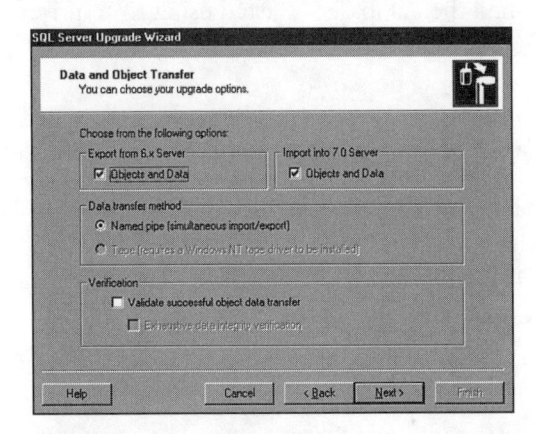

FIGURE 2.9
The SQL Server Upgrade Wizard.

Configuring SQL Server 7

After completing the initial installation of SQL Server 7, you'll probably have several optional components that you want to configure. Here are the exam objectives for this section:

- Configure SQL Mail.
- Configure default ANSI settings.

Configuring SQL Mail

SQL Mail was designed to use any MAPI (Messaging Application Programming Interface)-compliant messaging system to send messages to other users. For example, a database administrator can configure an alert to send an e-mail message when the transaction logs are more than 80 percent full. Setting up alerts is covered in more detail in Chapter 5. You can also send messages by using built-in stored procedures. Before using SQL Mail, you'll need to establish a mail profile for a user in the same domain as the server. This can be done by logging on to the operating system as any user and configuring the mail application to automatically send mail immediately. To configure SQL Mail, you first need to assign an account to the SQL Mail service by right-clicking the service in Enterprise Manager and selecting Properties. Select the mail profile that you set up earlier. To make sure that SQL Mail is always available, be sure to set the service to start automatically when the database is started using Enterprise Manager.

Configuring Default ANSI Settings

The ANSI (American National Standards Institute) settings specify how SQL Server will manage queries and other transactions that require both client and server processing. To configure the properties, right-click the server in Enterprise Manager and select Properties. Figure 2.10 shows the various options available.

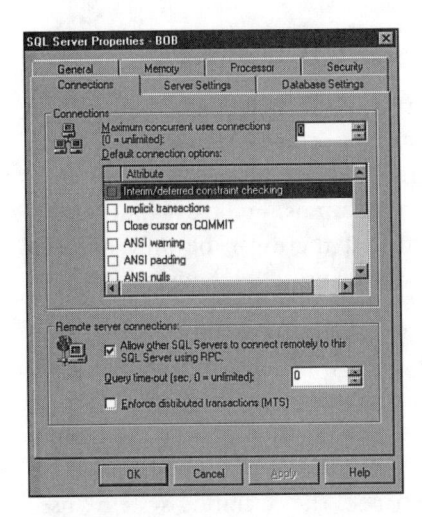

FIGURE 2.10
Setting ANSI defaults in Enterprise Manager.

Changing the defaults allows SQL Server parameters used to handle concurrency and locking issues to be handled differently. To enable default settings, from within a query or a transaction, you can type SET ANSI_DEFAULTS ON;.

INSTALLING AND CONFIGURING THE FULL-TEXT SEARCH SERVICE

The Full-Text Search Service in SQL Server 7 allows users to perform advanced queries on character-based fields. Although basic searching functions are available in standard SQL, certain operations, such as searching for words that are located near each other or searching for different forms of the same word, can't be performed. The Full-Text Search Service functionality frees application developers and end-users from having to use third-party tools for advanced searching. For the exam, you should know how to do the following:

- Install the Full-Text Search Service.
- Enable the Full-Text Search Service for specific columns and tables.
- Create and manage indexes for the Full-Text Search Service.

Installing the Full-Text Search Service

The Full-Text Search Service allows users to perform enhanced queries on VARCHAR and TEXT column types. For example, information on author, subject, and type of data contained in these fields can be obtained after a Full-Text Index is created for those columns. Full-Text Indexes differ from normal SQL Server indexes in that there can be only one per table. They must also be updated manually or using a scheduled job.

The Full-Text Search Service can be installed during setup only by specifying the Custom setup type. If you've already installed SQL Server, you can add or remove the Full-Text Search Service by rerunning SQL Server 7 Setup. Select the Custom installation type and then place a checkmark in the Full-Text Search box under the Server Components section. This service requires an account with "Act as part of the operating system" user permissions.

Customizing Full-Text Search

A Full-Text Search can only be performed on columns that have been indexed. You can configure the Full-Text Search service by right-clicking Full-Text Search and selecting Properties in the Enterprise Manager. Figure 2.11 shows the General tab, which shows the default file locations for the service. The system resource usage slider bar on the Performance tab allows you to set the priority that this service will receive. Also, by right-clicking the service, you can choose the Clean-Up Catalogs option, which removes unused space in the index. Table 2.7 shows the default locations of Full-Text Search files.

TABLE 2.7

FULL-TEXT SEARCH SERVICE DEFAULT PATHS

Files	Default Path
Catalog files	c:\mssql7\ftdata
Temporary files	c:\winnt\temp
Error LOG Files	c:\mssql7\ftdata

Installing and Configuring the Full-Text Search Service   65

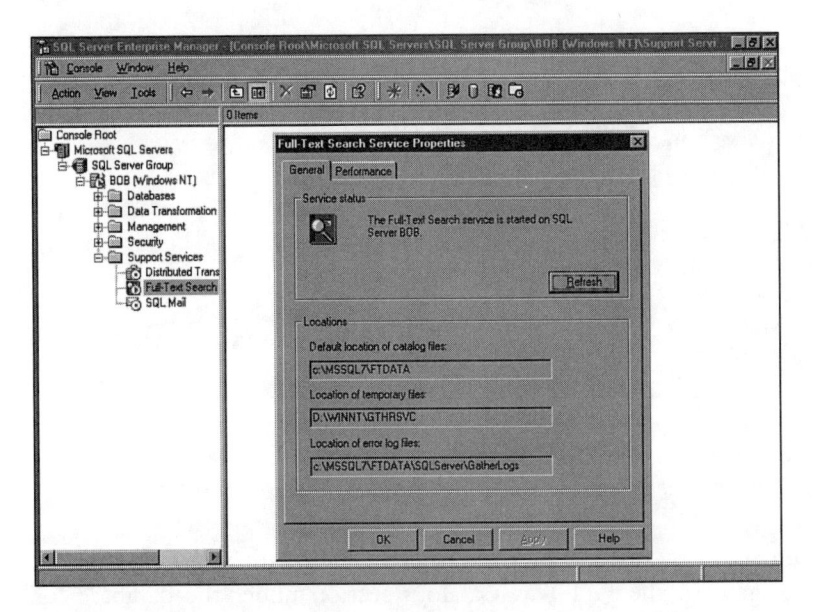

FIGURE 2.11
Viewing the Full-Text Search Service configuration.

Creating and Managing the Full-Text Search Indexes

In order to create a Full-Text Search Index, you must be the database owner (a SQL Server role described in Chapter 5). By default, the user who creates a database is the object's owner. The easiest way to create the index is to use the wizard. To do this, highlight a database and select Tools | Full-Text Indexing. Figure 2.12 shows the Full-Text Indexing Wizard that can be used to set up a Full-Text Search Index. Follow the prompts to specify which database, table, and columns you want to index.

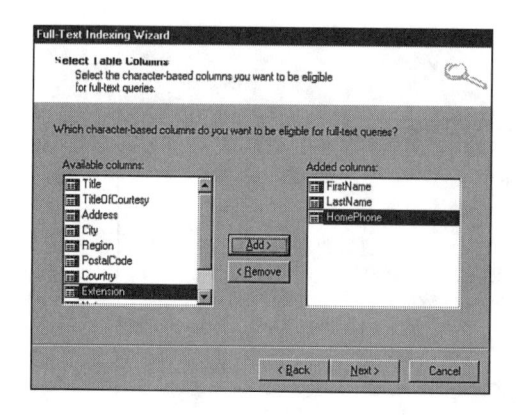

FIGURE 2.12
The Full-Text Indexing Wizard.

After the index is created, you need to populate it with actual data. To do this, navigate to the Full-Text Catalogs section under the database for which you set up the index. Right-click the name of the catalog, and select Start Population | Full Population. You can also set up a job to regularly repopulate the database. A full population will reindex all selected columns. Incremental populations will record only changes that occurred since the last indexing operation. Incremental populations generally require less processing and are better for large databases. Multiple full-text indexes within the same database are grouped into a single catalog.

Instead of being created and modified by SQL statements like regular indexes, Full-Text Indexes are administered using stored procedures. A complete list of these commands is available in the SQL Server Books Online, found in the Microsoft SQL Server program group.

NOTES

If Setup encounters any problems while installing SQL Server on your system, you can find more information in the \mssql7\install\Cnfgsvr.out file or the \mssql7\log\errorlog file. If you didn't choose the defaults, these files will be located in the subdirectory of the program files path.

By default, Setup uses Mixed security, allows any member of the Administrators group to log on as SA, and leaves the SA password blank. For more information on changing these settings, see Chapter 3, "Configuring and Managing Security."

What Is Important to Know

The following bullets summarize the chapter and accentuate the key concepts to memorize for the exam:

- The character set, Unicode collation sequence, and sort order specify the types of characters that will be available for use within the database. If you want to use options other than the defaults, you'll need to choose the Custom installation type.
- Network Libraries specify communications protocols that clients can use to access the SQL Server. They can be configured using the SQL Server Network Configuration and the SQL Server Client Configuration utilities.
- SQL Server uses several services, each of which can be controlled using the Control Panel, Enterprise Manager, the Service Manager, or the command line.
- You can perform an unattended setup by using the `sqlsetup` command-line command, together with an installation options text file.
- The SQL Server Upgrade Wizard can be used to automatically import data and settings from a SQL Server 6.x database server. The original database is left intact.

SQL Server configuration

- SQL Mail can be configured in Enterprise Manager to specify e-mail recipients. Messages can be sent using stored procedures or via alerts. The requirements include a MAPI-compliant e-mail system and at least one valid e-mail account.
- Default ANSI settings specify how SQL Server manages locking and distributed transactions. They can be modified in Enterprise Manager or per transaction.

Installing and configuring the Full-Text Search Service

- Full-Text Searches allow users and application developers to perform enhanced pattern-matching queries using SQL Server. You can install the Full-Text Search service as part of a Custom installation or by rerunning Setup. These indexes are managed using stored procedures, not standard SQL commands. The Full-Text Index Wizard can help you create indexes that are specific to certain columns in a table. All indexes in a database make up a single catalog.
- Full-Text Indexes must be populated manually or through the use of scheduled tasks. Population jobs can be full or incremental.

OBJECTIVES

An important aspect of managing any database is security. Only authorized users should be able to access information contained in a database. Once they have access, they must be permitted to only view and/or modify certain data. SQL Server 7 provides an extremely powerful yet easy-to-administer security system that you'll need to understand for the Configuring and Managing Security portion of the exam. The goals for this section include the following:

▶ Assign SQL Server access to Windows NT accounts, SQL Server login accounts, and built-in administrator accounts.

▶ Assign database access to Windows NT accounts, SQL Server login accounts, the Guest user account, and the DBO user account.

▶ Create and assign SQL Server roles, including fixed server, fixed database, public, user-defined database, and application.

▶ Grant to database users and roles the appropriate permissions to database objects and statements.

▶ Audit server and database activity by using the SQL Server Profiler.

CHAPTER 3

Configuring and Managing Security

An Overview of SQL Server Security

SQL Server 7 was designed to make managing one of the most tedious yet important areas of database administration—maintaining security—simpler and more powerful. Before a user can gain access to data stored on a SQL Server, he or she must meet three requirements:

- Have a database login
- Be assigned permissions to access specific databases
- Be given permissions on a specific database object to perform operations

If a user fails to meet any of these three requirements, he or she will be unable to perform any functions on a database object.

Logins map to database users, who may be created in Windows NT or SQL Server. These logins must then be given permissions to access specific databases. Database users can then be placed in roles or be directly granted permissions on database objects such as tables, views, and stored procedures. Figure 3.1 shows the relationships between the various levels of SQL Server security. In this chapter, we'll look at how you can configure the various levels of permissions and see how they fit into the overall security of a database.

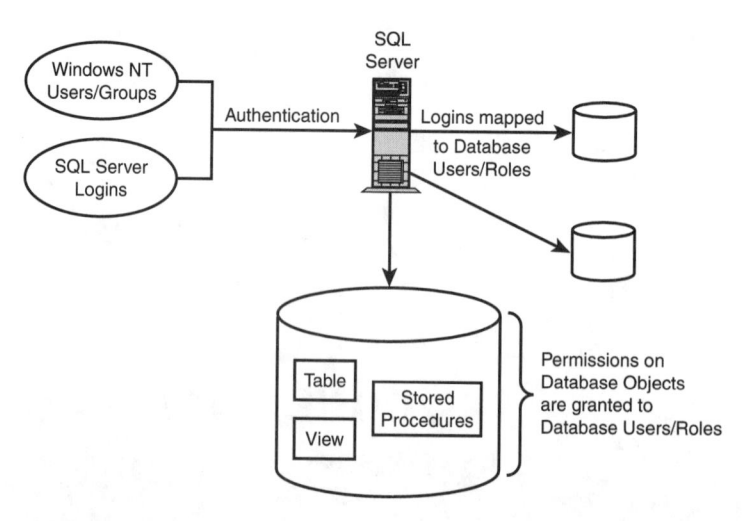

FIGURE 3.1
An overview of SQL Server security.

Managing SQL Server Logins

Before a user is allowed to have any interactions with a SQL Server database, he or she must have a login account for the server. In this section, we'll look at two ways to allow login permissions. The first decision you'll make is whether to allow only Windows NT-based authentication or to allow Mixed authentication (see Table 3.1).

TABLE 3.1
TYPES OF SQL SERVER LOGINS

Login Type	Account Information Source
Windows NT authentication	Windows NT users and groups
Mixed authentication	SQL Server logins or Windows NT users and groups

> **NOTE:** If you change security settings for a user in Windows NT, these changes will not take place until the user performs another login to the database.

> **WARNING:** The default password for the SA account is blank. One of the first steps you should perform after installing SQL Server is to assign a password to this account.

Windows NT authentication requires users to have a SQL Server login mapped to their Windows NT account for access. If Mixed security is selected, users may log in using a username and password if a login does not exist for their Windows NT account. Do the following to set the Server Authentication option in Enterprise Manager:

1. Right-click the name of a server and select Properties.
2. On the Security tab, shown in Figure 3.2, select either SQL Server and Windows NT or Windows NT only for the authentication type.

CHAPTER 3 Configuring and Managing Security

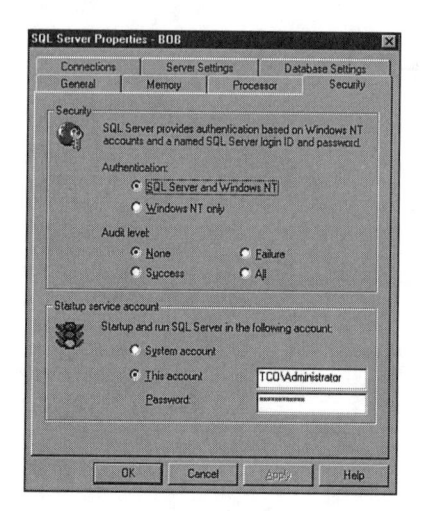

FIGURE 3.2
Setting SQL Server authentication options.

3. Next, choose what kind of auditing you want to enable for authentication. The default option is None, but you can choose Success, Failure, or All events. Click OK to accept the configuration.

   If SQL Server is running on a Windows 95/98 machine, users will not be able to use trusted connections. Therefore, Windows NT Authentication is not an available option and all users that connect to that server will be required to provide a valid login and password.

Creating SQL Server Logins

If you're using Mixed security, you can create logins and passwords that users can use to access the SQL Server database. Authentication will require the input of a password that matches the one stored by SQL Server.

To create a SQL Server login based on a Windows NT user or group in Enterprise Manager, do the following:

1. Select the server for which you want to create a login. Expand the Security folder. Right-click Logins and select New Login. You see the dialog box shown in Figure 3.3.

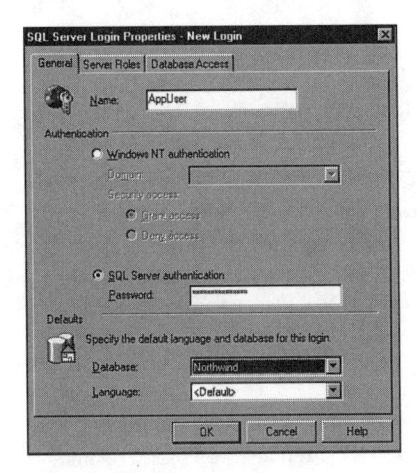

FIGURE 3.3
Creating a new SQL Server login.

2. In the Name field, specify a unique name for the new login. This is the name a user must use to connect to the database server.

3. For authentication, select SQL Server Authentication and enter a password to be used by a user or application to log in to the database.

4. Specify a default database to which the user will connect. Note that you may need to grant database permissions (described later) separately.

5. Click OK and then verify the password to create the new login.

You can optionally specify server roles and database roles using the other tabs in this dialog box (described later). SQL Server login information is stored in the syslogins system table. When a user attempts to authenticate, SQL Server verifies that a login and password are present in this table and, if so, allows the login.

Mapping Windows NT Accounts

Windows NT accounts (groups and users) can be directly granted permissions to access a Microsoft SQL Server database if you're using Windows NT Security or Mixed security. When a user logs on to the database using Windows NT authentication, he or she doesn't need to enter a password since SQL Server trusts that Windows NT has already authenticated the user. In most cases, it will be preferable to grant access to an entire group to make administration easier. Consider placing all SQL Server users in a new Windows NT group. This prevents the tedious process of having to manage individual accounts and permissions for logins. If you're working in a domain-based environment, you can assign logon permissions to either global or local groups. Windows NT Authentication is supported by both Windows 95/98 and Windows NT clients. Other client types can only use SQL Server Authentication.

> **NOTE** By default, members of the Windows NT Administrators and Domain Administrators groups are granted system administrator (SA) access to the database. Since the default password for this account is blank, you should change it immediately after installation.

Follow these steps to create a SQL Server login based on a Windows NT user or group in Enterprise Manager:

1. Select the server to which you want to create a login. Expand the Security folder. Right-click Logins and select New Login. You see the dialog box shown in Figure 3.4.

2. In the Name field, specify the name of a Windows NT user or group to which you want to grant login permissions. If you're working in a multi-domain environment, you'll also need to specify the domain name (such as Engineering\JoeUser).

3. Leave the Authentication setting as Windows NT Authentication. Users will not need to enter a username or password to gain access. For Security Access, choose whether this group should be granted or denied access.

4. Specify a default database to which the user will connect. Click OK to create the new login.

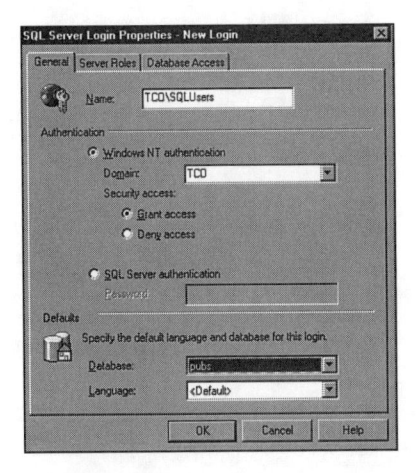

FIGURE 3.4
Creating a SQL Server login for the SQL Users group.

You can optionally specify server roles and database roles using the other tabs in this dialog box (described later). When a user attempts to log into a database using Windows NT authentication, SQL Server attempts to find a matching login in the syslogins table. If a Windows NT user attempts to log in from a nontrusted domain, he or she will be required to enter a username and password for the domain in which the SQL Server resides. In either case, if a login exists, the user is allowed to connect; otherwise, an error message is returned and the user is given a chance to provide a SQL Server login (if Mixed security is enabled).

ADDING USERS TO DATABASES

A user must be added to a database before he or she can access any information in that database. There are two ways to add these permissions. To add database permissions when creating a login, do the following:

1. In the New Login dialog box, click the Database Access tab, shown in Figure 3.5.
2. Place a checkmark next to the database(s) the user should be able to access.

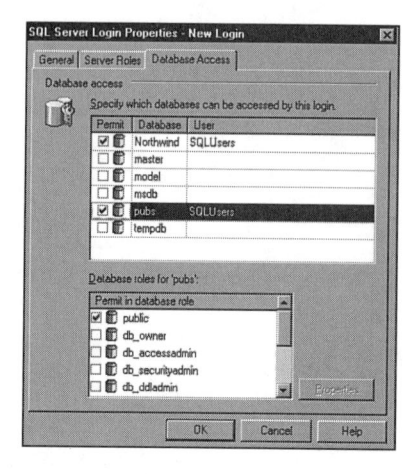

76 CHAPTER 3 Configuring and Managing Security

FIGURE 3.5
Assigning database access when creating a new login.

3. Optionally, you can assign database roles (described later) for these users.

If you already have user logins created, you can add them to a database by doing the following:

1. Expand the database for which you want to add users.

2. Right-click the Database Users folder and select New Database User. You see the dialog box shown in Figure 3.6.

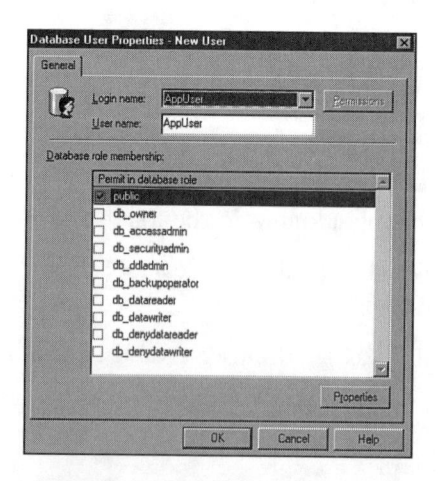

FIGURE 3.6
Creating a database user from an existing login.

3. Select a Login Name. You can use the login name as the user name within the database, or you can assign a unique name.

4. Add the users to any existing database roles (described later).

Managing Roles

It's easier to assign permissions to groups of users that have similar functions than it is to manage individual accounts. SQL Server includes roles to make assigning permissions easier. Roles work much like groups in Windows NT but are defined based on the specific function of an individual. For example, if you have several users who can view but not modify employee records, you may want to create a role called Employee Record Viewers. Roles can also contain other roles. The overall process is to define roles, assign users to roles, and then grant permissions to these roles, as shown in Figure 3.7.

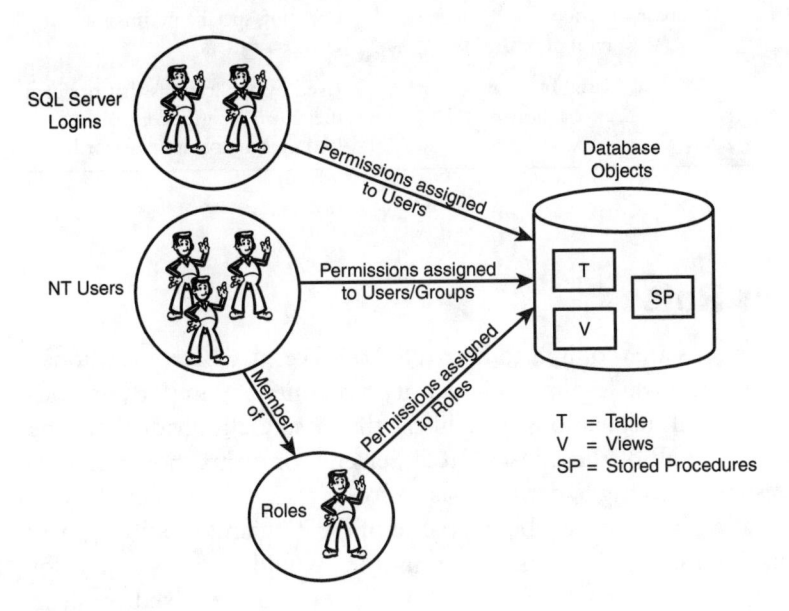

FIGURE 3.7
Managing permissions using roles and users.

SQL Server supports several different types of roles. Table 3.2 lists the different types of roles and describes the purpose of each.

TABLE 3.2

TYPES OF SQL SERVER ROLES

Role Type	Purpose	Usage
Fixed Server	Managing SQL Server Configuration, including objects, alerts, tasks, and devices	Configuration and maintenance of the database server.
Fixed Database	Allows specific database functions	Configuration and maintenance of databases.
Public	All users with permissions to access a database are members of the Public group	Default access permissions for any user who can access the database.
User-Defined Database	Group-based database-level permissions	Granting specific permissions to groups of users.
Application	Used by a single application	Used by applications that perform their own security control. Requires a separate password.

Server Roles

Many functions are required to keep a SQL Server database operational. Managing backups, logins, and security accounts are important concerns. For small installations, it is likely that a single individual will be responsible for all of these tasks. In larger environments, however, it is more desirable to assign specific tasks to specific users. For example, one database administrator may be in charge of creating and modifying user accounts for multiple servers, while another would be responsible for managing backups on all servers. SQL Server provides fixed, built-in server roles that have been created for making this process much easier. Table 3.3 lists the different system roles and their functions.

TABLE 3.3

SERVER ROLES

Database Role Name	User Name	Purpose
Database Creators	Dbcreator	Creates, alters, and resizes databases
Disk Administrators	Diskadmin	Manages database storage files
Process Administrators	Processadmin	Kills (stops) processes running on the server
Security Administrators	Securityadmin	Creates and manages server logins and auditing
Server Administrators	Serveradmin	Changes server configuration parameters and shutdown server
Setup Administrators	Setupadmin	Manages replication and extended procedures
System Administrators	Sysadmin	Completes control over all database functions

By default, only the System Administrators role contains accounts. The members are the Windows NT Administrators group and the SQL Server SA account. Also, note that members of each of the roles are allowed to assign the permissions of their role to another user account. For example, a user who is a member of the Setup Administrators role can add another user to this role. You can add user accounts to logins when they are created by accessing the Server Roles tab. To add existing logins to server roles, follow these steps:

1. In Enterprise Manager, expand the Security folder for the server you want to modify.

2. Double-click the name of a Server Role in the right panel, as shown in Figure 3.8, and click Add. Highlight users to assign them to this role.

3. Optionally, you can click the Permissions tab to see the permissions available for this user (but you won't be able to change the settings).

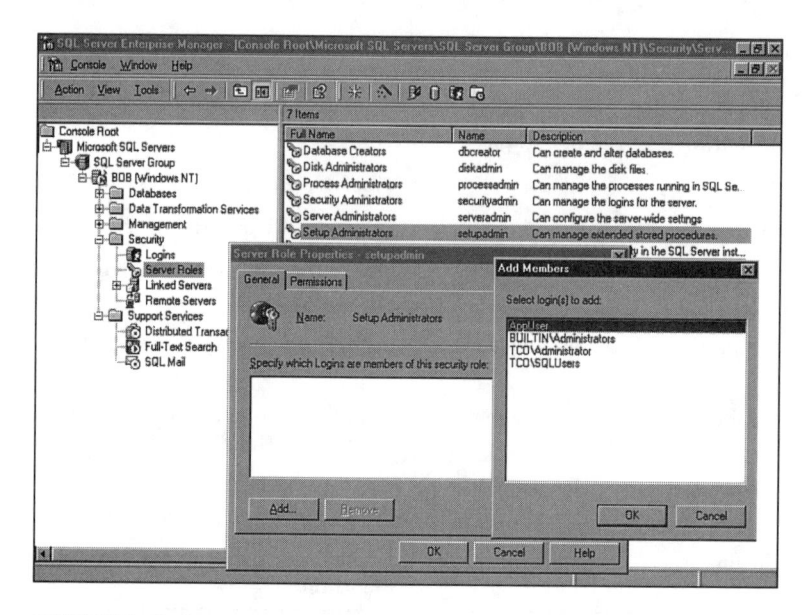

FIGURE 3.8
Assigning a user to a server role.

Application Roles

Specific database-dependent programs can use application roles to gain access to the SQL Server. Large database applications often enforce their own security based on the application logic. For example, an accounting package might enforce security permissions that allow a specific user to update a database only during specific hours. The application itself will use a single login and password that have access permissions to obtain and modify any data within a database. This prevents the administrator from having to manage multiple accounts on the database level and allows more complex security management within the application logic.

Database Roles

Within databases, users will be required to carry out specific functions. For small databases, a single individual might be responsible for all maintenance and administration. Large databases, on the other hand, will require multiple users to manage specific aspects of the configuration. To make managing permissions easier, SQL Server includes built-in database roles that allow administrators to easily assign only the permissions necessary for completing specific tasks. Table 3.4 lists the built-in database roles generated for new databases.

TABLE 3.4

SQL SERVER DATABASE ROLES

Database Role	Permissions
db_owner	Can perform the activities of all database roles, as well as other maintenance and configuration activities in the database
db_accessadmin	Can add or remove Windows NT groups, Windows NT users, and SQL Server users in the database
db_datareader	Can see any data from all user tables in the database
db_datawriter	Can add, change, or delete data from all user tables in the database
db_ddladmin	Can add, modify, or drop objects in the database
db_securityadmin	Can manage roles and members of SQL Server database roles, and can manage statement and object permissions in the database
db_backupoperator	Can back up the database
db_denydatareader	Cannot see any data in the database, but can make schema changes
db_denydatawriter	Cannot change any data in the database

Users can be assigned to any of these roles based on the requirements of their job functions. By default, whenever a user creates a database object, he or she is defined as the owner of that object. Other users with appropriate permissions may change database ownership. In order to remove a database owner, you must first either drop any objects owned by the user or transfer ownership to another user or role.

Creating User-Defined Database Roles

Although the built-in database roles handle permissions for common database management tasks, it's likely that you will want to group users who have access to perform specific database functions. To create a new user-defined database role, do the following:

1. In Enterprise Manager, expand the database for which you want to create a role.
2. Right-click Roles and select New Database Role. You see the dialog box shown in Figure 3.9.
3. For the Database Role Type, select Standard Role. Click Add to assign existing database users to this role. Alternatively, if you choose to make this an Application Role, it may be assigned a password or left blank.

Adding Users to Roles

Once a role is created, you can assign users to it. Users can be assigned to multiple roles based on their permissions. To add users to an existing role, expand the Database Roles folder within a database. Double-click an existing role and use the Add and Remove buttons to change assigned users. All users who are members of a role will inherit any permissions assigned to the role itself.

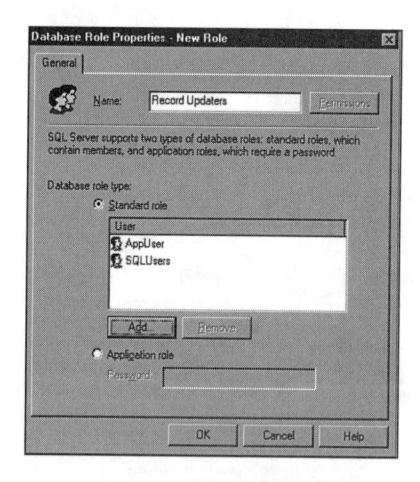

FIGURE 3.9
Creating a new database role.

Managing SQL Server Permissions

For managing security on database objects and actions, SQL Server supports three types of permissions, described in Table 3.5.

TABLE 3.5

SQL SERVER PERMISSION TYPES

Permission Type	Effects
Statement permissions	Database creation and modification
Object permissions	Executing queries that view and modify database objects
Predefined (role-based)	Permissions assigned to fixed roles and object owners

Assigning Object Permissions

Before user accounts and roles can be useful, you must assign them permissions on specific database objects. The types of permissions possible for database objects are described in Table 3.6.

TABLE 3.6

SQL SERVER PERMISSION TYPES (DATABASE OBJECTS)

Statement	What It Applies To	Purpose/Notes
Select	Tables and views	Reads data from an existing database row.
Update	Tables and views	Modifies the data in an existing database row.
Insert	Tables and views	Creates a new database row.
Delete	Tables and views	Removes an existing row from a database.
Declare Referential Integrity (DRI)	Tables	Allows users of other tables to refer to a key in this table without being able to view or modify that key directly.
Execute	Stored Procedures	Statements will execute with the permissions of the stored procedure's owner, not the executing user account.

For more detailed security, you can also place Select and Update permissions on specific columns within a database object. All database users will be members of the Public role by default, and this membership cannot be changed. This role permits them to perform functions that do not require specific permissions and to access any database via the Guest account (unless it is removed). You can define permissions by viewing user information or by viewing database object information. To add or modify permissions for a specific database object, follow these steps:

1. Expand the database for which you want to modify permissions.

2. Expand the folder for the type of object you want to assign permissions (such as Views).

3. Right-click the name of an object and select Properties.

4. Click Permissions. You see the dialog box shown in Figure 3.10. You can choose to list all users and roles, or just those that currently have access to the database.

5. Place a check mark next to the permissions you want to grant to these database users. Table 3.7 lists the meanings of the possible setting options. Figure 3.10 shows the permissions options available for a view.

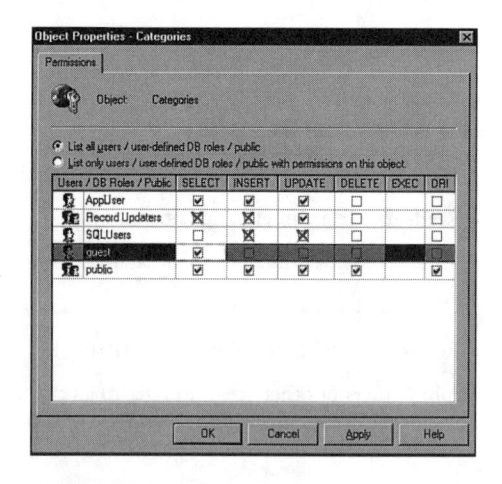

FIGURE 3.10
Assigning database permissions to a view.

TABLE 3.7

SQL SERVER PERMISSION TYPES (MEANINGS)

Setting	Symbol	Meaning
Grant	Check mark	The user has permissions.
Deny	Red X	The user does not have permissions.
Revoke	Blank	Unspecified (the user can inherit permissions).

To modify permissions on a per-user basis, double-click a username in the Database Users folder within a database. Click Permissions to view the security settings for this user. In general, permissions are additive. That is, if a user is a member of one group that is allowed SELECT permissions and another that is allowed INSERT and DELETE permissions, he or she will effectively have all three of these rights. However, if a user is a member of any group that is explicitly denied permissions to a resource, this setting overrides any other permissions. In this case, the user will not be able to perform the action until he or she is removed from the group that is denied access.

Permissions can also be set with the GRANT, REVOKE, and DENY statements using a SQL query tool. By default, the sysadmin, db_securityadmin, and db_owner roles have permissions to perform these functions. All permissions information is stored in the sysprotects system table. When a user executes a query or transaction, SQL Server checks for appropriate permissions in this table. Permissions are cumulative, unless they are specifically denied. For example, if John is a member of Group1 (which has Select permissions) and Group2 (which has Update permissions), he will be able to perform both functions. However, if he is also a member of Group3 (which has Denied Select permissions), he will be unable to query information from the object. In this case, he will receive an error message stating that he does not have sufficient permissions to execute the query or transaction.

In general, there are several good practices for managing permissions in databases of any size:

- Grant permissions on roles. Managing roles is much easier than granting permissions to individual users. Roles should be designed based on specific job functions and should provide only necessary permissions.

- Create a hierarchical role system. Some users may require basic read access to specific tables, while others will require full access to some tables and read access to others. Since roles can be contained in other roles, it might be worthwhile to create groups such as **DB - Basic Access**, **DB - Intermediate Access**, and **DB - Full Access**. The intermediate role could contain Basic Access permissions plus additional permissions.

- **Assign permissions on views and stored procedures.** If your database contains an employee information table that includes basic information (employee name, employee number) and sensitive information (such as salary), you may choose to create a view or stored procedure that obtains only nonsensitive data. As long as the view owner has access to the table, the user of the view will be able to access the data. You can remove all access to the table except for the view or stored procedure's owner. You can then grant users access to these objects without worrying that they will query sensitive information.

- **Use stored procedures.** Apart from security management benefits, **stored procedures execute much faster than the same SQL statements executed manually and can cut down on network traffic.** They also make interactions with database objects easier for developers and end-users.

AUDITING DATABASE ACTIVITY

SQL Server 7 lets you automatically log actions performed by users on specific database objects. Although technically it won't prevent wrongdoing or protect data directly, auditing is a vital function of any secure database server implementation. To view auditing information, do the following:

1. Expand the Management folder for the server for which you want to view the audit logs.

2. In the SQL Server Logs folder, click the Current log to view the most recent information or an Archive log to view older data.

3. You can modify the view by clicking the log name and selecting View. You can also click a column heading to sort by that value. Figure 3.11 shows a view of auditing information.

Auditing Database Activity 87

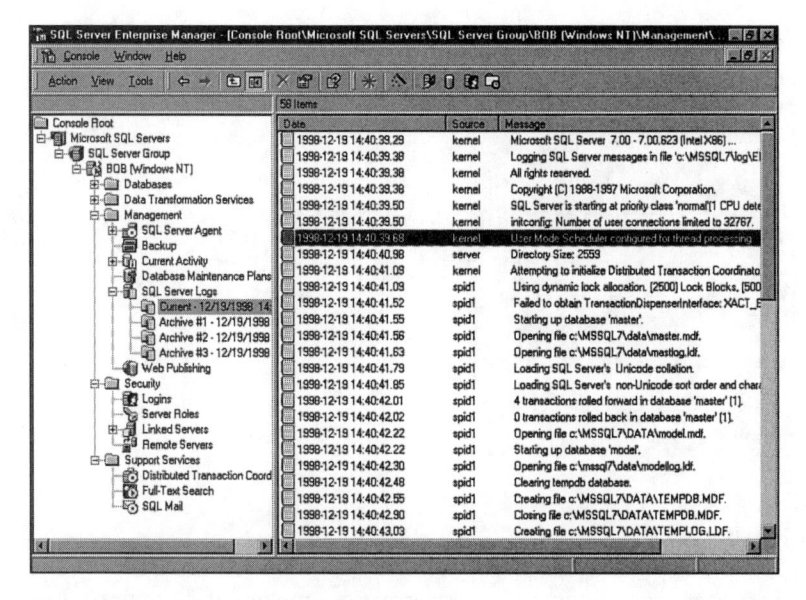

FIGURE 3.11
Viewing audit information.

The information displayed includes the date and time of the logged item, the process ID that generated the event, and the text of the logged message.

In addition to the default alerts, you can track other actions of interest. You can log specific information by configuring SQL Server alerts in the SQL Server Agent alerts option. To set an alert, do the following:

1. Expand the Management folder. Expand the SQL Server Agent folder, right-click Alerts, and select New Alert. You see the dialog box shown in Figure 3.12.

2. Name the alert and choose SQL Server event alert for the type. Check the Enabled box.

3. To define the alert condition, choose to report on an error message number (which may be user-defined) or on all events that have a specific severity. You can also assign the alert to only a specific database. Finally, enter the text for the error message.

4. Optionally, you can use the settings on the Response tab to notify database administrators of problems. Click OK to accept the settings.

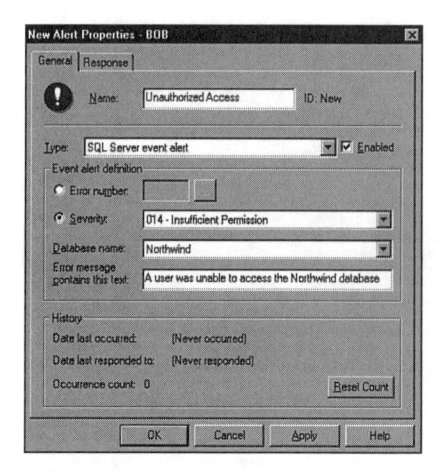

88 CHAPTER 3 Configuring and Managing Security

FIGURE 3.12
Setting SQL server alerts.

The activity logs can contain a lot of information, making it difficult to find exactly what you're looking for. To find a specific event, do the following:

1. Select Tools | Manage Server Messages. You see the dialog box shown in Figure 3.13.

2. In the Message text contains box, you can type in text you're searching for. You can also enter a specific error number and/or specify a certain severity.

3. Click Find to start the search.

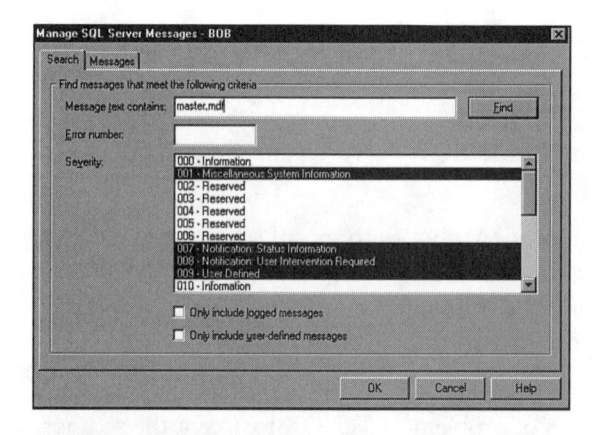

FIGURE 3.13
Searching server messages.

Server messages are also written to the Windows NT Application Log and can be viewed using the Event Viewer application.

You can view current database activity by selecting Management | Current Activity | Process Info. From this view, shown in Figure 3.14, you can find out which users are logged into the database server, what operations are being performed, and which objects are currently locked. There are options to send a message to a connected user and to kill a specific process (if you have permissions).

SQL Server Profiler

The SQL Server Profiler allows you to graphically view important database information. It can display information about user logins, connections to the server, and specific details related to queries.

The Profiler works by using *traces*—files containing events that you want to monitor. It can store this information in a trace file or in a SQL Server database table. You can launch the SQL Server Profiler directly from the SQL Server 7 program group or from within Enterprise Manager by using the Tools menu.

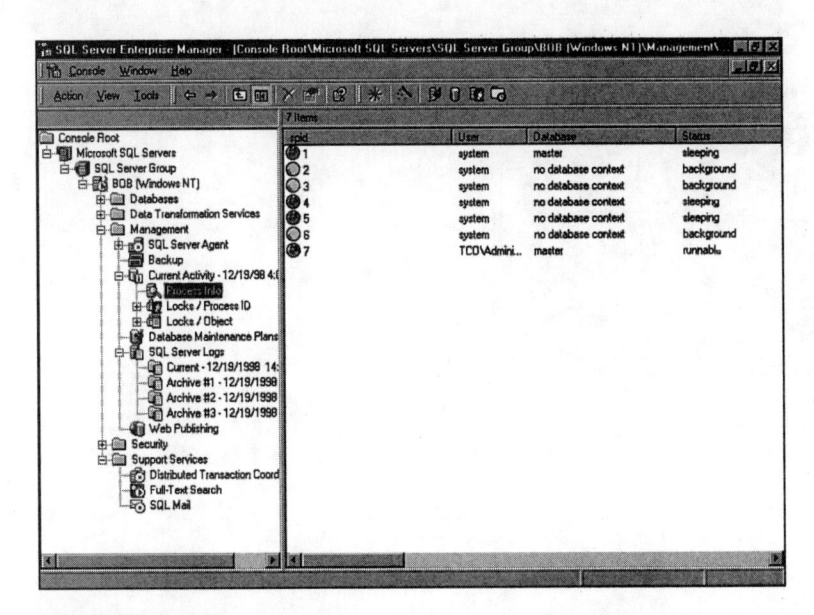

FIGURE 3.14
Viewing current server activity.

Follow these steps to create a trace:

1. Open the Profiler in the Microsoft SQL Server program group.

2. Select File | New | Trace. You see the dialog box shown in Figure 3.15. Enter a Trace Name and select the server you want to monitor.

3. Choose to save the collected information to a text file or to a SQL Server database.

4. On the Events tab, shown in Figure 3.16, add the events you want to monitor. The lower portion of the dialog box gives you a brief description of each item.

5. On the Data Columns tab, choose the type of information you want to view for each event. Again, a brief description of each column type is provided.

6. Finally, on the Filters tab, you can select specific criteria to include and exclude in events for this trace.

7. Click OK to save the trace file you've created.

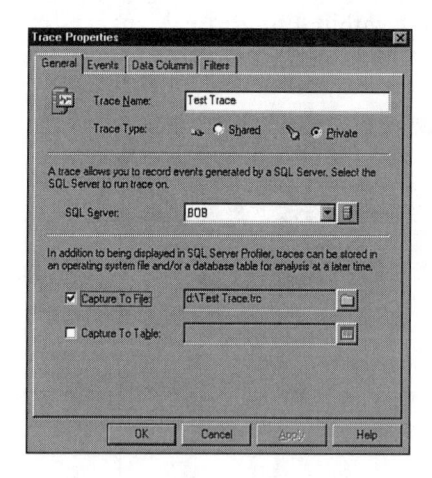

FIGURE 3.15
Creating a new trace in the SQL Server Profiler.

Auditing Database Activity 91

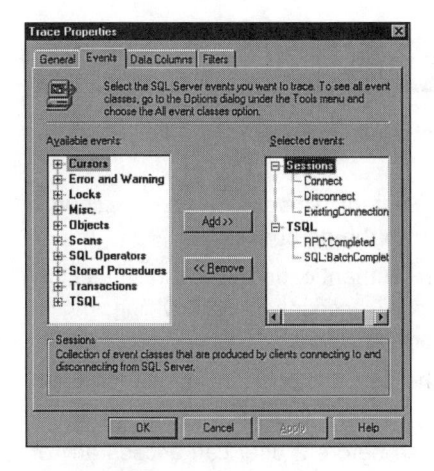

FIGURE 3.16
Adding events to a profile trace file.

To execute the trace you just created, select File | Run Traces and select a sample trace or one you created. A display will show information related to monitored events (see Figure 3.17). You can run multiple traces at the same time to record different kinds of information. To simulate the recorded information later, you can replay a trace by using the Replay menu. Finally, to view captured information, you can select File | Open and then choose Trace File (if you saved to a file) or Trace Table (if you saved to a SQL Server table).

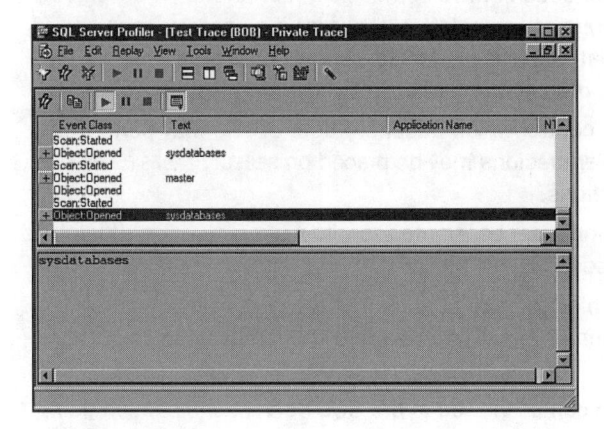

FIGURE 3.17
Running a trace in SQL Profiler.

What Is Important to Know

The following bullets summarize the chapter and accentuate the key concepts to memorize for the exam:

- If Windows NT Authentication is selected, Windows NT user accounts must be given permissions to log in to the database.
- The Windows NT and SQL Server authentication mechanisms allow users to log in using their Windows NT account or by providing a valid SQL Server user name and password.
- Login auditing can be specified in the Server properties using Enterprise Manager.
- A login must be added to a database before a user can access any of that database's objects.
- SQL Server roles let you easily manage groups of users. Users are assigned to roles. Roles can be granted permissions on database objects.
- Fixed server roles are used to manage database server functions. Fixed database roles allow for the management of database objects. All users with permissions to access a database are members of the public role. Application roles are protected by passwords and can be created for programs that enforce their own security. Finally, you can create user-defined roles to more easily assign permissions to multiple users.
- SQL Server permissions may be set to grant (the user is allowed permissions), deny (the user doesn't have permissions), or revoke (unspecified). In general, permissions are cumulative. However, if a user is a member of any group or role that is explicitly denied permissions, he or she will not be able to access a resource regardless of other permissions.
- Object permissions control which actions a user or role may perform on database objects. Permissions may be placed on SELECT, INSERT, UPDATE, and other SQL functions.
- Statement permissions can be granted to allow users to create, delete, and modify databases.
- Auditing can be enabled to track actions that are performed on database objects. The SQL Server Agent can be used to identify specific auditing events.
- Auditing information can be viewed in the SQL Server Logs section using Enterprise Manager.
- SQL Server Profiler can be used to view specific database information, including logon, logoff, and object access events. The collected data can be stored for later analysis.

OBJECTIVES

Managing and maintaining a reliable database is one of a database manager's most important tasks. The data stored in a SQL database is by far the most costly portion of the server. It would have the most adverse affect on your company if lost. Having said this, expect the topics covered in this chapter to make up a significant portion of the test.

The SQL Server 7.0 Administration test deals more with the implementation of a database than with the database's design. Here are the test objectives covered in this chapter:

▶ Create and manage data:
  - Create data files, filegroups, and transaction log files.
  - Specify growth characteristics.

▶ Load data using various methods, including the INSERT and SELECT INTO statements, bcp, DTS, BULK INSERT, and Transfer Manager.

▶ Back up and restore system and user databases, performing a full backup, a transaction log backup, a differential backup, and a filegroup backup.

▶ continues...

CHAPTER 4

Managing and Maintaining Data

OBJECTIVES continued

- Manage replication:
  - Configure distribution, publishing, and subscribing servers.
  - Create publications.
  - Set up and manage subscriptions.
- Automate administrative tasks:
  - Define jobs.
  - Define alerts.
  - Define operators.
  - Set up SQL Server Agent Mail for job notification and alerts.
- Enable access to remote data:
  - Set up linked servers.
  - Set up security for linked databases.

CREATING AND MANAGING DATA

This portion of the chapter looks at creating and managing databases by creating data files, filegroups, and transaction log files. Then it reviews the options for growing the database.

Creating Files, Logs, and Filegroups

When a database is created in SQL Server 7 (see Figure 4.1), a primary data file is created and is given an .mdf file extension. A copy of the *model* database, which includes the system tables, is copied to the new database. Therefore, the new database must be as large as or larger than the model database.

At least one transaction log file is also created, with an extension of .ldf. A secondary file can, but does not have to, be created for the database. If a secondary file is created, it will have an .ndf extension.

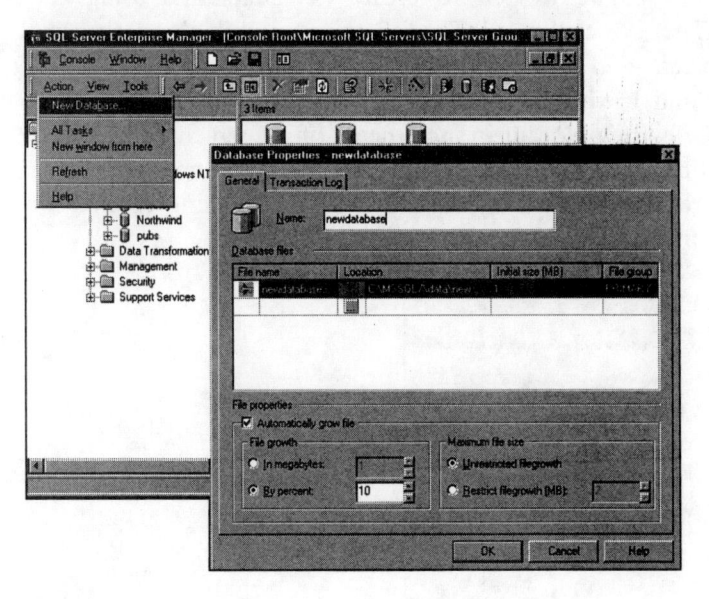

FIGURE 4.1
Database files created with a new database.

There are several ways to create a database in SQL Server 7, including, from most automated to least, the Create Database Wizard, the SQL Server Enterprise Manager, and the CREATE DATABASE statement. With the Create Database Wizard, shown in Figure 4.2, you simply answer the questions as they come up.

The Create Database Wizard can be started from the SQL Server Enterprise Manager, as shown in Figure 4.3. Click the server that will host the database, and then select Tools | Wizards | Database | Create Database Wizard.

To create a database from SQL Server Enterprise Manager without the aid of a wizard, right-click the server you want to create the database on and select New and Database. You will see a dialog box in which you can enter the primary database filename and location, growth characteristics, and log filenames and locations. It is recommended that the log files and primary database file be placed on different physical drives for added fault tolerance and better performance.

Script files can also be written to create new databases using the CREATE DATABASE command. The following example shows the syntax and commands used to create the monkey database with a 50MB primary data file and 15MB log file. The maximum size the file can grow to is 75MB. Growth will occur in increments of 10 percent. The transaction log will be set to grow in increments of 2MB to a maximum size of 20MB. Note that the primary file and log file are being created on two different drives.

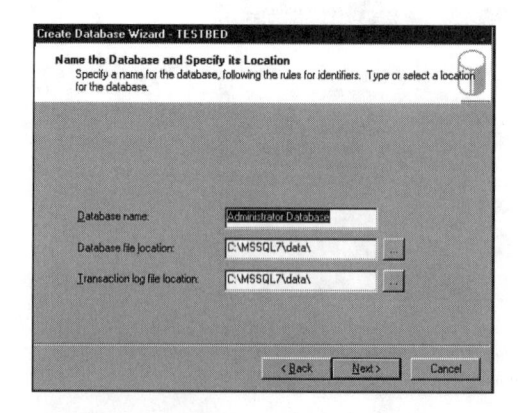

FIGURE 4.2
The Create Database Wizard.

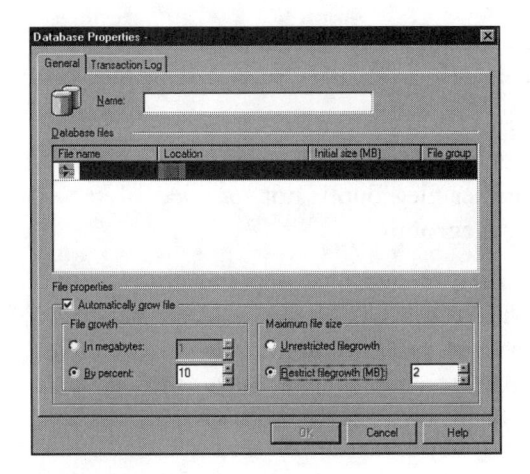

FIGURE 4.3
SQL Server Enterprise Manager database creation.

```
CREATE DATABASE monkey
ON
  Primary (NAME=monkey_data,
  FILENAME='d:\mssql7\data\monkey.mdf',
  SIZE=50MB,
  MAXSIZE=75,
  FILEGROWTH=10%)
LOG ON
  (NAME=monkey_log,
  FILENAME='e:\data\logfiles\monkey.ldf',
  SIZE=15MB,
  MAXSIZE=20MB,
  FILEGROWTH=2MB)
```

The ALTER DATABASE statement can be used to create new log files or modify existing ones, as well as add secondary data files. The following example shows a secondary data file being added to the monkey database:

```
ALTER DATABASE monkey
ADD FILE (NAME='monkey_data2',
FILENAME='f:\data\monkey2.ndf',
SIZE=35MB,
MAXSIZE=50MB)
GO
```

Filegroups allow the administrator to place different objects on specific disk drives if multiple drives are available. When configured properly, this technique can increase overall system performance, even though disk striping can be implemented to achieve the same affect with less administrative overhead.

A filegroup doesn't include the log file, only the database files, because log disk space is managed separately from data space. Also, files can belong to only one filegroup.

When a database is created, a default filegroup is created that contains the primary data file and, if another filegroup is not specified, all tables and indexes not placed in other filegroups.

The administrator can create a user-defined filegroup and place specific objects in it. This is done with the ALTER DATABASE statement specifying the FILEGROUP keyword, as shown in the following example. Here, a new filegroup named bananagroup is created, and the new secondary data file is added to the filegroup:

```
ALTER DATABASE monkey
ADD FILEGROUP bananagroup
GO

ALTER DATABASE monkey
ADD FILE
  (NAME='monkey_data3',
  FILENAME = 'f:\data\monkey3.ndf',
  SIZE=30MB,
  MAXSIZE=40MB)
TO FILEGROUP bananagroup
GO
```

It is important to note that if the automatic growth option is not configured, or the disk drive runs out of space, no new data can be added to the system tables.

Growing Your Database

Database size and growth characteristics and log file size and growth characteristics can be configured separately. The maximum size and incremental growth rate can be configured using the SQL Server Enterprise Manager, shown in Figure 4.4, or the ALTER DATABASE statement.

The growth can be configured to be incremented in megabytes of space or percentage of space. If an amount of space is configured, the database will grow by that amount each time more space is needed. If a percentage is configured, the database will grow by a percentage of the current size of the database. The following example shows the log file just shown being set to 18MB using the ALTER DATABASE statement.

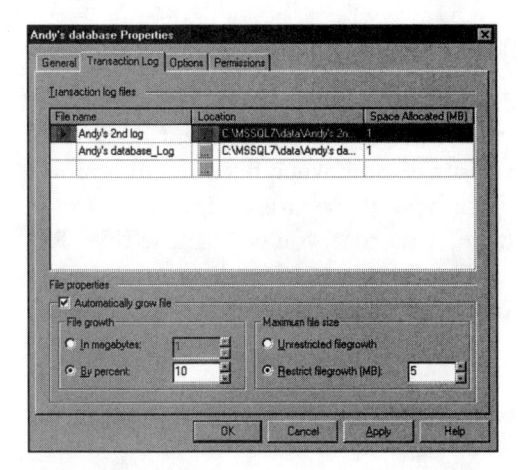

FIGURE 4.4
SQL Server Enterprise Manager growth configuration.

```
ALTER DATABASE monkey
  MODIFY FILE (NAME='monkey_log',
  SIZE=18MB)
GO
```

> ### At A Glance: Creating, Enhancing, and Growing Your Database
>
> To create a database, use the Create Database Wizard, the SQL Server Enterprise Manager, or the CREATE DATABASE statement.
>
> To enhance performance, create a filegroup. This allows you to place specific files of a database on specific physical drives. If multiple drives are used, the default filegroup is automatically used.
>
> You can grow your database manually or automatically. If you grow it automatically, you can set the growth characteristics to increment by a percentage of the current size of the database or by a specific size. The database and transaction log growth characteristics are configured separately.

LOADING DATA

Several methods are available for loading a database. The tools discussed in this section can be used to populate a database from various sources. Some of the methods provide a GUI-based interactive user interface, and others are Transact-SQL statements that can be used in scripting.

The INSERT Statement

The INSERT statement can be used to add new rows to a new or existing table. By default, the right to use the INSERT statement is given to the sysadmin fixed server role and the db_owner fixed database role. When using this command, you will typically test to see if the table exists and then retrieve or create the table. After that, you will use the INSERT command to add a row of data. The following example creates a table called Tree with two columns, one an integer and the other a string, and adds a row:

```
CREATE TABLE Tree(column_1 int, column_2 varchar(10))
INSERT Tree VALUES(1, 'row#1')
```

The SELECT Statement

The SELECT statement can be used with several different clauses to provide a powerful scripting tool for populating a database. You will be expected to know how to combine the SELECT statement with the INTO clause to load data into a database. The online documentation for SQL 7 comes with detailed information about the SELECT statement and its use with the various clauses.

You must have the CREATE TABLE permission in the destination database in order to use SELECT and INTO. Typically, you will run a query and then use SELECT INTO to dump the results into a new table. The new table will be a local or global temporary table unless you execute sp_dboption to enable the select into/bulkcopy option prior to the SELECT statement. If the table is a temporary table, the table name must begin with a #.

Remember, when you name SQL Server objects, the fully qualified name has four identifiers: the server name, database name, owner name, and object name, each separated by a period. Fully qualified names are written in the following format:

```
servername.databasename.ownername.objectname
```

Each object created must have a unique name. When an object is referenced, the complete fully qualified name doesn't have to be provided, but the periods must be in place if an intermediate identifier isn't used. The following example uses the SELECT statement to load the table tree column1 to a temporary database tree2:

```
USE monkey
SELECT column_1
INTO #tree2
FROM Tree
```

BCP

The Bulk Copy Program (BCP) utility is a command-line utility that provides a useful tool for transferring large amounts of data to and from a SQL Server database to a heterogeneous environment that uses the ODBC API. With SQL 6.x, the API used to provide this capability was the DB_Library API. The functions available with the Microsoft SQL Server BCP utility are different from the functions available with non-Microsoft SQL Server ODBC bulk copy utilities, so be sure to review the functions available in the online help before using this tool.

BULK INSERT statements provide similar capabilities but are used only to import data, not export it. When using the BCP utility to transfer SQL 6.x to another format, the datetime and smalldatetime are converted to ODBC-format date stamps.

DTS

Several Data Transformation Services (DTS) utilities are available. Each is used to provide different capabilities. DTS utilities can be used to do the following:

- Copy a table schema and data between SQL Server and a heterogeneous database
- Build custom data warehouses and custom transformation objects for moving data to and from SQL Server and various data sources on a schedule

DTS utilities can't be used to copy constraints, defaults, rules, stored procedures, triggers, or user-defined data. When multiple steps are joined by a user, a DTS package is created and can be run. The DTS packages

data to be imported, manipulated, and stored. The source and destination can be heterogeneous, so these utilities can be used to transfer data even when a SQL database isn't the target or destination.

The DTS engine is known as a *DTS data pump* and provides a COM-based structure for importing and exporting to a wide range of relational and nonrelational databases. A brief description of each of the DTS utilities follows, with an example when each would be used:

- The DTS Import and Export Wizards are interactive utilities that can be started from the SQL Server Enterprise Manager or from the command prompt. The Import and Export Wizards can be used for simple import and export tasks. To start the DTS Wizard from the SQL Server Enterprise Manager, select a server, select Tools | Data Transformation Services, and then select Import Data or Export Data, as shown in Figure 4.5. When the Wizard starts, you will be allowed to select the data source and what type of data is being imported, as shown in Figure 4.6.

  To start the Import or Export Wizard from the command prompt, type `dtswiz` and press Enter. This will start the wizards without using the SQL Server Enterprise Manager. You can also start the Import or Export Wizard by selecting Start | Programs | Microsoft SQL Server 7.0 | Import and Export Data.

- DTS Package Designer is a scripting tool that allows DTS packages to be created and executed. DTS Package Designer should be used if more complex workflows need to be designed. This tool is typically used when designing data warehouses where data will be imported from multiple sources. Use dtsrun to run a previously created DTS package.

- The DTS Transfer Manager is used to migrate a SQL Server database from one server to another. This is usually done when the platform is changed, such as from an Intel-based computer to a DEC Alpha computer, or if the code pages or sort order are changing.

Loading Data 103

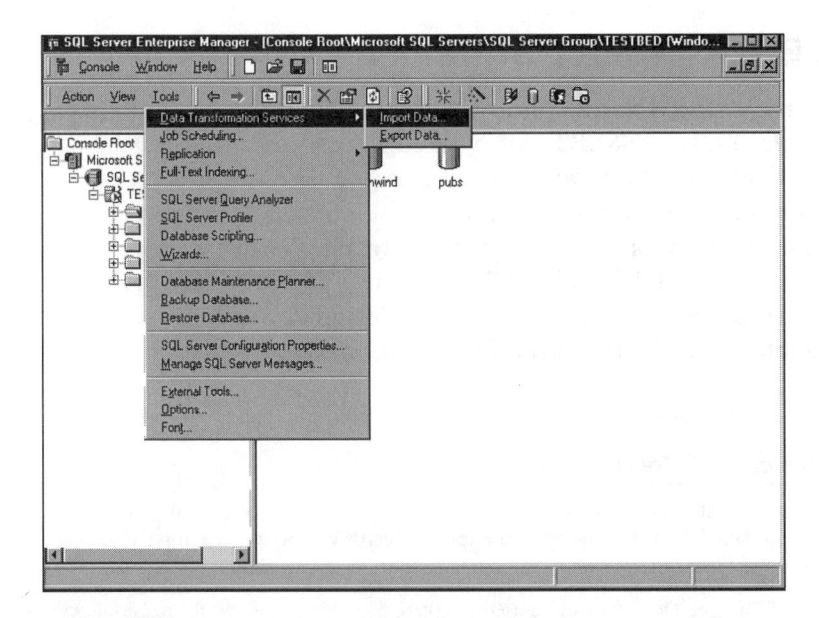

FIGURE 4.5
SQL Server Enterprise Manager DTS Data Transformation Wizards.

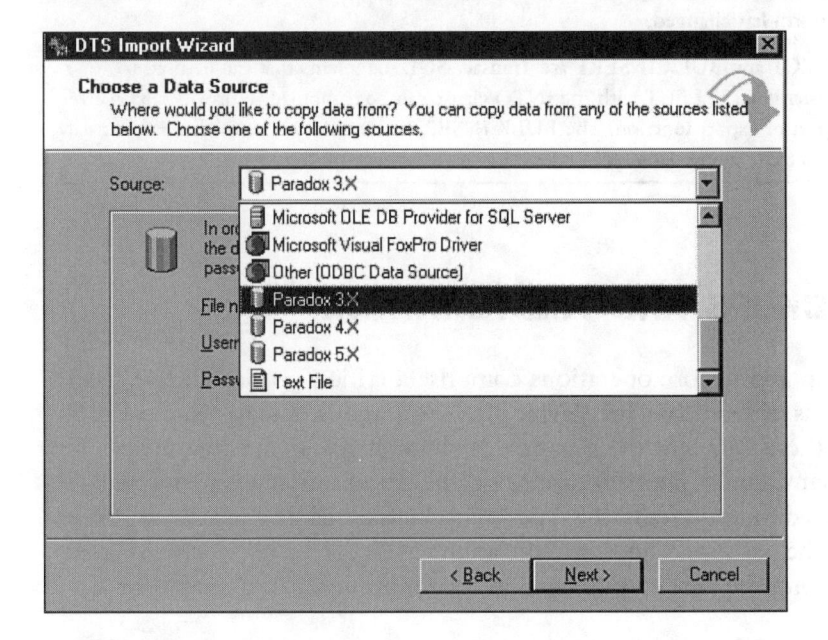

FIGURE 4.6
DTS Import Wizard data source type.

The BULK INSERT Statement

To use the BULK INSERT utility, you must be in the sysadmin fixed server role. BULK INSERT can be used to load data into a database table or view. This utility would be used to populate a SQL Server table or view rather than export data from a SQL server to a heterogeneous environment. Most of the 4800 series of errors indicate a problem with performing the BULK INSERT statement. The following example inserts the data from a tab-delimited text file andy.txt with two columns of data into the table tree of the database monkey:

```
BULK INSERT monkey.dbo.tree
FROM 'c:\temp\andy.txt'
```

At A Glance: DTS Tools

The Data Transformation Services (DTS) offer several tools for importing and exporting data. The DTS Import and Export Wizards can be used to import and export large blocks of data when the operations are relatively simple.

The DTS Package Designer can be used to create complex workflows for manipulating data as it is being transferred.

The DTS Transfer Manager is used to import data between SQL Servers when the platform has changed.

SELECT and BULK INSERT are Transact-SQL statements that can be used to transfer data. SELECT with the INTO clause can be combined to provide a powerful import or export function. The BULK INSERT statement can be used to import data into a SQL Server database.

Backups and Restorations

Backup and restore operations comprise a critical portion of the tasks a DBA is responsible for. Typically, the data is much more valuable than the equipment the database is running on. If the data is lost, the company could go bankrupt. For the certification test, you will be expected to understand the types of backups available and how to restore from the backups. Figure 4.7 shows the SQL Server Enterprise Manager displaying the backup information for the Andy's database.

Here are the types of backups SQL Server performs and the relative impacts on the system:

- Uses the industry-standard "fuzzy" backup
  - Writes an inconsistent set of pages
  - Includes a transaction log to be consistent
- Minimal impact on running transactions
  - Online backups
  - About 5 percent degradation in system throughput during backups
- Fast, noncached, no transformations to data

Here are some of the new features of SQL Server 7 backup/restore:

- Automatic database creation/alteration on restore
- Differential backups
- Backup/restore files and filegroups
- Microsoft Tape Format (MTF)
- Resume interrupted operation near point of failure
- List files in a backup set
- Assisted restoration
- Verify a backup set without having to restore it
- Simplified configuration

SQL Server 7 offers many utilities. Two of the more important ones are the backup and restore utilities, which allow "online" backups that have little impact on the performance of the databases.

Incremental backups can greatly reduce backup times because they back up only the data that has changed since the last incremental or complete backup. This can eliminate the time the server spends rolling transactions forward. When restoring a backup, the restoration process automatically creates the databases and all necessary files, making the restoration process very easy.

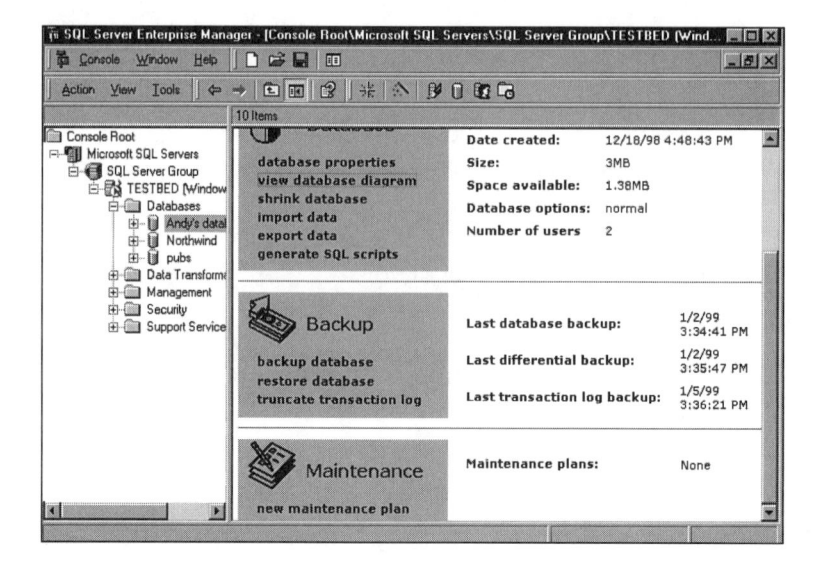

FIGURE 4.7
SQL Server Enterprise Manager showing backup information.

Planning a Backup Strategy

One of the most important troubleshooting tools you will have at your disposal is a well-documented plan that is kept up-to-date. Backup strategies and restoration procedures are no different. With a well-thought-out plan, you can be proactive rather than reactive. If you can prevent failures before they happen, you're doing your job well.

When developing your backup plan, answer the following questions. Your answers should help you decide on the best SQL Server backup methods, devices, and media to use in your environment:

- How large is each database?
- How often does the data in the database change?
- Are some tables modified more often than others?
- If data is lost, how vital is your database to the daily operation of the enterprise?
- How important is it to never lose a change?
- How easy would it be to re-create lost data?
- What are your critical database production periods?

- When does the database experience heavy use, resulting in frequent insertions and updates?
- Will users access the database during backup operations?
- How long can you go between transaction log truncations?
- Do you need to keep a rotating series of backups?

> **NOTE:** A rotating series of backups allows you to restore some data if a backup is lost. It also lets you restore further back in time if a problem isn't detected for some time after it occurs.

- Is your SQL Server in a cluster?
- Is your SQL Server system in a multiserver environment with centralized administration?

Some factors that play a role in backups and restorations include the speed of the devices that you're backing up to and the type of devices (tape, disk, or Jaz). One method you can use to determine the time it will take to back up and restore your database is to perform a realistic backup and then attempt to restore the database. Notice the time it takes to accomplish both the backup and the restoration. This is the best method to use. It also makes you familiar with the process and ensures that you're getting the information you expected to get.

Here are the steps you can use:

1. Create a database backup of the real system and time the operation.
2. Create a transaction log backup and time the operation.
3. Restore a database backup and time the operation.
4. Apply the transaction log backup and time the operation.

As you plan your backup strategy, you need to consider where your database files and transaction logs are. The recommended strategy is to place your transaction logs on a disk separate from the database files (probably on the faster disks). This can increase performance, efficiency, and your ability to recover up to the point of failure rather than to the last backup.

Other common problems that you might experience with backups and restorations include a corrupt or nonexistent backup. The best way to overcome this is through prevention. It takes only one catastrophe to drive home this point. Make sure you view backup logs to see if any errors were encountered, and periodically do a trial restoration to ensure that you have a good tape.

How long should you use tapes to back up important data? You might hear many different answers regarding this topic. Here are a few simple tips to follow that might keep you out of trouble:

- Rotate your tapes frequently.
- Inspect your tapes before and after a backup. Look for cracks, broken tape, and dry rot.
- Check the catalog for each tape to ensure that it contains what you backed up.

Here are some things to consider when restoring a database and its transaction log:

- When a database is restored from a backup, the database must not be in use.
- In the case of a media failure, drop the database before attempting to restore it.
- When you restore the transaction logs, they must be restored in the same sequence in which they were backed up.
    - SQL Server checks the time stamps on each backed-up database and transaction log to see that the sequence is correct.
    - When the entire sequence of transaction log backups has been restored, the database is restored to its state at the time of the last transaction log backup.
- If you need to recover the *master* database and you don't have a valid backup, you can use DISK REINIT and DISK REFIT to accomplish the restoration.

If your *master* is corrupt, you can recreate it by

- Running the SQL Server 7 Setup program

and

- Rebuilding the *master* database. When rebuilding the *master*, you must use the same
  - Character set
  - Sort order
  - Installation path and location name
  - Size for the *master* device as in the original installation
- Starting SQL Server in single-user mode
- Executing DISK REINIT to reinitialize each device in the sysdevices table

The DISK REINIT statement can be used to restore device entries to the system tables when

- The device exists
- The entry in the sysdevices table no longer exists

Once this has been accomplished, you can execute DISK REFIT to rebuild the tables for

- sysusages
- sysdatabases

Full Backups

A full backup is used to create a baseline for disaster recovery. All original files, objects, and data are backed up, as well as any activity that takes place during the backup. Also, any uncommitted transactions in the transaction log are backed up. To back up a specific database using the SQL Server Enterprise Manager, right-click the database being backed up and select All Tasks | Backup Database. You see the SQL Server Backup dialog box, shown in Figure 4.8.

110 CHAPTER 4 Managing and Maintaining Data

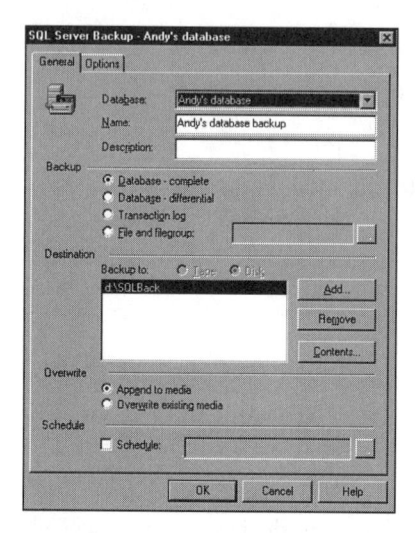

FIGURE 4.8
The SQL Server Backup dialog box.

Transact-SQL statements can also be used to perform a backup or restore of databases, files, filegroups, or log files. The BACKUP DATABASE statement can be used to back up an entire database to tape or a disk drive, or through named pipes, as shown in the following example. In the example, the monkey database is backed up to the monkeyback.dat file on the D drive:

```
BACKUP DATABASE monkey
TO DISK='d:\backups\monkeyback.dat'
```

Backups created using these statements can only be restored to a SQL Server 7 server. If backing up to a CD, be sure to specify a BLOCKSIZE of 2048. You can also restore using Transact-SQL statements. To restore the database monkey that was just backed up, the syntax would be as follows:

```
RESTORE DATABASE monkey
FROM DISK='d:\backups\monkeyback.dat'
```

There are several options available for customizing backups using Transact-SQL statements to limit the backup to transaction logs or specific files. Backups can be scheduled to start at predefined times.

Transaction Log Backups

Transaction log backups back up any changes made to the database since the last full or differential backup. In the event of loss of data, a transaction log backup requires a full backup, just as a differential backup does.

When a failure occurs, the full backup is applied, and then each transaction log, from oldest to most recent, is applied. Transaction logs store all changes made to the database, even if one particular item was modified a second or third time.

Differential Backups

A differential backup is used to back up the data that has changed since the last full backup. As with the full backup, any changes made during the differential backup, as well as the uncommitted changes to the transaction log, are backed up.

During a restoration, the full backup is applied, and then the differential backup is restored. Differential backups speed up the restoration process in the event of failure and are more effective in restoring a single file, because the backup is smaller.

Filegroup Backups

Filegroups are used when multiple physical drives are installed in a SQL Server computer. A default filegroup is used if the administrator doesn't specify a filegroup and multiple drives are in use. You can enhance performance on large databases that span multiple drives by placing specific files on specific drives.

In a case where filegroups are used to increase performance, increasing backup performance and minimizing the need to perform full backups should be considered. A filegroup backup can be used to back up specific files or filegroups rather than the entire database.

You can back up to 16 files or filegroups, but you must be sure to perform a transaction log backup to use in conjunction with the filegroup backup.

Backup Strategy

Here are two examples of a backup/restoration strategy:

Example 1

- Every Saturday night at midnight, a full backup is performed.
- Every Thursday morning at 2 a.m., a differential backup is performed.
- Every weeknight at midnight, a transaction log backup is performed.

If the data is corrupted on Friday afternoon, you would do the following to restore it:

- Restore the full backup from the previous Saturday.
- Restore the differential backup from Thursday morning.
- Restore the transaction log backup from Thursday night at midnight.

Example 2

- Every Saturday night at midnight, a full backup is performed.
- Every weekday morning at 2 a.m., a differential backup is performed.
- Every weekday during business hours (8:00 to 5:00), a transaction log backup is performed.

If the data is corrupted on Tuesday afternoon at 2:45 p.m., you would do the following to restore it:

- Restore the full backup from the previous Saturday.
- Restore the differential backup from Tuesday morning at 2 a.m.
- Restore the transaction log backups in order from Tuesday 8:00 a.m. through Tuesday 2:00 p.m. Before performing the restore, you could back up the transaction log using the NO_TRUNCATE option, then after completing the restore of the regular transaction log backups, restore the transaction log created at the beginning of the restoration process.

At A Glance: Backups and Restorations

The sysadmin fixed server role, db_owner fixed database role, and db_backupoperator fixed database role have the ability to perform backups.

Backups can be stored on a hard disk or tape device or through named pipes.

Always back up the system database files after modifying the master database, the msdb database, or the model database.

Backups can't be performed while you're creating a database or index, while the database is growing, or while operations that are not logged are being performed. Examples include SELECT INTO and UPDATE TEXT.

When performing a restoration, restore the full backup first, and then any differential or transaction log backups that have been created since the full backup. Perform the restorations in order from oldest to most recent.

Managing Replication

Replication provides the ability to place data on several SQL servers across your network to provide SQL clients with local data access rather than access across a WAN. The data is maintained on a publisher SQL Server, then a distributor SQL Server provides the updated information to a Subscriber SQL Server. The publisher and distributor can be the same SQL Server, or the tasks can be separated onto different machines.

Replication can require having permission to write information to a stand-alone server or a server that belongs to a different domain than the publishing or distribution server. Make sure the sending SQL Server's user account and password used to perform the update has rights on the receiving SQL Server. When planning a replication strategy, be sure that the following are true:

- Adequate memory is available for the distribution server.
  - The server designated as the distribution server requires a minimum of 32MB of RAM, with at least 16MB of RAM dedicated to SQL Server. (With SQL Server, the more RAM, the better.)
  - For larger SQL databases on a server, the rule of thumb is to give much of the RAM to SQL and never let the operating system have more than 40MB.

- The working directory is available to the publication server.
- When upgrading enterprise servers in replication, you must upgrade the distribution server before upgrading any other servers.
- Make sure that all SQL Servers are running SQL Server 7 or 6.5. Servers running 6.5 and participating in replication with 7 servers should have the most recent service pack for SQL Server.

SQL Server 7 automatically supports both publisher and subscriber servers from SQL Server 6.5 and SQL Server 7 replication servers. Before you set up replication between different versions of SQL Server, you need to ensure that the following criteria have been met:

- Run Replp70.sql (found in \mssql7\install) on the SQL Server 6.5 subscriber server, then sp addpublisher70. This allows the 6.5 server to incorporate 7 servers' information.
- In order for a SQL Server 6.5 publisher server to use a SQL Server 7 distribution server, the two servers must be on different computers.
- SQL Server 7 pushes subscriptions to SQL Server 6.5 servers.
- The default protocol should be either named pipes or MultiProtocol.
- If you're using SQL servers in different domains, you must establish a trust between the different domains so the account used for authentication has rights to perform the replication.
- You need to ensure that there is enough disk space for both databases and transaction logs.
- You need to have the appropriate service account created in Windows NT.

As with anything dealing with network design and implementation, you should come up with a solid plan for replication. A good plan helps prevent problems before they have a chance to materialize.

The replication plan can be complex, depending on the needs of the organization and the size and locations of the SQL Servers. With SQL Server 7's Graphical User Interface (GUI), the implementation becomes pretty easy. To determine the appropriate replication scenario, you should look at the following:

- Determine the purpose of the replicated data.
- Assess network connections:
  - Slow, unreliable connections
  - Reliable and steady connections
  - WAN connections
  - LAN connections
  - Connections across domains
- Is load balancing of information required?

Plan the implementation:

- Determine the size of the database and transaction logs.
- Determine an appropriate schedule for replication (frequency).
- Determine an appropriate schedule for synchronization (frequency).
- Which synchronization method will you employ?
  - Distributed Transactions - Microsoft Distributed Transaction Coordinator (MS-DTC), which is part of the Microsoft Transaction Server (MTS), can be used to perform distributed updates. This component uses a two-phase commit protocol to make sure that all sites are updated at the same time. This method of synchronization provides the highest degree of synchronization, but relies on all systems being available for updates. If one server is down, the update will fail. This is not a replication method, but a product that provides a vehicle to update information in a timely manner and provides the highest degree of synchronization. It requires all servers that are part of the distribution group. With MS-DTC, all sites can contain read/write copies of the information being distributed.
  - Transactional Replication - With this method, only changes are replicated. One site has the read/write copy of the information that is maintained and distributed, and the other sites have read-only copies that are updated by the single site. This keeps information consistent, but limits the update ability to one server.

- Transaction Replication with Updating Subscribers - This type of replication allows all sites to perform updates. The modified information is eventually replicated to all other sites, but does not occur as quickly as it does with MS-DTS. With this method of replication, the information can be updated at all sites, but chances for conflicts increase.

- Snapshot - With this method, the entire database is replicated (regardless of whether the information has changed) on a timed basis or on demand.

- If you have local data that needs to be updated, establish a method to uniquely identify local data from data that is replicated:
  - Set up location-specific codes so that data is not overwritten.
  - Create a composite primary key with a location code.

Determine the number of subscribers. Estimating the number of subscribers will help you determine:

- The load on the particular server
- The appropriate size for the transaction log

Estimating the frequency of replication will help you determine:

- The appropriate time for each subscriber to receive replicated data
- The appropriate backup strategy
- The appropriate size for the transaction log
- Load balancing requirements

Finally, you want to consider some maintenance issues:

- The frequency and method used to clean up old jobs
- Database and transaction log backup strategies

Remember, a good, well-thought-out plan generally will produce the results you're looking for.

Configuring Servers

Three different types of servers are created for replication: publishing, distribution, and subscriber. To configure replication, from the SQL Server Enterprise Manager highlight the server that replication is being configured on and select Tools | Wizards. The Select Wizard window should appear.

From the Wizard selection box, you can configure a publisher or distribution server, as well as configure push or pull subscribers. Another way to configure replication is to highlight the server being configured, select Tools | Replication, and then configure the type of replication needed, as shown in Figure 4.9.

Creating Publications

From the Replication Wizard, start the Create Publication Wizard to publish information. You can choose the type of publishing you want and the objects that will be published, as well as decide which server will be the distributor.

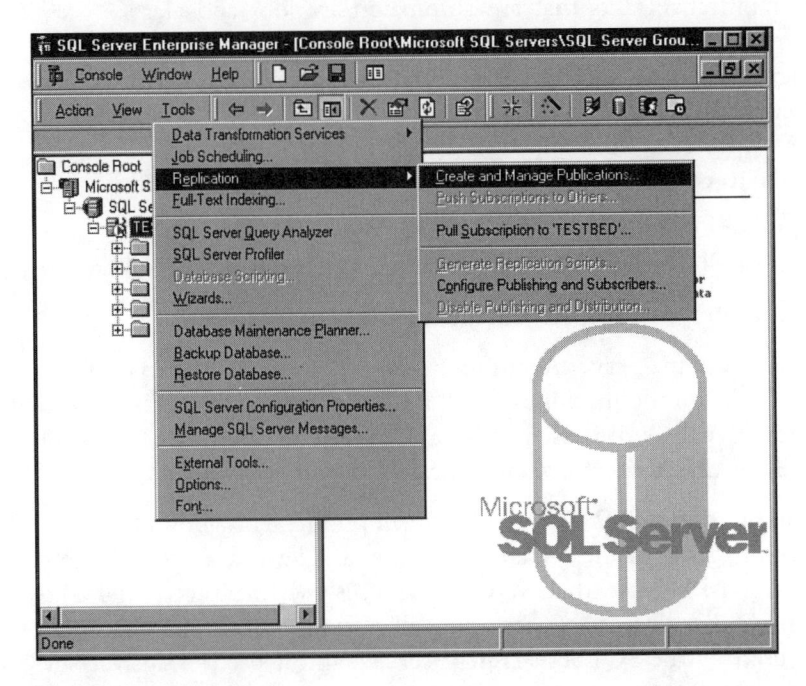

FIGURE 4.9
Creating and managing publications.

Subscriptions

From the Replication Wizard, select the Push or Pull Subscriber Wizard, depending on which type you want. Select the distribution servers you want to get the published data from.

At A Glance: Server Configuration and Filtering

The three types of servers configured in replication are the publisher server, distribution server, and subscriber server.

Subscription can be configured as push from the distribution server or pull from the subscriber server.

Filtering can be used to limit the amount of data provided to the subscriber server. This can be set up as horizontal (row) or vertical (column) filtering.

The types of server replication available are snapshot, distribution, log reader, and merge agent.

AUTOMATING ADMINISTRATIVE TASKS

The administrative tasks that are automated are jobs and alerts. A job is a sequence of functions that the server performs at a given time. Alerts are configured reactions to the jobs that are running. Operators are user accounts or roles that are configured to receive notification from an alert. As with most configuration items for SQL Server 7.0, a wizard is available to configure jobs, alerts, and which operators to notify.

To use these capabilities, the SQL Server must be configured properly. In order for all of these capabilities to work, you must do the following:

- Make sure the SQL Server Agent is running.

- Make sure the Server Agent user account has the ability to perform the tasks on the machines it will need to perform the tasks on. If a local user account is used on a stand-alone computer, the agent will only be able to perform tasks locally.

- Configure the SQL Server agent mail profile. This allows the SQL Server agent to send e-mail notification and have access to the messaging API. Note that SQL Server uses two mail accounts. The MSSQLServer service uses one mail session, SQL Mail. The other is used by the SQLServerAgent service and is used exclusively by the SQL Server Agent.

Defining Jobs

The Create Job Wizard, shown in Figure 4.10, takes you step by step through a SQL Server job configuration. The types of jobs that can be configured include backing up databases and maintaining indexes.

To start the Create Job Wizard using the SQL Server Enterprise Manager, highlight the server the job will run on, and then select Tools | Job Scheduling. This will start the Job Scheduling Wizard and allow a job to be configured at predefined times.

Defining Alerts

An alert can be configured to execute a procedure or secondary job in the event of a job's failure. The alert procedure can execute a given set of tasks or send an error alert message to a pager or an e-mail address. This provides a greater degree of error handling.

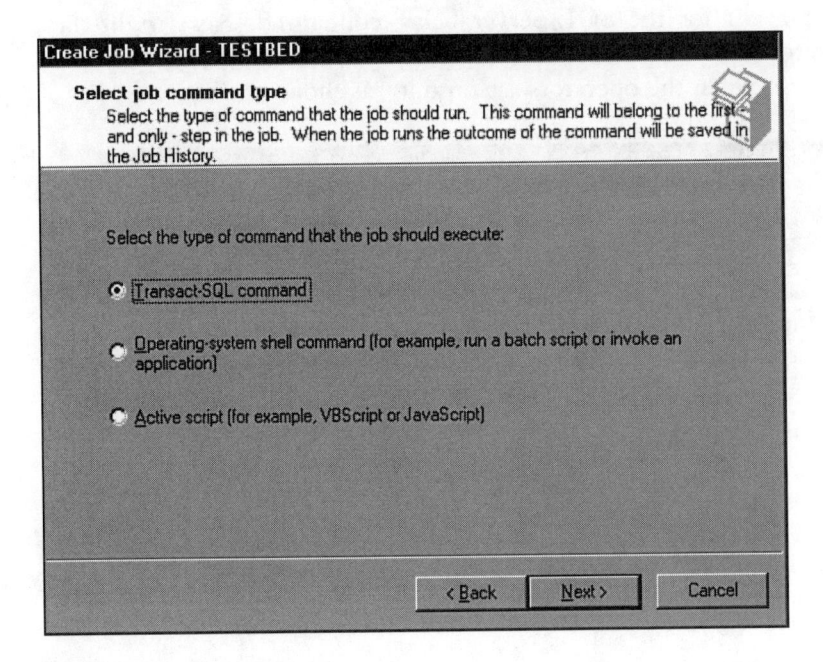

FIGURE 4.10
The SQL Server Create Job Wizard.

To configure an alert from the SQL Server Enterprise Manager, expand the server that the alert will be configured for. Expand the Management subfolder, and then expand the SQL Server Agent. Finally, right-click the Alerts subfolder.

A menu will appear that lets you configure a new alert or create a script from all the alerts (see Figure 4.11). Each alert can be configured with notification information for what user should be notified and the method of notification.

Defining Operators

Each alert can be configured to notify an operator through e-mail, pager, or a NET SEND command. Schedules can be configured that allow the alert process to notify different people at different times of the day. This allows flexibility in configuring who will be notified in the event of an anomaly. To configure the operator that will be alerted, expand the SQL Server agent for the SQL Server being configured. Next, right-click Operators. You can choose to configure the operators, mode of contact, and times when the operators are on duty, as shown in Figure 4.12.

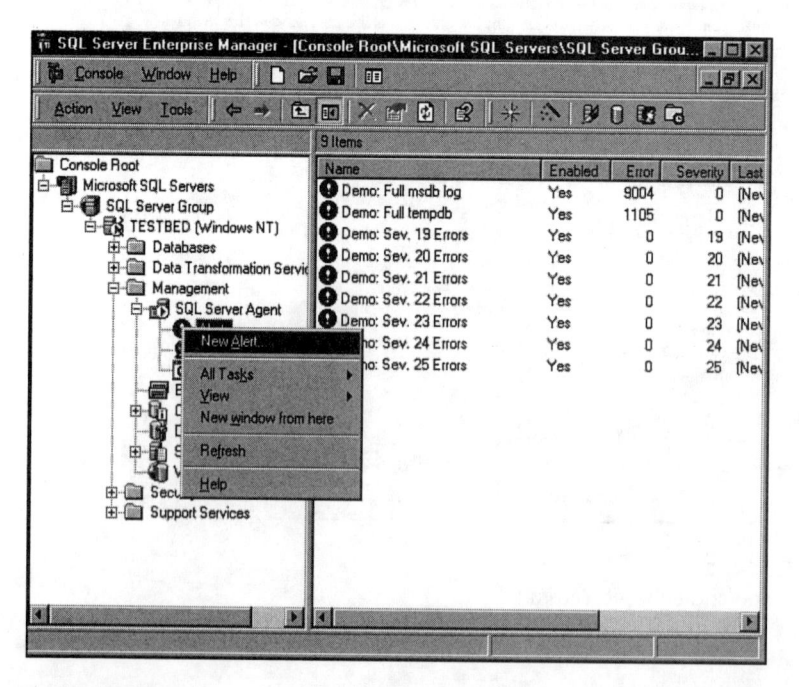

FIGURE 4.11
Alert configuration.

Automating Administrative Tasks 121

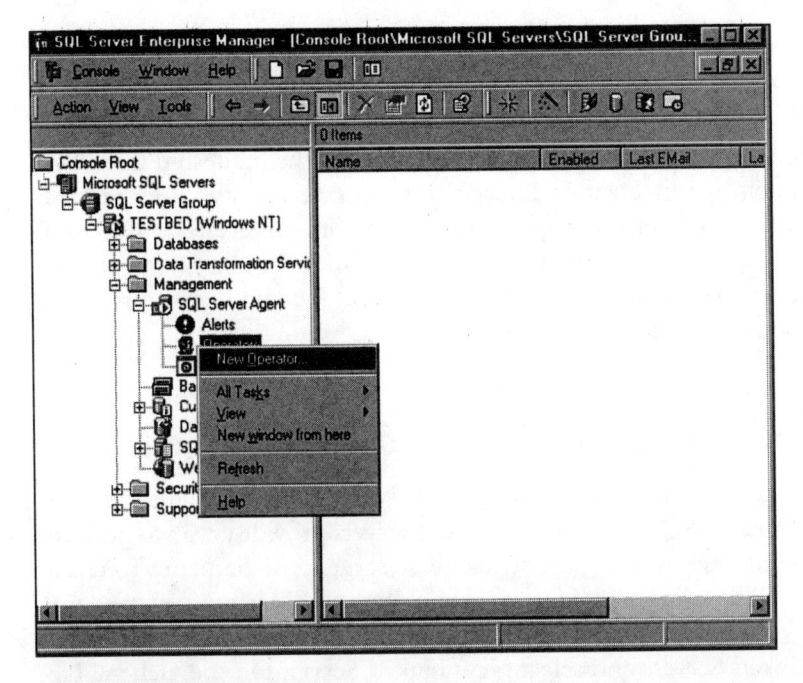

FIGURE 4.12
Operator alert scheduling.

At A Glance: Jobs, Alerts, and Mail Accounts

Jobs are tasks that can be grouped and then scheduled to be performed at certain times or when certain thresholds or predefined conditions are met. Examples include performing backups and moving data.

Alerts are scheduled to execute a task or series of tasks in the event of an anomaly. This might be a particular error during a scheduled backup. The task might restart the backup procedure.

Operator notification allows the SQL Server to notify a user or users when a preset condition is met. This notification can be through the NET SEND command, e-mail notification, or pager notification.

Two mail accounts are configured and used by SQL Server. The MSSQLServer service uses one mail session (known as SQL Mail), and the SQLServerAgent service has its own mail account defined, which is used exclusively by the SQL Server Agent.

Remote Data Access

SQL Server 7 has the ability to take an incoming client request and reroute the query to a remote server that stores the requested data. This is accomplished by creating linked servers. Linked servers use the OLE DB DLL to reform the request for the remote servers. The OLE DB DLL must be present on both servers in order for this to work. The remote server doesn't have to be a SQL Server 7 computer; it can be any database that provides OLE DB support.

Linked Server Configuration

Servers can be linked using the SQL Server Enterprise Manager or by using Transact-SQL statements. Linked servers provide a way to perform distributed queries in a multiple database server environment. To create a server link using the SQL Server Enterprise Manager, expand the server you're linking, and then expand the Security subfolder. Right-click Linked Servers and select New Linked Server. On the General tab, shown in Figure 4.13, provide the name of the server that will be linked to, and select either SQL Server or Other data source.

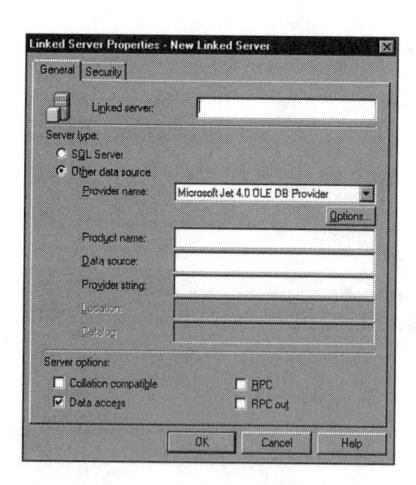

FIGURE 4.13
The General tab of the Linked Server Properties dialog box.

The stored procedure sp_addlinkedserver can be used to create the link if desired. To view linked server information, use the sp_linkedservers stored procedure. To drop a link, use the sp_dropserver stored procedure.

Linked Database Security

Authentication—that is, a valid username and password—are provided by the sender rather than the receiver, as is the case with RPC connections. The authentication can be configured using the SQL Server Enterprise Manager or through stored procedures. To configure authentication through the SQL Server Enterprise Manager, expand the server you're linking, and then expand the Security subfolder. Right-click Linked Servers and select New Linked Server. On the Security tab, shown in Figure 4.14, configure which form of authentication and which user account will be used.

The stored procedure sp_addlinkedsrvlogin can be used to configure login mappings. The sp_droplinkedsrvlogin stored procedure can be used to drop the login mappings if you would rather not use the SQL Server Enterprise Manager.

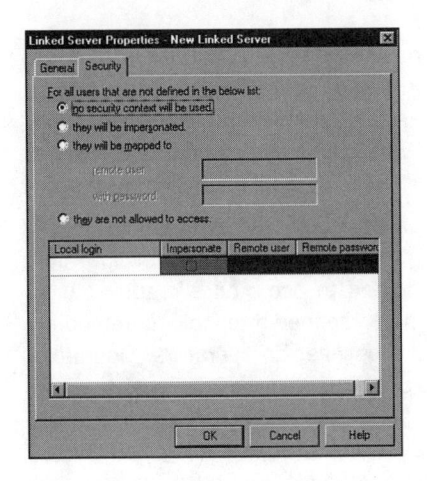

FIGURE 4.14
The Security tab of the Linked Server Properties dialog box.

What Is Important to Know

The following bullets summarize the chapter and accentuate the key concepts to memorize for the exam:

- You need to know how to manage and maintain data. You will be expected to know how to create data files, filegroups, and transaction log files. The two primary options for creating these files are through the SQL Server Enterprise Manager and by using Transact-SQL statements. When the new databases and transaction logs are created, you can specify the growth characteristics for each. They can be configured to grow to a maximum size. They can grow by a percentage of the database or log's current size or grow in megabytes.

- After the database, filegroups, and transaction logs are created, you will need to display a knowledge of the various methods available for populating the databases. These include using Transact-SQL statements such as INSERT, SELECT INTO, and BULK INSERT, as well as using bcp, the DTS utilities, and the Transfer Manager.

- Backing up and restoring data provides a safety net for the data stored on the SQL Servers. You will be tested on your ability to identify when full backups, differential backups, incremental backups, and transaction log backups should be performed, as well as how to do a filegroup backup.

- You will need to understand the terms involved with and tools used to configure replication. The distribution server is the server where data is maintained. The distribution server is the server responsible for providing updated data to subscriber servers. Subscriber servers provide a server located near the end user for providing published information.

- The operations of the SQL Server can be automated by creating jobs. A job is a scripted group of tasks to be performed by a SQL Server. Jobs can be configured to occur once or scheduled to occur on a regular basis. Alerts are scripts that are triggered when a defined threshold is exceeded. The alert can spawn a job and send messages to operators. Operators can be configured through the SQL Server Enterprise Manager to send e-mail messages, net messages, or phone calls to different defined users at various times of the day. This messaging is done through the use of two different mail accounts—one used by the MSSQLServer service, and the other used by the SQLServerAgent service.

- Linked servers can be configured to distribute data to several different machines. The client can then query one server, which can access linked servers to gather the information requested. Servers can be linked using stored procedures or through the SQL Server Enterprise Manager. The sending server sends the username and password for authentication.

OBJECTIVES

An important aspect of managing a SQL Server 7 database server is performance monitoring and optimization. Here are the test objectives for this part of the exam:

- ▶ Monitor SQL Server performance by using Performance Monitor and Profiler.
- ▶ Tune and optimize SQL Server memory and CPU usage.
- ▶ Limit resource use by queries by using the Query Governor.

CHAPTER 5

Monitoring and Optimization

Performance Monitoring Basics

Performance monitoring should be done with the same care as any other aspect of network and systems administration. First, before you can expect to improve performance, you need to have information about your current configuration. It's important to establish baseline measurements—averages of current activity—before making any changes. The overall goal will be to identify and *move* a performance bottleneck. A bottleneck is best defined as the slowest step in a given process, so it can't be eliminated. For example, suppose you're competing in a triathlon (that's 26 miles of running, 100 miles of cycling, and 5 miles of swimming), and your weakest skill is cycling. If you greatly improve your cycling abilities, your new weakness might be running. Despite the fact that a bottleneck is still present, you've realized an overall gain in your performance.

Although at first it might sound counterproductive, monitoring performance can have an impact on performance. For example, the Windows NT Performance Monitor uses memory itself, so running this application can affect memory-related statistics. However, if you consistently use the same tools to measure performance, the impact will be the same for all measurements.

After obtaining a reasonable picture of server activity, it's time to consider making changes. The most important rule when making performance tweaks is to change only one aspect of the system at a time. Otherwise, you might not be able to accurately gauge the effects of a change. For example, if you change network and memory settings on a single server and performance is unaffected, you can't be sure which change caused a performance increase and which one caused a decrease (thus evening each other out), or if these settings really made a difference at all. In this chapter, we'll look at methods for monitoring performance and ways you can apply this information to improve response times and throughput.

Monitoring SQL Server Performance

It can be very useful to know exactly what's going on with your server at any given time. For example, if you're supporting a transaction-intensive database application, you can determine at which times the server is experiencing the greatest load and identify overall trends. You can then use this information to answer questions such as when upgrades will be required.

Measuring SQL Server performance statistics has many benefits. It helps you do the following:

- Establish a baseline for predicting application performance and response times
- Maximize your hardware and software investment
- Plan hardware upgrades
- Troubleshoot performance problems

Using Performance Monitor

During installation, SQL Server Setup adds various counters that are available for use with the Windows NT Performance Monitor. Objects refer to a specific subsection of performance to be measured. One or more counters are available as part of an object. They measure a discreet aspect of this area. Objects may also have multiple instances, depending on the values being measured. For example, in measuring Windows NT CPU utilization, the object is Processor, the counter is % Processor Time, and the Instance is 0 for a single processor computer (multiprocessor machines will have instance options, including a Total instance). Table 5.1 lists some useful counters and describes their purposes.

TABLE 5.1

SQL SERVER PERFORMANCE COUNTERS

Object	Counter	Meaning
SQLServer:Block	Page Reads	Number of pages read from disk
SQLServer:Block	Page Writes	Number of pages written to disk
SQLServer:Buffer	Cache Hit Ratio	Percentage of information obtained from memory cache
SQLServer:Database Manager	Percent Log Used	Percentage of the log space currently used per database

continues

TABLE 5.1 continued

Object	Counter	Meaning
SQLServer:General Statistics	User Connections	Number of current user connections to the server
SQLServer:General Statistics	Total Server Memory (KB)	Total memory being used by the server
SQLServer:Locks	Lock Waits	Transactions that had to wait because of locks
SQLServer:Log Manager	Log Flushes	Number of times a log has been flushed per database
SQLServer:Replication Distribution	Delivered Transactions	Number of transactions from the last replication event

SQL Server includes a default Performance Monitor chart that displays vital information about the status of a SQL Server database. The Performance Monitor chart installed with SQL Server 7 provides useful basic information about the server (see Figure 5.1).

To run this chart, click Performance Monitor in the Microsoft SQL Server 7 program group. Memory information can be used to determine the optimal settings for a SQL Server 7 installation.

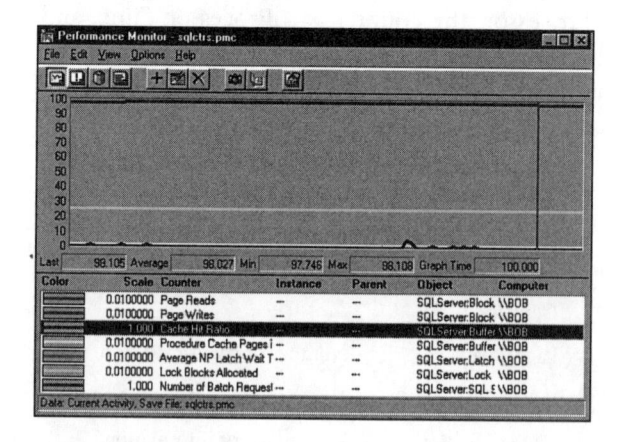

FIGURE 5.1
A basic SQL Server Performance Monitor chart.

In addition to the default SQL Server counters, all the standard Windows NT performance statistics may be used. Some of the more useful counters are described in Table 5.2.

TABLE 5.2

COMMON WINDOWS NT PERFORMANCE COUNTERS

Counter	Object	Meaning	Usefulness
Memory	Pages/sec	The number of times per second that the memory subsystem had to get information from the hard disk	If sustained greater than five, you might want to consider a RAM upgrade.
Logical Disk	% Free Space	Percentage of free space per volume or per all volumes	A value of less than 10% indicates that additional storage space is needed.
Physical Disk	Avg. Disk Queue Length	The number of tasks that had to wait for disk-based data	If high, disk performance might not be sufficient.
Server	Bytes Total/sec	The amount of data transferred by this server	High values indicate many and/or large file transfers to and from the server.
Server	Server Sessions	Number of active processes on this server	Indicates current activity. Use to compare loads on different machines.
Network Segment	% Network Utilization	What percentage of the total network bandwidth is in use	If sustained greater than 40%, this might be decreasing performance.
Redirector	Reads/Writes Denied/sec	Rejected requests for data transfer	Large file transfers might be occurring to and from this server.

To add counters to the Performance Monitor, do the following:

1. In Performance Monitor, select Edit | Add to Chart. You see the dialog box shown in Figure 5.2.

2. Enter the UNC name of the computer you want to monitor (the default will be the local machine).

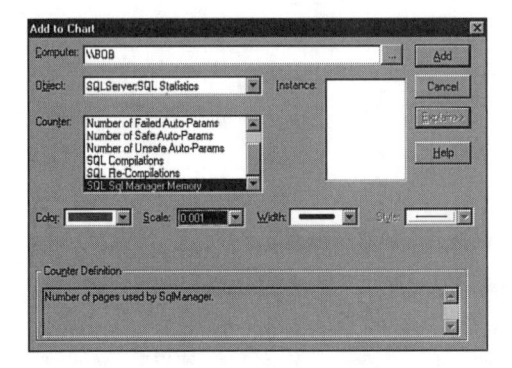

FIGURE 5.2
Adding a new counter to the Performance Monitor.

3. Select an object, counter, and instance (if applicable). To view a brief description of a value, click the Explain button.

4. Optionally, change the color, scale, and width of the chart options.

5. Click Add to include this value in the current chart.

Performance Monitor's vertical axis uses a logarithmic scale (based on powers of 10). Certain counters display percentage information (such as Cache Hit Ratio), and others report absolute numbers (such as Page Reads). Depending on the usage of your server, you might need to change the multiplier from the default. For example, if your database server frequently accepts more than 100 concurrent connections, this chart value will be off the scale. To change the scale, double-click the counter item and change the value for Scale. Numbers less than 1 will increase the range of the chart values, and numbers greater than 1 will decrease it.

Performance Monitor also offers other views:

- **Report view.** Reports are an alternative way of viewing performance information. Only average values over the sampling interval are displayed. This is useful if you want to view many different counters at the same time without having to interpret chart values individually (see Figure 5.3).

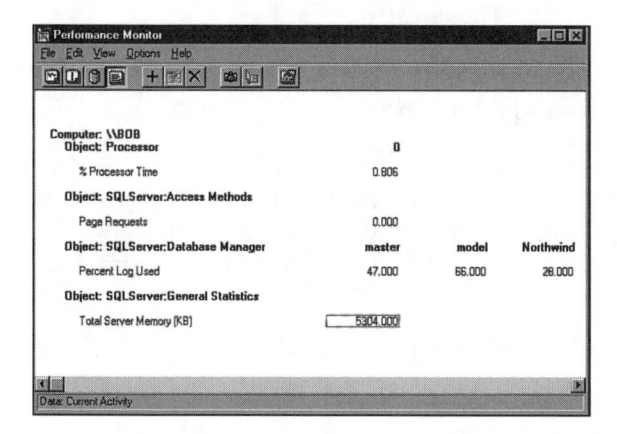

FIGURE 5.3
Using Report view in Performance Monitor.

- **Alert view.** Alerts can be used to notify a user or administrator when a specific value is exceeded. For example, I could add an alert that will send me a message when remaining disk space falls to less than 10 percent on any server hard disk. Later in this chapter, we'll look at using the SQL Server Agent to set up alerts.

- **Log view.** If you want to track server performance over time (to establish a performance baseline, for example), you can use Log view to collect information. Logs monitor entire objects at a time and can save the information for later analysis. You can also set the polling interval based on the level of detail required.

Each view retains its own counter and object settings. You can capture data to a text file that can be used to later report on information. To do this, simply select Options | Data From and choose to monitor either current activity or data stored to a specific file. Finally, Performance Monitor is a powerful tool that can be used to monitor statistics for remote Windows NT Workstation and Server computers from a single location.

Using SQL Profiler

SQL Profiler can be used to monitor the performance of queries as they occur. It can display information about user logins, connections to the server, and starting and completion times for database transactions. In

Chapter 3, "Configuring and Managing Security," we looked at ways to use the SQL Profiler to monitor security-related information. Here we'll use the same tool to monitor performance.

The SQL Profiler works by using *traces*—files containing events that you want to monitor. Information obtained from running a trace file can be stored in a text file or in a SQL Server database table. You can launch the SQL Server Profiler directly from the SQL Server 7 program group or from within Enterprise Manager using the Tools menu.

To create a new trace, do the following:

1. Open the Profiler from the Microsoft SQL Server program group.

2. Select File | New | Trace. Enter a trace name and select the server you want to monitor.

3. Choose to save the collected information to a text file or to a SQL Server database.

4. In the Events tab, shown in Figure 5.4, add the events you want to monitor. The lower portion of the dialog box gives a brief description of each item.

5. In the Data Columns tab, choose the type of information you want to view for each event. Again, a brief description of each column type is provided.

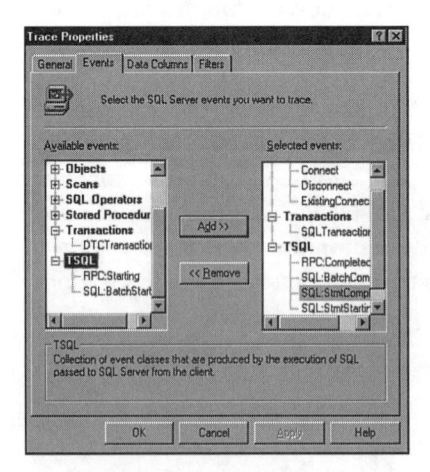

FIGURE 5.4
Adding events to a profile trace file.

6. Finally, on the Filters tab, you can select specific criteria to include and exclude in events for this trace.

7. Click OK to save the trace file you've created.

To execute the trace you just created, select File | Run Traces and select a sample trace or one you created. As shown in Figure 5.5, a display will show information related to monitored events. You can run multiple traces at the same time to record different kinds of information (for example, query performance and overall server statistics). To simulate the recorded information at a later time, you can replay a trace using the Replay menu. Finally, to view captured information, you can select File | Open and then select Trace File (if you saved to a file) or Trace Table (if you saved to a SQL Server table). Trace files can also be used with data reporting tools such as Microsoft Access and Microsoft Excel.

Using SQL Query Analyzer

The SQL Query Analyzer is a powerful new tool included with SQL Server 7. On a basic level, it provides a Transact-SQL command environment for executing SQL queries. However, it goes much further by color-coding queries and allowing users to display results in a grid format. For measuring the performance of specific queries, it can show the exact statistics for fulfilling a request. Finally, it can analyze queries and make recommendations as to which columns to place indexes in.

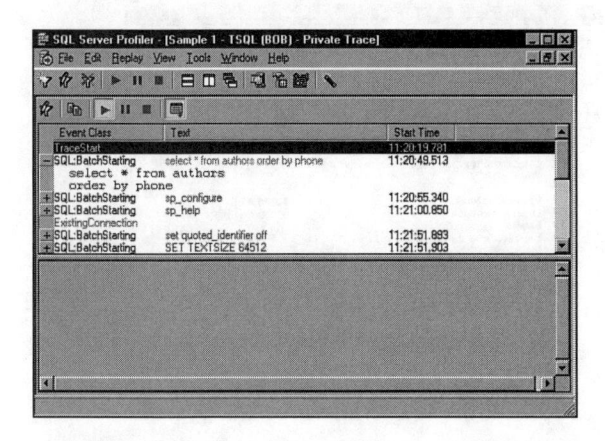

FIGURE 5.5
Using SQL Server Profiler to view query statistics.

136 CHAPTER 5 Monitoring and Optimization

Follow these steps to create and test a new query:

1. Open the SQL Query Analyzer from the Microsoft SQL Server 7 program group or by selecting Tools | Query Analyzer in Enterprise Manager.

2. If prompted, log on to a SQL Server database.

3. Type a standard SQL query in the main window.

4. Select Query | Display Estimated Execution Plan to execute the query and record statistics. You might have to maximize the query window to see all the information. The following query run against the Northwind sample database will present information similar to that shown in Figure 5.6 (more information on SQL syntax is available in the SQL Books Online):

```
SELECT productname, SUM(od.unitprice * quantity) AS total
FROM [order details] od inner join products p
ON od.productid = p.productid
GROUP BY productname
```

5. Hover the mouse over a specific step or arrow in the execution plan for the SQL Query to view performance information for that step. You'll see information similar to that shown in Figure 5.6.

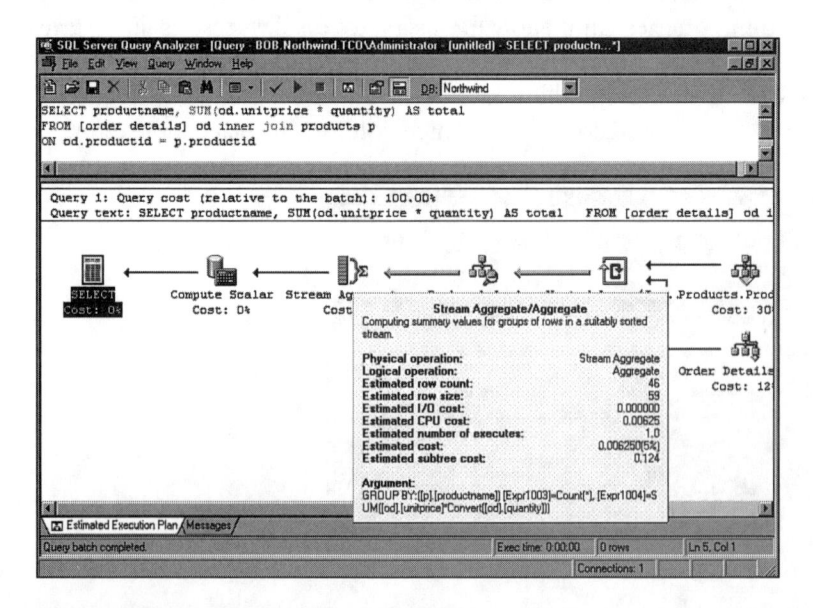

FIGURE 5.6
A SQL execution plan shown by Query Analyzer.

6. Optionally, select Query | Perform Index Analysis to rerun the same query and to make recommendations on index implementation. This option only works for certain types of queries that can be analyzed by the SQL Query Analyzer.

Summary of Performance Monitoring Tools

When monitoring performance on SQL Server 7, it's important to choose the right tool for the right job. In many cases, several tools may be able to provide useful information. Real world performance monitoring and troubleshooting experience can be very useful in this area. Table 5.3 lists some suggestions and examples of best uses for each of the SQL Server performance tools.

TABLE 5.3

BEST USES FOR SQL SERVER 7 PERFORMANCE MONITORING TOOLS

Tool	Best Use	Example
Performance Monitor	Measuring overall system performance	A server is being used for multiple purposes and overall system performance is too slow.
	Measuring overall database server performance over a given period of time	
SQL Profiler	Logging performance and object access information for later analysis	Database performance is exceptionally slow when many users run a specific application.
	Monitoring multiple queries occurring on a server over a given period of time	
SQL Query Analyzer	Analyzing the performance of a specific query	A specific SELECT statement seems to be running slowly.
SQL Server Alerts	Responding to a specific event of interest and notifying the appropriate personnel	A transaction log has become full and a system administrator should be notified.

Tuning and Optimizing SQL Server

Microsoft SQL Server 7 makes significant advances over previous versions by offering many automatically tuned parameters. In most cases, SQL Server 7 does an adequate job of managing hardware resources. However, SQL Server can be configured to optimize its usage of memory, processor time, and other system resources. You can make several changes in Windows NT Server and SQL Server configuration to improve performance. The overall goal of performance optimization is to decrease *response times* (the amount of time a client must wait to receive results from a query) and increase *throughput* (the number of completed transactions in a given unit of time).

Processor and Memory Settings

The SQL Server service is installed with default memory and CPU usage options that will be appropriate for working in most environments. If you need to make changes, however, you have options. To set SQL Server memory settings, do the following:

1. In Enterprise Manager, right-click the name of the server you want to modify and select Properties.

2. In the Memory tab, shown in Figure 5.7, you can modify the amount of memory the SQL Server will use. The default option—to dynamically configure memory usage—will be appropriate for most situations. If you have a large amount of RAM on the system, you might want to increase the minimum memory size. Alternatively, if your server will be running many other important applications, you might want to lower the maximum setting. If you have an accurate baseline of how much memory SQL Server will typically use, you can put the value at a fixed setting. This avoids the performance overhead caused by excessive paging of information to and from the hard disk.

3. You can check the Reserve physical memory for SQL Server option if you want Windows NT to set aside physical RAM for the service. This prevents the operating system from swapping this information to disk and can increase performance. The Maximum query memory option specifies the limit of RAM that can be allocated to any single-user transaction.

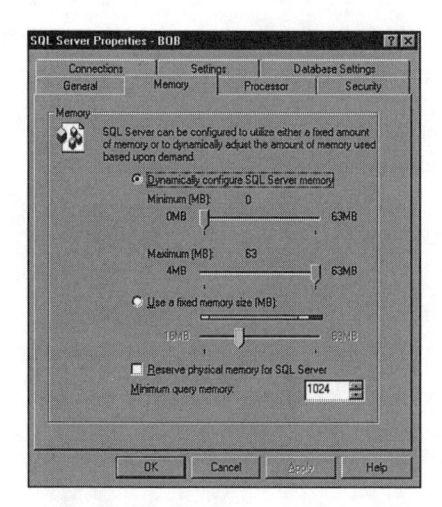

FIGURE 5.7
Viewing the SQL Server memory settings.

4. In the Processor tab, shown in Figure 5.8, you can specify which CPU(s) in a multiprocessor system can be used by SQL Server. This is often useful if you want to dedicate one or more CPUs to operating system functions and other applications. The Maximum worker threads setting specifies how many operations SQL Server can perform simultaneously. A higher number allows more users and processes to occur, but performance might decrease as SQL Server switches between threads. If the value is exceeded, users will receive an error message when trying to execute a command.

5. The Boost SQL Server priority setting should be used if the primary function of your machine is to act as a SQL Server. This will give the SQL Server service more CPU time when multiple tasks are competing for resources.

6. Finally, in the Parallelism section, you can specify whether you want SQL Server to distribute query processing between multiple processors. Multiprocessing generally incurs overhead, and the default setting for the minimum query plan threshold will determine whether it is efficient to use multiple CPUs for this task. "Costs" are based on the time required to process a transaction. Legal values are between 0 and 32,767.

7. To accept all changes, click OK. Dynamic memory changes will take place immediately, but others might require a restart of the SQL Server.

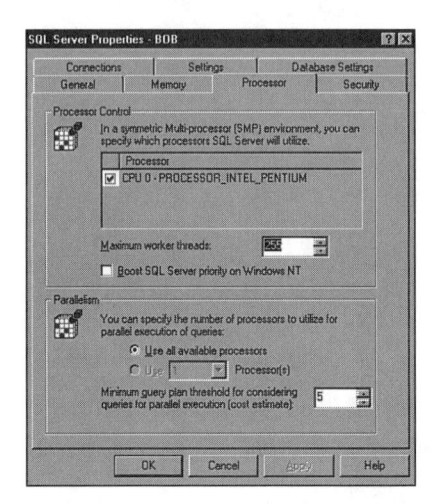

FIGURE 5.8
Viewing the SQL Server processor settings.

Setting SQL Server Configuration Settings

SQL Server 7 improves on previous versions of the product by managing more configuration settings automatically. Its self-tuning ability means that many settings should be left alone. As we've seen, you can modify several settings in Enterprise Manager by right-clicking a server name and selecting Properties. However, if you want to modify advanced settings, you can do so using the sp_configure stored procedure or the Enterprise Manager. To view the current settings, type sp_configure from a SQL Query Tool. Table 5.4 shows the meaning of each column of information.

TABLE 5.4

RETURNED COLUMNS FROM sp_configure

Column	Meaning
Name	The name of the configuration setting
Minimum	The minimum possible value setting
Maximum	The maximum possible value setting
config_value	The currently configured value
run_value	The value currently being used by the server

Figure 5.9 shows a listing of some of the configuration settings. For a complete list of available settings and their possible values, see the SQL Server Books Online.

> **WARNING**
> Don't make any configuration changes unless you're sure of the actions' exact ramifications. In a worst-case scenario, an incorrect setting can prevent SQL Server from starting.

Since some configuration parameters require the server to be restarted, the config_value and run_value settings might be different. To change a setting, you can type sp_configure `'setting_name', value`. To make a configuration change take effect, enter the command RECONFIGURE. Certain statements will require you to use the RECONFIGURE WITH OVERRIDE command. The GO command is used to execute a statement within a transaction before moving on to the next one. Some configuration options are considered advanced settings and can be viewed or changed only if you enable them by typing the following commands:

```
USE master
EXEC sp_configure 'show advanced options' , 1
GO
RECONFIGURE WITH OVERRIDE
GO
```

The first line specifies that you want to change from the active database to the master. Next, you execute the sp_configure stored procedure and specify that you want to change the value of the show advanced options setting to 1. The GO command executes this statement. Finally, you need to use the RECONFIGURE WITH OVERRIDE command to make this change and then execute it with a final GO command. The next time you run sp_configure, you will see all the advanced options in addition to the ones displayed without this setting.

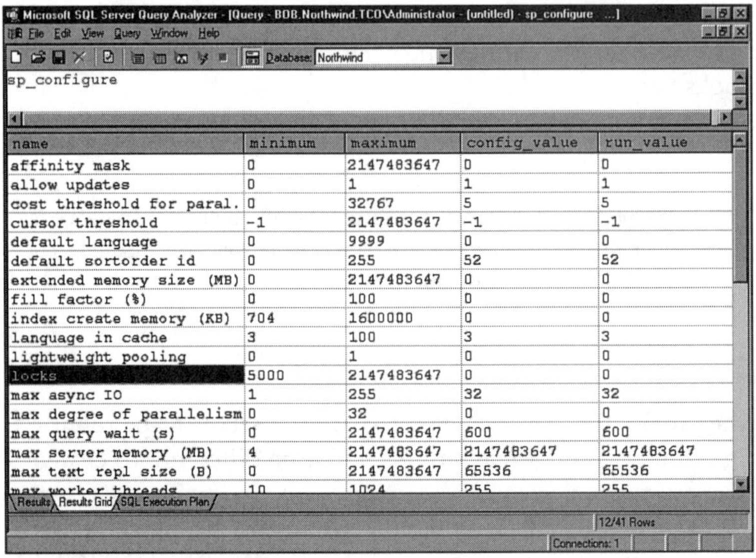

142 CHAPTER 5 Monitoring and Optimization

FIGURE 5.9
Using sp_configure to view configuration settings.

Tuning Windows NT Memory Settings

SQL Server can be affected by several Windows NT Server settings. Upon installation, SQL Server 7 automatically configures the Server service on Windows NT Server computers to Maximize Throughput for Network Applications. The settings are listed in Table 5.5.

TABLE 5.5

SETTINGS FOR THE WINDOWS NT SERVER SERVICE

Setting	Recommended Use
Minimize Memory Used	Stand-alone machines or a few network clients
Balance	Allocates memory for network connections and local applications
Maximize Throughput File Sharing	Allocates maximum memory for file- and network-level for cache
Maximum Throughput for Network Applications	Optimizes memory for applications that perform their own memory caching

In most cases, the default setting will be sufficient. If the primary purpose of your machine is to run SQL Server, this will be the ideal option. However, if your SQL Server has limited usage and other applications are competing for resources, it might be better to change the setting. To set the options, do the following:

1. Select Control Panel | Network.
2. On the Services tab, highlight Server and click Properties.
3. You see the dialog box shown in Figure 5.10. It lets you tune memory settings based on your usage of the server.

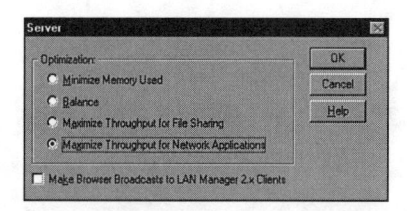

FIGURE 5.10
Windows NT Server service properties.

IMPROVING QUERY PERFORMANCE

The purpose of the database is to return information quickly and efficiently. However, in many cases, the way you ask a question to the database will affect how quickly and efficiently you'll receive a response.

Using Stored Procedures

You can improve the performance of common queries dramatically by using SQL Server stored procedures. You may have noticed that the sp_configure command is not a SQL statement but is a shortcut for a stored series of commands that refer to database objects in the system database. Stored procedures are precompiled collections of SQL statements that remain cached in memory and execute up to 20 times faster than the same statement run manually. They also have the following advantages:

- **Decreases in network traffic.** Instead of sending large queries with hundreds of lines, a single command can be executed on the server.

- **Sharing code.** Stored procedures can call each other, and common procedures can be written only once and shared throughout a database.

- **Enforced security rules.** Stored procedures can provide embedded security permissions logic. Since stored procedures execute with the permissions of the owner of the stored procedure, security implementation is simplified.

You can create a stored procedure in one of two ways. First, you can enter a query into the SQL Query Analyzer. The CREATE PROC statement is used to create a new stored procedure, as in the following example (for help with generating SQL queries, see *SQL Books Online*):

```
CREATE PROC Find_Rich_Employees AS
SELECT * FROM employees where Salary > 70000
```

To run the stored procedure, type `EXEC Find_Rich_Employees`. Stored procedures can accept command-line arguments and can process complicated statements. Alternatively, you can use Enterprise Manager to create a new stored procedure. Right-click the Store Procedures object in a database and select New Store Procedure. In the window, type the SQL query to execute when the stored procedure is run.

Setting the Query Governor Cost Limit

It is often useful to be able to limit the resources used by a single query or transaction in SQL Server. For example, if a user enters a query that asks for the sum of all values in a multigigabyte table, this would be quite costly to perform. Other users would suffer from slow response times, and the database server itself might be significantly slowed. In many cases, such a transaction might be executed by mistake. If the transaction must be carried out, it would be a good idea to schedule it to occur at a later time.

SQL Server 7 includes a server configuration parameter that can allow an administrator to limit the resources that can be used by a single operation. This option, the query governor cost limit, sets the longest time (in seconds) that a query may run. To set these options for all databases on a server, you can use the sp_configure stored procedure, as follows:

```
USE master
EXEC sp_configure 'query governor cost limit', '1'
RECONFIGURE
EXEC sp_configure
```

For the setting to take effect, you'll need to stop and restart the SQL Server. Finally, the query governor cost limit can be set on a per-transaction basis using the following statement as part of a transaction:

```
SET QUERY_GOVERNOR_COST_LIMIT
```

A value of 0 will set no limit on the maximum query execution time. Any values greater than 0 will specify the number of seconds that a query may run. Note that the same query might take differing amounts of time to complete, based on server hardware configurations.

OTHER WAYS TO OPTIMIZE PERFORMANCE

In addition to monitoring SQL Server performance and making configuration changes, there are several things database administrators can do to improve overall performance and manageability. In this section, we'll look at managing alerts and scheduling batch jobs.

Scheduling Jobs

The properties of the SQL Server Agent allow you to schedule tasks to occur when there is little or no activity currently on the database. Although it's often better to schedule jobs for times of the day or night when you know activity will be low, this isn't always possible. To set SQL Server Agent Properties, do the following:

1. Expand the Management folder, right-click the SQL Server Agent, and select Properties. On the General tab, shown in Figure 5.11, you can specify the account to be used by the SQL Server Agent, the mail profile to be used for sending messages, and the name of the file to save error information to. Optionally, if you want a user to see a pop-up dialog box when errors occur, enter the name of the user who should be alerted.

146 CHAPTER 5 Monitoring and Optimization

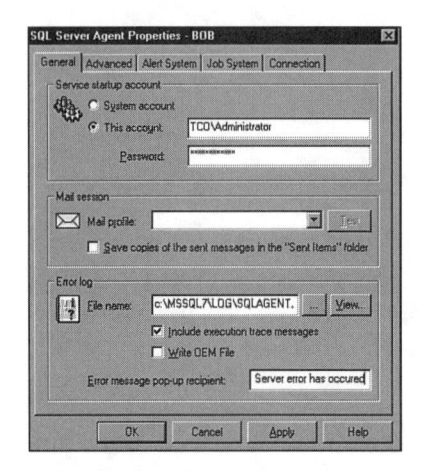

FIGURE 5.11
General properties of the SQL Server Agent service.

2. On the Advanced tab, you can set the Idle CPU conditions as desired. The percentage threshold specifies the maximum CPU usage, and the number of seconds specifies the duration of this level of activity (or less) before tasks are run. You can also configure whether you want the SQL Server Agent to restart when an unexpected stop occurs. Finally, you can choose to forward events to remote servers so that all information can be managed in a single location.

3. The Alert System tab allows you to send e-mail to a compatible pager. A fail-safe operator can also be set up as an alternative recipient when an error occurs.

4. The Job System tab allows you to configure settings for the maximum log size. Here, you can also restrict access to executing operating system commands to system administrator users. This option prevents users from running jobs under elevated privileges using the CmdExec procedure.

5. Finally, on the Connection tab, you can specify the account that SQL Server Agent will use to log on to SQL Server. When you're done with the configuration, click OK to accept the changes.

This will allow certain operations to occur when, for example, the staff is in a meeting or during lunchtime. Figure 5.12 shows the options available for scheduling jobs. Note that you should use this option only for noncritical jobs, because there is a chance that on a very busy server the task might not execute at all.

Other Ways to Optimize Performance   147

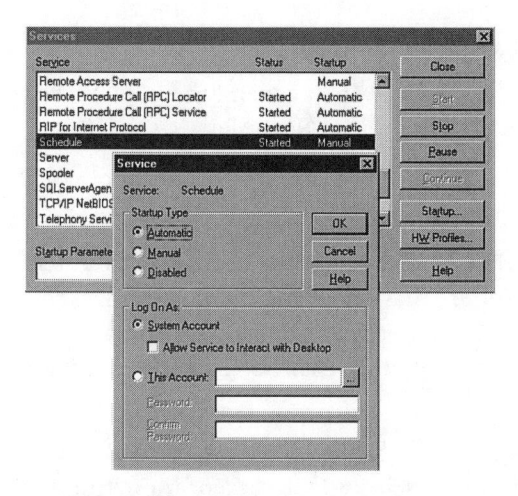

FIGURE 5.12
SQL Server Agent job-scheduling options.

Setting Alerts with SQL Server Agent

The SQL Server Agent can be used to send alerts based on performance data. For example, if the number of user connections exceeds a certain value (see Figure 5.13), a server administrator can be notified.

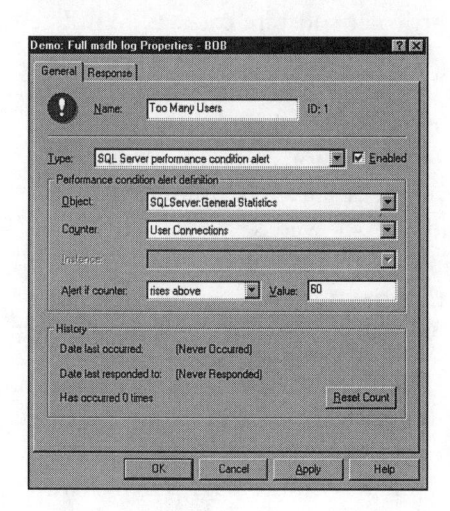

FIGURE 5.13
Setting performance alerts with the SQL Server Agent.

Follow these steps to set a performance-based alert:

1. Expand the Management folder, and then expand the SQL Server Agent item. Right-click Alerts and select New Alert.

2. Name the alert and set the type to SQL Server performance condition alert. Check the Enabled box.

3. To define the alert condition, choose an object and a counter. These are the same values that can be monitored by the Performance Monitor (described earlier). Finally, set the alert to fire when a value is lower than, higher than, or equal to a certain number.

4. Optionally, you use the settings in the Response tab to notify database administrators of problems. Click OK to accept the settings.

The alert must also be defined in the SQL Server Performance Monitor. In order for the alerts to function, the SQL Server Agent and the SQL Server Performance Monitor must be running.

Hardware Upgrades

Scalability refers to the ability of a particular software package to utilize hardware to its maximum potential. The scalability of SQL Server 7 has been greatly improved over past versions to take full advantage of processor power, memory, and network bandwidth. However, no matter how much tweaking and optimization you perform on a SQL Server installation, you will eventually hit a maximum based on hardware limitations. Tables 5.1 and 5.2 showed several performance counters that can be used to determine where performance problems are occurring. For example, if you find that the number of pages/sec value is consistently high on your server, you might have hit a performance ceiling based on your configuration.

At this point, you'll need to upgrade or replace hardware to increase performance. Although it might be tempting to replace older servers with entirely new machines, there might be a more cost-effective way. For example, if you find that your SQL Server Cache Hit Ratio is very low, you might want to add more memory. On almost any server, an increase in RAM can greatly increase the useful lifetime of the machine.

Similarly, if response times are low due to network problems, you might need to look at circumstances outside of the server, such as other network applications and overall network bandwidth. A final option would be to implement multiple servers and use replication to distribute transaction loads and storage requirements.

What Is Important to Know

Microsoft expects you to know how to measure and track the performance of SQL Server 7 and then apply this information by optimizing the way it works in your environment. Specifically, be sure to understand which performance monitoring tools are important for troubleshooting or monitoring a specific aspect of your server. For answering performance-related questions on the exam, be sure you know the following:

- The Performance Monitor icon in the Microsoft SQL Server program group starts the Windows NT Performance Monitor with useful statistics for monitoring.

- In addition to the SQL Server counters, administrators can add customer objects, counters, and instances to their Performance Monitor charts. The Performance Monitor can store captured data and display statistics in several different ways.

- SQL Profiler can be used to collect specific performance-related information for SQL Server. Using trace files, you can define the actions you want to monitor and view or store information for later analysis.

- SQL Query Analyzer can be used to display statistics and show the execution plan for standard SQL queries. It can also be used to make suggestions on database indexes. This information can then be used to optimize queries for better performance.

- Although SQL Server 7 is largely self-tuning, Enterprise Manager can be used to modify SQL Server hardware resource utilization settings.

- To modify advanced SQL Server settings, you can use the sp_configure stored procedure to view and change settings.

- On the Windows NT Server operating system, the Server service can be modified to optimize memory usage based on the tasks running on the server.

- Executing queries as stored procedures can dramatically increase performance. Stored procedures can be created using Transact-SQL or Enterprise Manager.

- The query governor cost limit option can be set to limit the amount of CPU time a query may use. Longer-running queries are aborted, and the user is notified of the error.

What Is Important to Know

- The SQL Server Agent can be used to schedule jobs and notify administrators via pager and/or e-mail when certain events occur on the server.
- Upgrading hardware—such as adding CPUs or more physical memory—is a good way to improve performance when tweaking settings doesn't result in acceptable performance.

OBJECTIVES

As a system administrator, you will spend some of your time troubleshooting problems with your servers. This usually involves finding, diagnosing, and resolving issues related to data, the network, or user access rights. This chapter helps tie together the rest of the information in this book about installation problems, boot failures, configuration errors, printer problems, RAS, connectivity problems, access and permission problems, and fault tolerance failures. Here are the test objectives covered in this chapter:

▶ Diagnose and resolve problems with upgrading from SQL Server 6.x.

▶ Diagnose and resolve problems with backup and restore operations.

▶ Diagnose and resolve replication problems.

▶ Diagnose and resolve job or alert failures.

▶ Diagnose and resolve distributed query problems.

▶ Use the Client Configuration Utility to diagnose and resolve client connectivity problems.

▶ Diagnose and resolve problems with access to SQL Server, databases, and database objects.

CHAPTER 6

Troubleshooting

Before You Begin

Upgrading to or installing SQL 7 can present some interesting challenges that require troubleshooting. One of the best ways you can have a successful, trouble-free installation or upgrade is through prior planning and prevention. As part of your planning phase, you should always come up with a plan of action and then follow that plan. Here is a checklist of things to consider before running SQL Server Setup:

- Back up your Microsoft SQL Server version 6.x installation if you are installing SQL Server version 7 on the same computer.
- Install the latest SQL Server Service Pack if you are upgrading servers to be used in replication.
- Set tempdb to at least 25MB in your SQL Server 6.x installation. Do not set the memory option to use much more than half the available memory.
- Shut down all services dependent on SQL Server.
- Shut down all unnecessary applications.
- Review the hardware and software requirements for installing SQL Server.
- Ensure that all database users have logins in the master database.
- Create a domain user account to assign to the MSSQLServer and SQLServerAgent services if you plan to perform any server-to-server activities. Do this before you begin the installation.
- Log on to the system under a user account that has administrative privileges.
- Ensure that you upgrade all databases with cross-reference dependencies.
- Stop replication and make sure the log is empty.

Here are some additional considerations before you run a custom installation:

- Select a character set, sort order, and Unicode collation. Great care must be taken when selecting a character set, because if you need to change it later, you must rebuild the databases and reload the data.

You should develop a standard within your organization for these options. Many server-to-server activities might fail if the character set, sort order, and Unicode collation are not consistent across servers.

- Review all other SQL Server installation options, and be prepared to make the appropriate selections when you run the Setup program.

Diagnosing and Resolving Problems with Upgrading from SQL Server 6.x

The Upgrade Wizard, as with most of Microsoft's newer wizards, is designed to be problem-free and easy to use. However, with any new product, there are likely to be a few potential problem areas. The number one problem is running out of disk space, resulting in a failure to create an object in SQL Server 7. The Upgrade Wizard generates detailed logs that describe any upgrade problems that were encountered. An Upgrade folder is created in the path \Mssql7\Upgrade whenever the SQL Upgrade Wizard is run. This folder will contain the server name and the current date and time.

This folder contains log files that describe very specific areas of the upgrade process, as well as folders for each of the upgraded databases that contain log files indicating the success or failure of creating the different objects. The two extensions that you will see are .ok and .err.

All .err log files are listed at the end of the Upgrade Wizard. They can be found in the following locations throughout your system:

- %systemroot%
- \Mssql7\Upgrade
- Database-specific directories

Disk Space

Disk space is the primary problem you will encounter when performing an upgrade from SQL Server 6.x to SQL Server 7. The Upgrade Wizard is designed to be automatic and easy to use and can estimate the amount of disk space that is required. The key word, though, is estimate. When upgrading, it is extremely important to ensure that you have plenty of free disk space. If you are debating whether you have enough, chances are you don't. Don't take the chance. Use the adage "If you have to ask how much it is, you can't afford it." This applies very well here. If you are unsure whether you have enough space, you don't.

Other Common Problems

Here are some other very common problems that you might encounter during an installation or upgrade:

- Improper permissions:
  - You must be part of the Domain Administrators group on the domain controller or have administrative rights on the member server that has the installation of the SQL Server.

- Failure of setup due to memory allocation error:
  - The PAGEFILE.SYS file needs more memory allocated to it.
  - PAGEFILE.SYS is growing during the installation process, causing a disk space problem.

- Failure to establish a connection, causing SQL Enterprise Manager not to start:
  - SQL Server might not be running.
  - The network might be down.
  - There might be a physical connection problem.
  - Incorrect transport protocol

At A Glance: Upgrading and Memory

The upgrade error log is stored in the \mssql7\upgrade directory.

The Upgrade Wizard estimates the free disk space needed for the upgrade, but this is only an estimate.

If the page file is too small, you will receive a memory allocation error.

DIAGNOSING BACKUP AND RESTORATION PROBLEMS

Backups are a staple of supporting an SQL implementation. With backups comes the need to restore information. Before you perform any other checks, you should verify that the media are in good shape. The physical tape should be in good repair and should be replaced on a regular, rotational basis. After the backup, view the backup logs to better identify what types of errors are occurring. Here are some of the error codes that can arise during a backup:

- Error 156. This is a severity level 15 error code that indicates a syntax error during a BACKUP or RESTORE statement. The BACKUP and RESTORE statements are available only when operating in SQL 7 mode. If you're running the SQL Server 7 product in SQL Server 6.5 mode, this error can occur.

- 3,000 through 3,999. Most of the other backup errors fall into the 3000 range of error messages and occur when the backup process attempts to perform an operation it isn't allowed to perform. Generally speaking, the following are true:

  - 3,000 through 3,099 can be caused by attempting a backup or restore operation while it can't be performed. Reissuing the command will typically cure the error.

- 3,100 through 3,199 can be caused by compatibility problems, such as an incorrect tape format or database/backup incompatibility. This type of error typically requires research to identify the problem and correct it. A full restoration and incremental or transaction log restorations may be required to cure these problems.

- 3,200 through 3,299 can be caused by media-related problems. This can be the tape media or the drive media, as when the backup or restoration spans multiple drives.

- 4,000 through 4,999 error messages aren't typically related to the backup and restoration process, but if these errors occur during a backup or restoration, they indicate a gap in data or a loss of pointers, indicating at what point the backup and restore processes are.

These are generalizations to give you an idea of what categories the error messages fall into. For more detailed information on backup and restore error messages, refer to the online documentation.

At A Glance: Backup and Restore Error Messages

Backup and restore error messages are logged when they occur.

Error Message Number	Definition
3000 through 3099	Indicates that the backup attempted an illegal operation. This type of message can often be fixed by reissuing the command.
3100 through 3199	Indicates a compatibility problem between the tape backup and live database.
3200 through 3299	Indicates media-related problems that can be caused by the tape or disk drive.
The 4000 range	Indicates a gap in the data or pointers (when they refer to a backup or restore operation)

The order of restoration is full backup, then incremental or transaction log backup in order from oldest to newest.

Diagnosing and Resolving Replication Problems

Replication problems can stem from many areas, but most have the same troubleshooting path. Replication involves transferring data from one computer to another, sometimes through an intermediary computer. These computers may be in a single domain or may be in different domains.

If replication is being set up and fails, check the physical network first to verify that you can communicate with the computers you are configuring. Next, verify that the account being used for replication has the proper rights to perform the tasks involved in replication.

Once these two checks have been performed, view the replication history to better understand where the failure is occurring. Once the indications are identified, use the Replication Monitor to view the current status and configuration information for the replication agent for the subscriber that has the replication problem. Verify that the steps involved in replication are functioning properly.

If no agent is running for a particular subscriber, check the Jobs folder for errors. If the problem appears to be with the account being used, configure the agent to use a local account on the subscriber, and verify proper operation. If this resolves the problem, verify that the trust relationships needed for replication are in place and that the account being used for replication has the authority to operate on all machines involved in the replication process.

If the problem indicated is a conflict, use the Replication Conflict Viewer on the publisher as an aid in troubleshooting. By default, the conflict table is stored on the publisher. If possible, configure the publisher to be a SQL Server 7 machine. If the problem appears to be only between SQL 7 publishers and SQL Server 6.5 subscribers, refer to the online documentation for a detailed troubleshooting procedure.

At A Glance: Troubleshooting the Replication Process

Check the physical connection for communications and the logical connection for rights to operate on all machines involved in the replication process.

Ensure that the account being used for replication has the proper rights and permissions on the machine it is responsible for. The sender is authenticated on the receiver.

Make sure all servers in the publication/subscriber process are running SQL 6.5 or newer and, if possible, set a SQL Server 7 computer as the publisher. Also, make sure that all SQL 6.5 servers have run replp70.sql and sp_addpublisher.

Use the Replication Monitor to verify that an agent is operational and to identify the point of failure.

Use the Conflict Viewer to resolve conflicts when data is merged from different sources.

DIAGNOSING AND RESOLVING JOB OR ALERT FAILURES

When diagnosing job or alert failures, start with the basics and then work toward the harder problems. The following are some simple problems and possible solutions. If an alert isn't firing, these are some simple things you can check:

- Make sure that the SQL Server Agent service is running:
    - Check the Services icon in Control Panel.
    - Check the Task Manager processes.
- Check the Event Viewer Application log.
- Make sure that the alert is enabled.

If you have an operator that is not receiving notification from an alert that is firing, do the following:

- Check the operator's notification information to ensure that it's correct. Check any syntax for e-mails, pagers, or net send addresses. Also check connectivity.

Diagnosing and Resolving Job or Alert Failures 161

- Check the operator's schedule. If you have a slow notification from an alert:

  - Check the complexity of the alert response. The more notifications it must send, the longer it will take for notifications to reach all their destinations.

  - You might have the Delay Between Responses set too high or for too long of a delay.

You can perform simple tests to see if the response time is due to network problems or complexity by sending notifications to one or two e-mail recipients and seeing how long they take to arrive. If the response time is still slow, you probably have a network physical layer problem. If the time is good, reduce the complexity of the alert notifications.

If you have a problem where your Windows NT Application Event Log rapidly fills up with the same error, you will generally also have an unusually high CPU usage time and a high number of alert responses.

A couple of job errors can be found in the online documentation that comes with SQL Server 7. Or you can find the support pages at Microsoft under the following URL:

http://www.support.microsoft.com/support

You may also want to search TECHNET.

At A Glance: The Application Event Log

Verify that the SQL Server Agent is running.

View the Application Log for error messages.

Make sure that the alert is enabled.

Verify that notification is configured properly.

If the alert is slow, simplify the alert process and reconfigure the Delay Between Responses setting.

Diagnosing and Resolving Distributed Query Problems

Before we discuss some specific problems with distributed queries, let's review what distributive queries are and how they are utilized through SQL Server 7.

SQL Server 7 supports distributed queries that access data from multiple data sources, which can be stored on one computer or multiple computers. SQL Server 7 uses OLE DB for distributed queries, which is the Microsoft specification. Distributed queries provide SQL Server users with access to

- Data stored on multiple SQL computers
- Different data stored in various data sources, both relational and nonrelational, so long as there is an OLE DB provider or ODBC driver

OLE DB exposes its data in *rowsets,* which are tabular objects. These rowsets can be referenced in Transact-SQL statements just as though they were a SQL Server table.

There are 11 common distributed query problems that you might encounter. The SQL Server 7 Online Books goes into great detail about each of these. Each is highlighted with a possible resolution below.

- Error 7303
    - Problem: Incorrect initialization parameters in the sp addlinkedserver
    - Solution: Verify parameter information and correct if necessary.
    - Problem: Incorrect login and password
    - Solution: Verify correct user account and password, and check for common login errors.
- Error 7306
    - Problem: Incorrect parameter or interface in the UPDATE, DELETE, or INSERT statement
    - Solution: Find the specific information and trace the errors on the missing OLE DB support.

- Error 7314
  - Problem: A missing table or column
  - Solution: Verify the existence of the specified table or column and make sure that the user's permissions are appropriate for the table.
- Error 7321
  - Problem: An error in the syntax string's parameter
  - Solution: Verify that the query string is free of syntax errors.
- Error 7356
  - Problem: Inconsistent metadata between the OLE DB that is present and that which is reported
  - Solution: Use the SQL Server Profiler to determine which table column caused the error.
- Error 7357
  - Problem: Missing table or incorrect login
  - Solution: Verify table and login parameters.
- Error 7391
  - Problem: Unsupported distributed transaction
  - Solution: Rewrite the data modification statement using an implicit or explicit statement rather than a distributed transaction.
- Error 7399
  - Problem: A problem with your access database
  - Solution: Either map a login to the SQL Server or make sure the pathname is correct in the Registry.
- Error 7403
  - Problem: An error in the Registry, or the OLE DB provider is not registered properly.
  - Solution: Verify that the provider has been registered properly.

- Error 7413
  - Problem: Invalid authentication login using a distributed query without an explicit login mapping
  - Solution: Create an explicit mapping using sp_addlinkedsrvlogin.

These are some of the common distributed query problems and their resolutions. A detailed list can be found in the Online Books help.

At A Glance: Verifying Task Authorities

Verify that the account being used for authentication has the authority to perform the tasks associated with the query process.

View the error log for specific error messages, and then troubleshoot following the procedures given in the online documentation.

DIAGNOSING AND RESOLVING CLIENT CONNECTIVITY PROBLEMS

Use the Client Configuration Utility to diagnose and resolve client connectivity problems.

In order for a client application to successfully connect to Microsoft SQL Server, two crucial pieces must be configured:

- A network protocol must be installed. This is normally done during Windows NT setup.

- The client and server must have a compatible set of Net-Libraries, and both the server side and the client side must match and correspond to a desired transport protocol.

During the SQL Server installation, the client Net-Libraries are installed, and the SQL Server is configured to "listen" on all the different Net-Libraries (Named Pipes, TCP/IP, Multiprotocol, and Shared Memory). You can also select additional Net-Libraries for the SQL Server to "listen" on.

Diagnosing and Resolving Client Connectivity Problems 165

You use SQL Server Client Configuration to configure the corresponding client Net-Libraries to any server Net-Libraries you activate. To start network configuration, go to the Start menu and select Programs | Microsoft SQL Server 7 | SQL Server Network Utility.

To load an installed server network library, do the following:

1. In the SQL Server Network Library Configuration dialog box, click Add.

2. In the Add New Network Library Configuration dialog box, specify the server name to load an installed server network library on.

3. Select the server network library to load. You may need to specify the necessary connection parameters.

Once the appropriate network libraries are installed and configured, you still have potential connectivity problems. This boils down to protocols and APIs.

The following components manage communication between SQL Server and its clients:

1. The client application calls the appropriate API, which in turn causes the OLE DB provider, driver, or DLL to be used for SQL Server communications.

2. From this point, the client Net-Library is called by the provider, driver, or DLL, which calls the appropriate IPC API.

3. This information is transmitted to a server Net-Library using the underlying IPC.

    - Named Pipes or Shared Memory are used if it is a local IPC.

    - The transport protocol stack is used if it is a network IPC.

4. Once the Server Net-Library has the request, it passes it to the SQL Server to be processed.

> **NOTE** The Microsoft Online Help provides useful information for this.

The Named Pipes Net-Library is not supported on machines running Microsoft Windows 95 or later as a server, but Windows 95 clients can use named pipes.

All server Net-Libraries are automatically listened to by the SQL Server by default. The one exception is SQL running on a Windows 95 machine, which doesn't listen on the TCP/IP Sockets Net-Library.

I stated earlier that all client Net-Libraries are installed by default during SQL Server setup. You can define which Net-Libraries a client uses to connect to a particular server by using the SQL Server Client Configuration. Using the Client Configuration Utility, you can do the following:

- Specify the default Net-Library used for all connections except those that use a server alias.
- For connections that use a server alias, you can specify connection parameters and specific Net-Libraries.

In order for a client to connect to a SQL Server, the following criteria must be present:

- The client must use a client Net-Library that the server is "listening" to.
- Both the client and the server must be running a common protocol stack supporting the network API.

When running an application on the same computer as SQL Server, you can use the following names to reference the SQL Server:

- Windows NT
  - Computer name of the SQL Server
  - (local)*
  - .*
- Windows 95 and 98
  - Computer name of the SQL Server
  - (local)

The preferred method is to use the computer name, which uses the Shared Memory Net-Library.

Tabular Data Streams (TDS) is an application-level protocol that is used for communication between SQL Servers and clients. TDS packets are encapsulated and used in the specific network Net-Libraries.

With this background and a few utilities, you will be able to troubleshoot common client connectivity issues. Two utilities that can be used to troubleshoot connection problems are makepipe and readpipe.

At A Glance: Troubleshooting Client-Related Problems

> Identify the scope of the problem and whether the problem involves one client or several.
>
> Use the Client Configuration Utility to troubleshoot client-related problems.
>
> Verify that the client has the proper protocol installed and configured and is running the proper network library.

DIAGNOSING AND RESOLVING ACCESS PROBLEMS

Most of the problems you will run into with accessing the SQL Server will involve permissions—or lack thereof. You can log in to Microsoft SQL Server from any of the graphical administration tools, or from a command prompt using `osql`.

When using the Enterprise Manager GUI to connect to a SQL Server, you are prompted for the server name, login ID, and password. After logging in to the SQL Server, you can perform various tasks, such as administering the server or querying a database.

SQL Server services are integrated with Windows NT services and therefore can be started, stopped, or paused the same way as any other Windows NT service. You can specify services to start automatically or manually. When you start SQL Server, two services must be running:

- MSSQLServer: the SQL Server service
- SQLServerAgent: SQL Server Agent

These two services must be running before any clients can connect or before you can administer the server. The SQL Server service can also be paused. This prevents new users from logging in. It also gives you time to send a message to current users, asking them to complete their work and log out before you stop the server. If you stop SQL Server without pausing it, all server processes are terminated immediately. Stopping SQL Server prevents new connections and disconnects current users.

If you can't start the two SQL services under a particular account, check the following:

- Make sure the service account has been granted the Log on as a service right and that the service account has administrative privileges:
  - Using an account on the domain controller as the service account, use the AGLP concept:
  - Create a global group on the domain controller and place the service account into the group.
  - Create a local group on the member server, and then move the global group that contains the service account from the domain controller into the local group.
  - Assign permissions to the local group.
  - Using an account from the SQL Member Server:
  - Create the Service account, and assign it permissions to log on as a service.
- Re-enter the password for the account in the startup parameters of both services through the Service icon in Control Panel.

Some problems that you might encounter while trying to access databases and database objects include problems with accounts and/or permissions. Consider some of the following principles when troubleshooting connectivity to either a database or a database object.

SQL Server logins, users, roles, and passwords can contain up to 128 characters. These characters can contain letters, symbols, and numbers (such as George_Brown, Betsie Collier 123456789, or #65C&58A=1998B&B). Be careful when using characters such as double quotes (") and square brackets ([]). Use delimiters in Transact-SQL statements when the SQL Server login, user, role, or password contains or begins with a space or begins with $ or @.

> **NOTE:** It isn't necessary to specify delimiters when entering logins, users, roles, and passwords into the text boxes of the SQL Server graphical client tools, such as SQL Server Enterprise Manager.

Additionally, a SQL Server login, user, or role cannot

- Contain a backslash (\) character, unless referring to an existing Windows NT user or group. The backslash separates the Windows NT computer or domain name from the user name.
- Already exist in the current database (or master, for logins only).
- Be NULL, or an empty string (" ").

When granting Windows NT local or global groups access to connect to SQL Server, specify the domain or computer name that the group is defined on, followed by a backslash and then the group name. However, to grant access to a Windows NT built-in local group, specify BUILTIN instead of the domain or computer name. For example, to grant access to a global group called SQL_Users in the Austin domain, specify Austin\SQL_Users as the group name to add to SQL Server. However, to grant access to the built-in Windows NT local group Administrators, specify BUILTIN\Administrators as the group name to add to SQL Server.

At A Glance: Identifying and Verifying Authentication

Identify the type of authentication being used (NT accounts or mixed).

Identify whether rights are obtained through NT domain groups or SQL Server roles.

Verify the authentication path.

Verify that the SQL Server service and SQL Server Agent are operational.

Use the sa account for testing.

What Is Important to Know

The following bullets summarize the chapter and accentuate the key concepts to memorize for the exam:

- When you're upgrading SQL Server 6.x to SQL Server 7, the upgrade error log is stored in the \mssql7\upgrade directory. A memory allocation error will occur if the page file is too small. Backup and restoration error messages are logged when they occur. The order of restoration is full backup, and then incremental or transaction log backup in order from oldest to newest.

- When configuring replication, check the physical connection for communications and the logical connection for rights to operate on all machines involved in the replication process. Make sure all servers in the publication/subscriber process are running SQL 6.5 or newer. If possible, set a SQL Server 7 computer as the publisher. Also, make sure that all SQL 6.5 Servers have run replp70.sql and sp_addpublisher. When troubleshooting jobs, verify that the SQL Server Agent is running, and then view the Application Log for error messages.

- When troubleshooting client configuration problems, verify that the account being used for authentication has the authority to perform the tasks associated with the query process. View the error log for specific error messages, and then troubleshoot following the procedures given in the online documentation. Use the Client Configuration Utility to troubleshoot client-related problems.

- When troubleshooting client/server connectivity problem, your first step should be to isolate the problem. If several clients are able to connect to a server but one is having problems, then chances are that the problem is occurring on the specific client. Similarly, if no users can connect to a SQL Server database, it's likely that the server isn't configured properly. To troubleshoot the problem, first check for network connectivity by ensuring that users can access a specific server and other workstations. If that fails, the problem is not SQL Server-related, but instead is a network configuration error.

- If basic network connectivity is possible between machines, but you can't connect to SQL Server, the most likely problem is a mismatch in the supported Net Libraries. Be sure that both the client and the server are using at least one compatible NetworkLibrary.

What Is Important to Know 171

- If you're importing data between databases, it's likely that some changes will be needed in data format. For example, your Human Resources database might include employee information in one format and your Sales and Marketing department might use another. The Data Transformation Services (DTS) can be very useful in allowing you to make changes to such items as column names, column definitions, and even data types. This is also useful for migrating between database platforms.

- If you're exporting data from Microsoft SQL Server to an Oracle database, for example, the graphic interface of the DTS will enable you to answer some simple questions in a wizard. Another major benefit of using DTS is that "packages"—definitions of the import/export operations and any parameters used—can be saved for later use or reuse. In the preceding example, this might mean that you could do a daily export of HR-related information into the Sales database. The main limitation of BCP is the inability to make any types of modifications to data.

Objectives

Think of this as your personal study diary—your documentation of how you'll beat the exam.

The Objective Review Notes section is provided so that you can personalize this book to maximum effect. This is your workbook, study sheet, notes section—whatever you want to call it. You will ultimately decide exactly what information you'll need, but there's no reason this information should be written down anywhere else. As I have learned from my teaching experiences, there's absolutely no substitute for taking copious notes and using them throughout the study process.

Each subobjective covered in this book has its own section (there are two on a page). Each subobjective section falls under the main exam objective category, where you would expect to find it. I strongly suggest that you review each subobjective, make note of your knowledge level, and then return to the Objective Review Notes section repeatedly and document your progress. Your ultimate goal should be to review this section by itself and determine if you are ready for the exam.

continues

Objective Review Notes

OBJECTIVES CONTINUED

Here is how I suggest you use the Objective Review Notes:

1. Read the objective. Refer to the part of the book where it's covered.
2. If you already know this material, check "Got it" and make a note of the date.
3. If you need to brush up on the objective area, check "Review it" and make a note of the date. While you're at it, write down the page numbers you check, since you'll need to return to that section soon enough.
4. If this material is something you're largely unfamiliar with, check "Help!" and write down the date. Now you can get to work.
5. You get the idea. Keep working through the material in this book and in any other study materials you have. The more you understand the material, the quicker you can update and upgrade each Objective Review Notes section from "Help!" to "Review it" to "Got it."

Most people who take certification exams use more than one resource. Write down the page numbers of where this material is covered in other books, software programs, and videotapes you're using.

OBJECTIVE REVIEW NOTES 175

Planning

▶ Objective: Plan a security strategy to determine user accounts, group structure, server roles, accounts used to run services, application security strategy, and requirements for linked databases.

☐ Got it ☐ Review it ☐ Help!
Date:____ Date:____ Date:____

Notes:
_____
_____
_____
_____
_____

Fast Track cross reference, see pages:
_____
_____

Other resources cross reference, see pages:
_____
_____
_____

▶ Objective: Develop a SQL Server capacity plan to include the physical placement of files, use of filegroups, hardware and communication requirements, and planning for growth over time.

☐ Got it ☐ Review it ☐ Help!
Date:____ Date:____ Date:____

Notes:
_____
_____
_____
_____
_____

Fast Track cross reference, see pages:
_____
_____

Other resources cross reference, see pages:
_____
_____
_____

176 OBJECTIVE REVIEW NOTES

Objective: Develop a data availability solution to include an appropriate backup and restoration strategy and use of a standby or failover server.

☐ **Got it**
*Date:*_____

☐ **Review it**
*Date:*_____

☐ **Help!**
*Date:*_____

Notes:
_____
_____
_____
_____
_____

Fast Track cross reference, see pages:
_____
_____

Other resources cross reference, see pages:
_____
_____
_____

Objective: Develop a migration plan to include upgrading from a previous version of SQL Server and migration of data from other data sources.

☐ **Got it**
*Date:*_____

☐ **Review it**
*Date:*_____

☐ **Help!**
*Date:*_____

Notes:
_____
_____
_____
_____
_____

Fast Track cross reference, see pages:
_____
_____

Other resources cross reference, see pages:
_____
_____
_____

OBJECTIVE REVIEW NOTES 177

▶ Objective: Develop a replication strategy, determining which replication model and replication type to use.

☐ Got it ☐ Review it ☐ Help!
Date:_____ Date:_____ Date:_____

Notes:
_____
_____
_____
_____

Fast Track cross reference, see pages:
_____
_____

Other resources cross reference, see pages:
_____
_____
_____
_____

Installation and Configuration

▶ Objective: Install SQL Server 7, selecting the character set, Unicode collation sequence, and sort order, and installing the proper network libraries, protocols, and services. Also, configure a SQL Server client, perform an unattended installation, and upgrade from a previous version of SQL.

☐ Got it ☐ Review it ☐ Help!
Date:_____ Date:_____ Date:_____

Notes:
_____
_____
_____
_____

Fast Track cross reference, see pages:
_____
_____

Other resources cross reference, see pages:
_____
_____
_____

178 OBJECTIVE REVIEW NOTES

Objective: Configure SQL Server. Configure SQL Mail and the default ANSI settings. Install and configure the Full-Text Search service.

☐ **Got it**
Date:

☐ **Review it**
Date:

☐ **Help!**
Date:

Notes:

Fast Track cross reference, see pages:

Other resources cross reference, see pages:

Configuring and Managing Security

Objective: Assign SQL Server access to Windows NT accounts, SQL Server login accounts, and built-in administrator accounts.

☐ **Got it**
Date:

☐ **Review it**
Date:

☐ **Help!**
Date:

Notes:

Fast Track cross reference, see pages:

Other resources cross reference, see pages:

OBJECTIVE REVIEW NOTES

▶ Objective: Assign database access to Windows NT accounts, SQL Server login accounts, the Guest account, and the DBO user account.

☐ Got it ☐ Review it ☐ Help!
Date:_____ Date:_____ Date:_____

Notes:
_____
_____
_____
_____

Fast Track cross reference, see pages:
_____
_____

Other resources cross reference, see pages:
_____
_____

▶ Objective: Create and assign SQL Server roles to include fixed server, fixed database, public, user-defined database, and application.

☐ Got it ☐ Review it ☐ Help!
Date:_____ Date:_____ Date:_____

Notes:
_____
_____
_____
_____

Fast Track cross reference, see pages:
_____
_____

Other resources cross reference, see pages:
_____
_____
_____

OBJECTIVE REVIEW NOTES

▶ **Objective: Grant to database users and roles the appropriate permissions to database objects and statements.**

☐ Got it ☐ Review it ☐ Help!
Date:_____ Date:_____ Date:_____

Notes:
_____
_____
_____
_____

Fast Track cross reference, see pages:
_____
_____

Other resources cross reference, see pages:
_____
_____
_____

▶ **Objective: Audit SQL server and database activity by using the SQL Server Profiler.**

☐ Got it ☐ Review it ☐ Help!
Date:_____ Date:_____ Date:_____

Notes:
_____
_____
_____
_____

Fast Track cross reference, see pages:
_____
_____

Other resources cross reference, see pages:
_____
_____
_____

Managing and Maintaining Data

► Objective: Create and manage databases, including creating data files, filegroups, and transaction log files, and specifying growth characteristics.

☐ Got it ☐ Review it ☐ Help!
Date:_____ Date:_____ Date:_____

Notes:

Fast Track cross reference, see pages:

Other resources cross reference, see pages:

► Objective: Load data using various methods, including the INSERT, SELECT INTO, and BULK INSERT statements, DTS, HDR, and the Transfer Manager.

☐ Got it ☐ Review it ☐ Help!
Date:_____ Date:_____ Date:_____

Notes:

Fast Track cross reference, see pages:

Other resources cross reference, see pages:

▶ Objective: Back up system and user databases, performing a full backup, transaction log backup, differential backup, and filegroup backup.

☐ Got it ☐ Review it ☐ Help!
Date:_____ Date:_____ Date:_____

Notes:
_____
_____
_____
_____

Fast Track cross reference, see pages:
_____
_____

Other resources cross reference, see pages:
_____
_____

▶ Objective: Restore system and user databases from a full backup, transaction log backup, differential backup, and filegroup backup.

☐ Got it ☐ Review it ☐ Help!
Date:_____ Date:_____ Date:_____

Notes:
_____
_____
_____
_____

Fast Track cross reference, see pages:
_____
_____

Other resources cross reference, see pages:
_____
_____
_____

OBJECTIVE REVIEW NOTES 183

▶ Objective: Manage replication by configuring distribution, publishing, and subscribing servers, create publications, and set up and manage subscriptions.

☐ Got it ☐ Review it ☐ Help!
Date:_____ Date:_____ Date:_____

Notes:
_____
_____
_____
_____

Fast Track cross reference, see pages:
_____
_____

Other resources cross reference, see pages:
_____
_____
_____

▶ Objective: Automate administrative tasks by defining jobs, alerts, and operators, and by setting up SQL Server Agent Mail for job notification and alerts.

☐ Got it ☐ Review it ☐ Help!
Date:_____ Date:_____ Date:_____

Notes:
_____
_____
_____
_____

Fast Track cross reference, see pages:
_____
_____

Other resources cross reference, see pages:
_____
_____
_____

184 OBJECTIVE REVIEW NOTES

Objective: Enable remote access to data by setting up linked servers and configuring security for linked databases.

☐ Got it ☐ Review it ☐ Help!
Date:_____ Date:_____ Date:_____

Notes:
_____
_____
_____
_____

Fast Track cross reference, see pages:
_____
_____

Other resources cross reference, see pages:
_____
_____
_____

Monitoring and Optimization

Objective: Use Performance Monitor and Profiler to monitor SQL Server performance.

☐ Got it ☐ Review it ☐ Help!
Date:_____ Date:_____ Date:_____

Notes:
_____
_____
_____
_____

Fast Track cross reference, see pages:
_____
_____

Other resources cross reference, see pages:
_____
_____
_____

OBJECTIVE REVIEW NOTES 185

▶ **Objective: Tune and optimize SQL Server memory and CPU utilization.**

☐ Got it ☐ Review it ☐ Help!
*Date:*___ *Date:*___ *Date:*___

Notes:
_____
_____
_____
_____
_____

Fast Track cross reference, see pages:
_____
_____

Other resources cross reference, see pages:
_____
_____
_____

▶ **Objective: Limit resources used by queries by using the Query Governor.**

☐ Got it ☐ Review it ☐ Help!
*Date:*___ *Date:*___ *Date:*___

Notes:
_____
_____
_____
_____
_____

Fast Track cross reference, see pages:
_____
_____

Other resources cross reference, see pages:
_____
_____
_____

Troubleshooting

Objective: Diagnose and resolve problems with upgrading from SQL Server 6.x.

☐ Got it ☐ Review it ☐ Help!
Date:_____ Date:_____ Date:_____

Notes:

Fast Track cross reference, see pages:

Other resources cross reference, see pages:

Objective: Diagnose and resolve problems with backup and restore operations.

☐ Got it ☐ Review it ☐ Help!
Date:_____ Date:_____ Date:_____

Notes:

Fast Track cross reference, see pages:

Other resources cross reference, see pages:

OBJECTIVE REVIEW NOTES

▶ Objective: Diagnose and resolve replication problems.

☐ Got it ☐ Review it ☐ Help!
*Date:*____ *Date:*____ *Date:*____

Notes:
_____
_____
_____
_____
_____

Fast Track cross reference, see pages:
_____
_____

Other resources cross reference, see pages:
_____
_____
_____
_____

▶ Objective: Diagnose and resolve job or alert failures.

☐ Got it ☐ Review it ☐ Help!
*Date:*____ *Date:*____ *Date:*____

Notes:
_____
_____
_____
_____
_____

Fast Track cross reference, see pages:
_____
_____

Other resources cross reference, see pages:
_____
_____
_____
_____

OBJECTIVE REVIEW NOTES

▶ **Objective: Diagnose and resolve distributed query problems.**

☐ Got it ☐ Review it ☐ Help!
*Date:*___ *Date:*___ *Date:*___

Notes:
_____
_____
_____
_____
_____

Fast Track cross reference, see pages:
_____
_____

Other resources cross reference, see pages:
_____
_____
_____
_____

▶ **Objective: Use the Client Configuration Utility to diagnose and resolve client connectivity problems.**

☐ Got it ☐ Review it ☐ Help!
*Date:*___ *Date:*___ *Date:*___

Notes:
_____
_____
_____
_____
_____

Fast Track cross reference, see pages:
_____
_____

Other resources cross reference, see pages:
_____
_____
_____
_____

► Objective: Diagnose and resolve problems regarding access to SQL Server, databases, and database objects.

- ☐ **Got it** Date:_____
- ☐ **Review it** Date:_____
- ☐ **Help!** Date:_____

Notes:
_____
_____
_____
_____
_____

Fast Track cross reference, see pages:
_____
_____

Other resources cross reference, see pages:
_____
_____
_____
_____

PART II

INSIDE EXAM 70-028

Part II of this book is designed to round out your exam preparation by providing you with chapters that do the following:

- "Fast Facts Review" is a digest of all "What Is Important to Know" sections from all Part I chapters. Use this chapter to review just before you take the exam: It's all here, in an easily-reviewable format.
- "Insider's Spin on Exam 70-028" grounds you in the particulars for preparing mentally for this examination and for Microsoft testing in general.
- "Hotlist of Exam Critical Concepts" is your resource for cross-checking your technical terms. Although you're probably up-to-speed on most of this material already, double-check yourself anytime you run across an item you're not 100 percent certain about; it could make a difference at exam time.
- "Sample Test Questions" provides a full-length practice exam that tests you on the actual materal covered in Part I. If you mastered the material there, you should be able to pass with flying colors here.
- "Did You Know?" is the last-day-of-class bonus chapter: A brief touching-upon of peripheral information designed to be helpful and of interest to anyone using this technology to the point that they wish to be certified in its mastery.

7   Fast Facts Review

8   Insider's Spin on Exam 70-028

9   Hotlist of Exam-Critical Concepts

10 Sample Test Questions

11 Did You Know?

OBJECTIVES

The exam is divided into six objective categories:

- ▶ **Planning**
- ▶ **Installing and Configuring**
- ▶ **Configuring and Managing Security**
- ▶ **Managing and Maintaining Data**
- ▶ **Monitoring and Optimization**
- ▶ **Troubleshooting**

CHAPTER 7

Fast Facts Review

What to Study

A review of the key topics discussed in the preceding six chapters follows. After you are certain that you understand the principles given in those six chapters, study these key points on the day of the exam prior to writing it.

Chapter 1: Planning

The SQL Server 7.0 Exam covers the details of planning for a SQL 7 installation. You must have solid knowledge of all aspects of SQL 7. The planning portion of the test is broken into the following five areas:

- Develop a security strategy
- Develop a capacity plan
- Develop a data availability solution
- Develop a migration plan
- Develop a replication strategy

In developing a security plan, you need to decide whether to use the Windows NT user accounts only or mixed mode using either NT accounts and/or SQL login accounts. Windows NT user accounts provide more control over the account, such as password lockout and better auditing. If non-Windows clients need access to the SQL Server, you should use mixed mode.

Windows NT groups can be assigned to fixed server roles, fixed database roles, and user-defined roles to provide permissions to perform tasks and access data on the SQL server. By integrating SQL Server access with Windows NT administration, you simplify administration.

Capacity planning deals with making sure the equipment and network can support the users who are accessing the database. When you're planning a SQL deployment, the equipment capability is important, as well as the placement of data on physical drives and servers. It is suggested that the database files and log files be placed on separate physical drives, if possible.

A filegroup is a named collection of files that is used when a SQL Server computer has multiple physical drives. There are two types of filegroups: default and user. Using filegroups to place specific objects and files on different drives can increase system performance.

By default, databases are configured to grow automatically. You can manually add secondary database and log files, manually increase the size of database and log files, or set the database and log files to increase automatically, in specified increments.

It is expected that SQL databases will always be available. For this reason, you might want to create a standby server or failover server. A standby server is a server that is always running. The production server updates the standby server's database files. In the event of a failure, the administrator can switch the users over to the standby server. This doesn't happen automatically. A failover server shares drives with the production server. If the production server fails, the failover server automatically takes over, picking up where the production server left off.

When performing backups, you can select a full backup, a differential backup, or a transaction log backup. A full backup backs up the entire database and transaction log, including any uncommitted transactions. A differential backup backs up any changes to the database since the last full backup, along with any changes to the transaction log that occurred during the full backup. A transaction log backup is used to back up the transaction log only. It requires a full backup to perform a restoration.

Data can be imported into the SQL 7 database using several different methods. Data can be imported to most major databases. A Migration Wizard is available for upgrading from SQL Server 6.x only. This wizard will upgrade any or all databases and will transfer all catalog data, users, and user data, along with most SQL 6.x Server configuration information. This upgrade can be performed using named pipes or tape backup.

Replication can be implemented to allow SQL Servers to share and update information between each other. During this process, the server or servers that maintain the data are known as the publisher. The publisher provides the updated information to a distributor SQL Server computer. The distributor is responsible for providing the updated information to the subscriber SQL Server computer or computers, which service the user's requests for data.

With replication, four different configurations can be used:

- Single-Publisher/Multi-Subscriber. One publisher supports several subscribers.
- Multi-Publisher/Single-Subscriber. One subscriber is updated by several publishers.
- Multi-Publisher/Multi-Subscriber. Several publishers update several subscribers.
- Remote Distribution. A distributor receives a complete update from a publisher across a high-speed data link and then updates subscriber SQL servers with only the data each subscriber needs.

Three types of replication can be configured:

- Snapshot. A snapshot of the data on the publisher is taken periodically and then transferred to the distributor.
- Transactional. Incremental changes are replicated out.
- Merge. All subscribers can makes changes to the data, and then the publisher merges the data. Predefined priorities are used to settle data conflicts.

Chapter 2: Installing and Configuring SQL Server 7

The SQL Server 7.0 Exam covers the details of installing and configuring the product. In most cases, the default choices will be fine. However, for the exam, you'll need to know the significance of each option.

- The character set specifies the types of characters that will be available for use within the database.

- The Unicode collation sequence tells SQL Server how to sort only Unicode data.
- The sort order is a separate setting that specifies rules for sorting.
- Network libraries specify communications protocols that clients can use to access the SQL Server:
  - Named pipes (Windows clients only) works on TCP/IP NetBEUI or IPX/SPX networks.
  - TCP/IP (all TCP/IP clients) works on TCP/IP NetBEUI or IPX/SPX networks.
  - Multi-protocol (all clients) uses any protocol type. Data and authentication encryption are possible.
  - NWLink IPX/SPX (Novell NetWare clients and servers) can connect to the NetWare Bindery.
  - AppleTalk ADSP (Macintosh clients) uses the local AppleTalk zone for communications.
  - Banyan VINES (VINES clients) supports SPP communications. Available only on the Intel platform.
- SQL Server uses several services, including the following:
  - SQL Server 7 (sqlservr.exe) is the database server.
  - SQL Server Agent (sqlagent.exe) schedules SQL Server 7 batch jobs.
  - MS Distributed Transaction Coordinator (msdtc.exe) allows real-time transactions involving multiple servers.
  - Full-Text Search (mssearch.exe) allows users to perform searches without knowing SQL.
- An unattended setup can be performed using the `sqlsetup` command-line command, together with an installation options text file.
- The SQL Server Upgrade Wizard can be used to automatically import data and settings from a SQL Server 6.x database server.
- The SQL Server services can be configured using the Control Panel, the SQL Service Control Manager, or the command line.
- SQL Mail can be configured to specify e-mail recipients. Messages can be sent using stored procedures or via alerts.

- Default ANSI settings specify how SQL Server manages locking and distributed transactions. They can be modified in Enterprise Manager or per transaction.
- Full-text searches allow users and application developers to perform enhanced pattern-matching queries using SQL Server.
- The Full-Text Search service can be installed as part of a custom installation or by rerunning Setup.
- The Full-Text Index Wizard can aid in creating indexes.
- Full-Text Indexes must be populated manually or through the use of scheduled tasks. Population jobs can be full or incremental.
- Full-Text Indexes are managed using stored procedures, not standard SQL commands.

Chapter 3: Configuring and Managing Security

Providing access to data for valid users while limiting a user's capabilities and keeping out intruders is an important part of administering SQL Server. You must know the following items to pass the exam and function as a SQL administrator:

- SQL Server can use Mixed or Windows NT authentication methods for logins. Mixed security allows the use of Windows NT or SQL Server authentication, while Windows NT authentication requires that a Windows NT user account have permissions to access the server.
- A login must be added to a database before the user will be able to access any information in that database.
- Roles are groups of users created based on database and server functions. Users are placed in roles, and then roles are granted permissions. Roles may also contain other roles. Here are the types of roles:
    - Fixed server provides the rights needed to maintain and manage a SQL Server configuration, including objects, alerts, tasks, and devices.

- Fixed database provides the rights to configure and maintain a specific database.
- Public provides the default access rights for users when accessing a SQL database.
- User-defined database provides group-based database-level permissions that are defined by the administrator.
- Application provides rights to a specific application for accessing a database. Requires a separate password.

♦ All database users belong to the Public built-in role.

♦ SQL Server supports three different kinds of permissions:
- Statement permissions permit database creation and modification.
- Object permissions permit the execution of queries that let you view and modify database objects.
- Predefined (role-based) permissions are assigned to fixed roles and object owners.

♦ SQL Server can be configured to audit specific actions on a database. Alerts can be created to track custom actions. Auditing information can be viewed through the Enterprise Manager or in the Windows NT Event Viewer.

♦ SQL Profiler can use traces that store information on specific database actions, such as logons and logoffs.

Chapter 4: Managing and Maintaining Data

For the exam, you will need to have an understanding of the following techniques:

♦ Creating and managing databases

♦ Loading data

♦ Performing backups and restorations

♦ Managing replication

♦ Automating administrative tasks

♦ Configuring remote data access

You can create a database using the Database Creation Wizard, SQL Server Enterprise Manager, or a CREATE DATABASE statement. Information about each database is stored in the sysdatabases table in the master database. To create a new database, you must be using the master database. When a new database is created, it is a duplicate of the model database, so any options or settings in the model database are copied.

The database can be configured to automatically increase the size of the database and transaction log files as needed. You can configure the growth increment through the SQL Server Enterprise Manager or through the ALTER DATABASE statement.

There are several ways to populate a database in SQL Server 7. You must understand the operation of each of these methods:

- INSERT SELECT adds data to an existing database.
- SELECT INTO creates a new table.
- BULK INSERT copies a complete database to a different SQL Server.
- BCP, the Bulk Copy Program, can be used to import or export data between a SQL Server table and a data file, such as an ASCII text file.
- DTS, the Data Transfer Service, is comprised of several tools used for various purposes:
  - DTS Import and DTS Export Wizards. Interactive tools used to import, export, and transform heterogeneous data.
  - DTS Package Designer. Complex data workflows can be defined to import, export, and transform heterogeneous data.
  - DTS Transfer Manager. Used to move schema, objects, and data from one server to another. This tool is typically used when the source and target platforms are dissimilar, such as an Intel-based server and a DEC Alpha server.
- HDR, Host Data Replication, is not a utility, but the process of configuring the publisher, distributor, and subscriber to transfer data.

Backups and restorations are an important part of the SQL Server administrator's responsibility. Here are the types of backups that can be performed:

- A full backup backs up the activity that took place during the backup and any uncommitted transactions in the transaction log.

- A differential backup backs up the changes to the database since the last full backup and the transactions that took place during the backup.

- With a transaction log backup, the transaction log can be backed up separately from the database, and it provides a backup of any database changes, but it requires a full database backup to restore.

The replication process has three functional components: publisher, distributor, and subscriber. The configurations that can be used include single publisher/multiple subscriber, multiple publisher/single subscriber, multiple publisher/multiple subscriber, and remote distributor. The three types of updates that can be performed by the publisher are snapshot, transactional, and merge.

Commands can be grouped into jobs, which can be scheduled to run at selected times. A job is a collection of commands or tasks that can be performed on the SQL Server computer. Alerts can be configured to trigger and perform various tasks, as well as send a message when a defined threshold is exceeded.

Chapter 5: Monitoring and Optimization

One of the key benefits of SQL Server 7 is the server's ability to tune itself and increase the size of the databases automatically. You must understand the configuration options and how to best configure and tune your SQL Server environment.

- The purpose of performance monitoring is to identify a bottleneck—the slowest step in a given process—and to fix it.

- SQL Server includes a default Windows NT Performance Monitor chart that can be used to view real-time memory, CPU, cache, and user logon statistics. Useful counters include the following:

- SQLServer:Block:Page Reads
- SQLServer:Block:Page Writes
- SQLServer:Buffer:Cache Hit Ratio
- SQLServer:Database Manager:Percent Log Used
- SQLServer:General Statistics:User Connections
- SQLServer:General Statistics:Total Server Memory (KB)
- SQLServer:Locks:Lock Waits
- SQLServer:Log Manager:Log Flushes
- SQLServer:Replication Dist.:Delivered Transactions

- SQL Query Analyzer can be used to measure statistics as a specific query executes. This information can then be used to optimize performance and find bottlenecks.
- On multiprocessor systems, SQL Server can be specified to use one or more CPUs.
- The default memory settings for SQL Server are automatically tuned, but these settings can be overridden based on the server's purpose.
- The sp_configure stored procedure can be used to tune SQL Server settings.
- Stored procedures greatly increase the performance of a query or transaction.
- The Query Governor Cost Limit option can be set to limit the amount of server resources that a transaction may consume.
- The SQL Agent can be used to schedule jobs to occur at a specific time or when server utilization is low.

Chapter 6: Troubleshooting

The exam groups troubleshooting questions into seven major areas:

- SQL 6.x upgrade problems. Available with SQL 7 is an Upgrade Wizard that can be used to upgrade SQL 6.x to SQL 7. This tool should copy the majority of the server configuration information and import any selected databases to SQL 7. When run, the Upgrade Wizard generates a number of log files that can help you troubleshoot upgrade problems.

- Backup/restoration problems. With backup and restoration, you need to make sure that the user account performing the backup has proper permissions to be able to perform the backup and that the tape or tape set has the available storage capacity to hold the information being backed up. Three different types of backups can be performed:
    - Full backup backs up the activity that took place during the backup, as well as any uncommitted transactions in the transaction log.
    - Differential backup backs up the changes to the database since the last full backup.
    - Transaction log backup backs up only the transaction log. When restoring, you must restore a full backup and then restore each of the transaction logs to effectively recover from a catastrophic event.
- Replication problems. With replication, the account used to transfer the data from the distributor to the subscriber must have adequate rights to write the information on the destination. This is an issue in a multidomain environment.
- Job and alert failures. If a job doesn't run as expected, verify that the job script is written with the proper syntax. With alerts, problems can include an alert's not firing or slow alert notification. For an alert that isn't firing, make sure that the alert is being written in the Event log and that the alert history is changing. If the alerts are firing but the notification is slow, make sure that the alert response isn't too complex and that the alert's setting for the delay between responses isn't too high.
- Distributed query problem. The operation of performing distributed queries with SQL 7 is much simpler than with SQL 6.x, but there are still several errors that can arise, causing the query to fail. The most common of these problems are listed in Chapter 6. You will want to review these errors before taking the test.

- Client configuration problems. To troubleshoot client configuration problems, use the Client Configuration utility. Two of the more common problems that are encountered with clients are the client's not having a transport protocol installed and configured properly, and the client's not having the correct network library for accessing the SQL Server.

- Access problems. The most common problem for clients attempting to access a SQL database is not having permission to perform the task being attempted. Two tools that can be used to verify proper permissions for performing a function are SQL Server Enterprise Manager and SQL Server Query Analyzer. The user account that can be used for authentication can be a SQL login account or an NT domain user account. If the NT domain user account is used, the account could be a member of a group that is added to a fixed server or database role. The more apparent problem is finding a user who has too few rights to perform a task on a SQL Server. The harder-to-find rights problem involves the user's having too much capability. The user won't complain, because he can perform the task at hand, but he could jeopardize the SQL Server by using permissions greater than his knowledge base.

The Insider's Spin gives you the author's word on information specific to exam 70-028, as well as information you possibly didn't know—but could definitely benefit from—about what's behind Microsoft's exam preparation methodology. This chapter is designed to deepen your understanding of the entire Microsoft exam process. Use it as an extra edge—inside info brought to you by someone who teaches this material for a living.

CHAPTER 8

Insider's Spin on Exam 70-028

At A Glance: Exam Information

Exam Number	70-028
Minutes	90
Questions	TBD*
Single-Answer Questions	Yes
Multiple-Answer Without Correct Number Given	Yes
Objective Categories	6

* At the time of publication, this information was unavailable.

Microsoft is migrating to adaptive testing for the MCP exams, and simulations are used to verify your ability to navigate the interface. By this time, you probably have experienced a Microsoft adaptive test, so not much here will be new. The adaptive tests aren't nearly as long as the old tests, but the amount of knowledge covered is the same.

With a standard *x*-question exam, the number of questions on each topic is about the same. The emphasis is more on knowing conceptually how the product works rather than knowing specific product details. When studying for the test, determine what you feel is most important to understand in each objective area. For instance, when configuring an Enterprise environment, locating servers on local networks is an important task, as well as ensuring that unwanted users can't access your system's data files.

Here are the six objective areas for SQL Server 7, along with the types of questions that might be asked for each area, based on past testing:

- Planning. This area runs the gamut of the SQL Server 7 product. You should know the terminology used when configuring the SQL Server. The types of user accounts you use are determined by the types of users who access the SQL Server, the number of SQL Servers used, and the domain model in use. When you're planning, user rights play a key role in ensuring that SQL Server can interact properly.

- Installation and configuration. The questions covering this portion of the test will challenge your knowledge of automating the client installation process and choosing the correct installation options for a given scenario. You are expected to know how many mail accounts are needed for a given scenario and what services use which mail account for messaging, job execution, and alert notification. You also have to know how to upgrade from SQL Server 4.x and 6.x to SQL Server 7.

- Configuring and managing security. This portion of the test quizzes your knowledge of service accounts and auditing capabilities. You will be tested on the use of roles for assigning server rights as well as database rights. Know what rights a user has if he's using an application that has application roles configured.

- Managing and maintaining data. This portion of the test makes sure you understand the best way to import or export data to and from a SQL Server 7 computer, configure replication, and automate administrative tasks, such as jobs and alerts. You need to know the difference between the available tools and how each works. Since the data on the server and server uptime are two critical issues for a database administrator, you have to know how and when to use the different backup and restoration methods and how to configure fault tolerance into your SQL Server design using standby servers and failover servers.

- Monitoring and optimization. As always, performance is key, so you can expect some questions on Performance Monitoring. Two critical points to remember concerning bottlenecks are that queue lengths should be less than two, and capacity counters should be less than 75 percent utilized on a regular basis. SQL Server is self-tuning, but you will see questions on how to grow files in SQL Server.

- Troubleshooting. Typically, these questions are masked as planning or configuration questions. Normally, you don't need to remember every error message that can arise, but you need to know the difference between a bad error message and a critical error message through severity levels. You need to know where to look for errors and have an idea of what the problem might be when something doesn't seem to work right. An example of this might be not receiving alert messages or only receiving the messages sometimes. Look for these to provide an error indication and list a number of possible solutions. You have to select the one that is most likely to fix the problem.

Although Microsoft no longer releases specific exam information, at one time they said that 85 percent of those who take a certification exam fail. Common logic then indicates that only 15 out of every 100 people, who think they know a product, know it well enough to pass—a remarkably low number.

Quite often, administrators who *do* know a product very well and use it daily fail certification exams. Is it because they don't know the product as well as they think they do? Sometimes. More often than not, however, it's because of other factors:

- They know the product from a real-world perspective, not Microsoft's perspective.

- They are basing their answers on the product as it currently exists, not on when it was first released.

- They are unaccustomed to so many questions in such a short time, or they are unaccustomed to the electronic test engine.

- They don't use all the testing tools available to them.

GET INTO MICROSOFT'S MINDSET

When taking the exam, remember that Microsoft was responsible for writing the exam. Microsoft employees don't write the exam. Instead, experts in the field are hired on a contract basis to write questions for each exam. However, all questions must adhere to certain standards and be approved by Microsoft before they make it into the actual exam. What this translates into is that Microsoft never puts anything in an exam that reflects negatively on them. They also use the exam as promotional marketing as much as possible.

To successfully answer questions and pass the exam, you must put yourself into the Microsoft mindset and see questions from their standpoint. Take the following question, for example:

1. Which network operating system is the easiest to administer in a small real estate office?

   A. NetWare 3.12

   B. SCO UNIX

   C. Windows NT 4.0

   D. LAN server

Although you could make a sincere argument for at least three of the answers, only one will be correct on the exam. Don't try to read too much between the lines, and don't think that you can put a comment at the end of the exam, arguing why another choice would be better. If you answer anything other than C, you might as well write this one off as a missed question.

UNDERSTAND THE EXAM'S TIME FRAME

When you take an exam, find out when it was written. In almost all cases, an exam goes "live" within three months of the final release of the product it's based on. Prior to the exam's release, it goes through a beta process in which all the questions that can be on the exam are written. It is then available for a short time (typically a week), during which scores on each question can be gathered. Questions that exam-takers get right every time are weeded out as being too easy, and those that are too hard are also weeded out.

When you take something like a major operating system (which will remain nameless in this example) and create an exam for it, you end up with a time frame similar to the following:

1. The product goes into early beta.

2. A survey is done (mostly of beta testers) to find out which components of the product they spend the most time with and consider the most important. Their findings are used to generate the objectives and the weighting for each.

3. The product goes to final beta.

4. Contract writers are hired to write questions about the product, using the findings from the survey.

5. The product goes "live."

6. The exam is beta-tested for one to two weeks. After that, the results of each question are evaluated, and the final question pool is chosen.

7. The service pack for the product is released.

8. The exam goes "live."

9. Another service pack is released. It fixes problems from the first service pack and adds additional functionality.

10. Yet another service pack comes out.

11. An option pack that incorporates service packs is released.

12. You take the exam.

Now suppose the product happens to be Windows NT Server 4, and you see a question such as this:

1. What is the maximum number of processors that Windows NT Server 4.0 can handle?

    A. 2

    B. 4

    C. 8

    D. 16

In the real world, the answer would be D. When Windows NT 4.0 first came out, however, the answer was B. Because the original exam questions were written to the final beta, the answer then was B, so the answer now is B. Microsoft has maintained that they will only test on core products, not add-ons. Service packs, option packs, and the like are considered something other than core product.

With this in mind, you must *always* answer every question as if you were addressing the product as it exists when you pull it from the box, and before you do anything else with it—because that is exactly what the exam is written to. You must get into this mindset and understand the time frame in which the exam was written, or you will fail the exam consistently.

Get Used to Answering Questions Quickly

Every exam has a different number of questions, and most stick with the 90-minute time frame. If you run out of time, every question you haven't answered is graded as a wrong answer. Therefore, keep the following in mind:

- Always answer every question; never leave any unanswered. If you start running out of time, answer all the remaining questions with the same letter (such as C or D), and then go back and start reading them. Using the law of averages, if you do run out of time, you should get 25 percent of the remaining questions correct. If you are taking an adaptive exam, this strategy will not work because each question is scored as you move on to the next question. You are unable to mark questions and return to them later.

- Time yourself carefully. A clock runs at the top right of each screen. Mark all questions that require a lot of reading, or that have exhibits, and come back to them after you have answered all the shorter questions. Remember, you do not have the opportunity to mark questions in an adaptive exam.

- Practice, practice, practice. Get accustomed to electronic questioning and answering questions in a short period of time. With as many exam simulators as there are available, there is no reason for anyone not to run through one or two before plunking down $100 for the real test. Some simulators aren't worth the code they're written in, and others are so close in style to the actual exam that they prepare you very well. If money is an issue, and it should be, look for demos and freebies on Web sites. For a great sample that is accessible over the Web, go to http://www.MeasureUp.com, where you can try some sample exams online. Be careful when visiting "braindump" Web sites. The people who add information to the braindump have attempted to remember what the questions were and what they think are the right answers. Sometimes one question will have three or four answers listed as the correct answer. Other times, one word is left out that changes the question's meaning.

If you do run out of time, spend as much time as you want on the last question. You will never "time out" with a question in front of you. You will "time out" only when you click Next to go from that question to the next one.

Taking the Test

An enormous amount of common sense is important here, and much of that common sense only comes as you get more used to the testing procedure. Here's a typical sequence of events:

1. You study for an exam for a considerable period of time.
2. You call Sylvan Prometric (1-800-755-EXAM) and register for the exam.
3. You drive to the testing site, sit in your car, and cram on last-minute details.
4. You walk into the center, sign your name, show two forms of ID, and walk to a computer.
5. Someone enters your ID in the computer and leaves. You're left with the computer, two pieces of plain paper, and two #2 pencils.
6. You click the button on the screen to begin the exam, and the 90 minutes begins.

When you call Sylvan, be certain to ask how many questions are on the exam so that you know before you go in. Sylvan is allowed to release very little information (for example, they can't tell you the passing score). This is one of the few pieces of information they can pass along.

The exam begins the minute you click the button to start it. Before that, the 90-minute time frame hasn't started. After you walk into the testing center and sit down, you're free (within reason) to do whatever you want to. Why not dump everything from your brain (including those last-minute facts you studied in the parking lot) onto those two sheets of paper before you start the exam? The two sheets provide you with four sides—more than enough to scribble down everything you remember and refer to it during the 90 minutes.

When working with an adaptive exam, you can't mark questions and return to them, and the number of correct answers isn't displayed. However, if you select all the answers, a message will appear in the lower-left corner, stating that only x number of answers are needed. You can then deselect the answers you feel are incorrect.

Sometimes, when there are four possible answers, one will be so far off the mark as to not even be worth considering, and another will be too much of a gimme to be true. So you're left with two possibilities. Here's an example:

1. In Windows NT Server 4.0, to view the Application log, what tool must you use?

    A. Application Viewer

    B. Event Viewer

    C. Event Observer

    D. Performance Monitor

In this case, choice A is the gimme of a nonexistent tool that fits the question too perfectly. Choice D is the blow-off answer—so far away from what's possible as to not be considered. That leaves choices B and C.

Even if you knew nothing about Windows NT Server, a clue that B and C are legitimate possibilities is the closeness in the wording of each. Anytime you see two answers worded so closely, assume them to be the ones to focus on.

If you fail an exam, and everyone will occasionally, *never* be lulled into a false sense of confidence by the Section Analysis. If it says you scored 100% on a particular section, you should still study that section before retaking the exam. Too many test-takers study only the sections they did poorly on. That 100% in Monitoring and Optimization could be because the first question pool contained only one question, and you had a 25 percent chance of guessing correctly. What happens next time, when there are three questions in the random pool in that category, and you don't know the answers? You're handicapping yourself right off the bat.

A good rule of thumb if you do fail an exam is to rush back to your car and write down all the questions you remember. Have your study materials in the vehicle with you so you can look up the answers then and there. If you wait until later, you will forget many of them. Chances are, you will remember what you didn't know rather than what you knew.

The new policy from Microsoft allows you to retake an exam that you fail once without waiting (other than the time it takes you to register, and so on). If you fail it again, however, you must wait 14 days before you can take it a third time (and 14 days from that point for the fourth try, and so on). This is to prevent people from actually memorizing the exam. Do your best to never fall into this category. If you fail an exam once, start over and study anew before trying it the second time. Make the second attempt within a week of the first, however, so that the topics are fresh in your mind.

WHERE THE QUESTIONS COME FROM

Knowing where the questions come from can be as instrumental as knowing how to prepare for the exam. The more you know about the question-creation process, the better your odds of passing. Earlier, I discussed the time frame used to create the exam, and I told you that contract writers are hired for the exam. The contract writers are given a sizeable document that details how questions must be written. If you really want to pursue this topic with more fervor, contact Microsoft and inquire about a contract writing position. For now, here are a few tidbits that can be gleaned from multiple-choice authoring:

- No question should have an "all of the above" answer. When you see this choice, it's almost always the correct answer, so it isn't a fair representation of a valid multiple-choice question.

- For the same reason, there should never be a "none of the above" answer.

- Scenarios should be used when they will increase the value of the question.

- No subjective words (such as best and most) should be used.

- Negative words (such as not and cannot) should be avoided.

- Although there can be only one correct answer for the question, all other possibilities should appear plausible and avoid all rationale or explanations.

- All single-answer questions must be mutually exclusive (no A+C, B+C, and so on).

DIFFERENT FLAVORS OF QUESTIONS

At one time, all questions were either single-answer or multiple-answer. There is a push today toward ranking questions and performance-based questions. Older exams have only the first two question types, but newer ones offer the latter two.

Ranking questions provide you with a scenario, a list of required objectives, a list of optional objectives, and a proposed solution, and then ask you to rank how well the solution meets the objectives. Here's a rudimentary example:

1. Evan is a teenager who just got his driver's license. He wants to buy a fast car and ask Betty Lou to the movies on Friday.

    Required objectives: Buy a fast car
    Ask Betty Lou to the movies

    Optional objectives: Earn money for the movies
    Earn money for a car

    Solution: Take a part-time job at the Qwik-E-Mart and buy a classic '67 Cougar

    Rank the solution in terms of the objectives:

    A. The solution meets all of the required and optional objectives.

    B. The solution meets both required objectives and only the first optional objective.

    C. The solution meets both required objectives and only the second optional objective.

    D. The solution does not meet the required objectives.

In this simple example, the answer is D. The solution doesn't include asking Betty Lou to the movies, so it doesn't meet the required objectives. With ranking questions, it is often the case that the required objectives are met in all but the last answer, so read the question backward, if you will, and see whether the required objectives are met. If they aren't, you can answer the question quickly without reading any further and go on to the next one.

Performance-based questions have been incorporated into electronic testing for a long time—just not with Microsoft testing. If I really wanted to test how well you knew a product before hiring you, the best way to do so would be to turn you loose with the product and tell you to do something. If you can, I'll hire you. If you can't, I won't.

Representing that scenario in the testing center becomes difficult. Why? First and foremost, you can't be given unrestricted access to the product within the confines of something (a shell) that grades your actions. Second, the stability of the antiquated machines in most testing centers is questionable at best. Last, the time allotted can't exceed a reasonable amount, or you will become exhausted, and the testing center won't be able to move as many people through each day.

The solution to many of these problems is to keep the number of performance-based questions to a minimum and to have you work with an emulator of some type. The emulator can come onscreen when you click the button and bring up something that looks similar to the configuration information in the real product, without the time and overhead involved in bringing up the real product.

How do you prepare for performance-based questions? Simple—know your product. Focus on the administrative side of it. If you know how to add new users, sites, servers, and directories, you should have no difficulties. If you're good at guessing multiple-choice answers, but you really don't know the product, these questions will ferret that out. On the other hand, if you know your product extremely well, but you aren't good at multiple-choice guessing, you will find these questions a godsend.

Regardless of your familiarity with the product (or lack thereof), be very careful with performance-based questions. Although the emulator can load much quicker than the actual product in question, it is still very time-consuming, and the amount of time required to answer each question is far from minute. These questions take *a lot* of time, and you need to budget for them accordingly.

In the Future

The study of test delivery and grading is known as *psychometrics,* and a good many people are employed in this profession. Microsoft uses these people to help design and implement their exams. It should come as no surprise (if you have any experience with other certifications, such as Novell's) that the next big push will be toward adaptive testing.

Under adaptive testing, the amount of time for each exam can be reduced from 90 minutes to somewhere near 30, and the number of questions can drop from between 50 and 70 down to 15 or so. This benefits you greatly and also allows more students to be tested each day at the training centers.

The premise behind adaptive testing is fairly simple. The first question you get is totally at random and pulled from a pool. After that first question, the rest of the questions are related to how well you answered the preceding question.

For example, suppose I want to give you a general exam on astronomy. The first question asks you how many planets are in our solar system. You answer correctly (nine). I now ask you to name the third planet from the sun, and again you answer correctly (Earth). I can now assume that you know your planets very well, so the next question will be about quasars. This continues for 15 questions. If you answer them all correctly, I will assume that you know astronomy well and pass you.

On the other hand, if you answered Mars to the second question, the next question will be about planets again, giving you a chance to redeem yourself. If you miss that one, I'll probably ask an extremely difficult question about planets to see if you can get it right. If you can't, you don't know planets, so you don't know astronomy, and you'll fail. In some versions of adaptive testing, you bomb out right then, because there is no chance of redemption. With others, you're given bogus questions for the remainder of the exam to make you feel like you're getting your money's worth, even though you're going to fail.

It differs according to style and vendor, but with most adaptive tests, if you answer the 15 questions and haven't passed but are very close to doing so, you can be asked additional questions. The additional questions give you an opportunity to redeem yourself and achieve a passing score.

The key to adaptive testing, besides each question's relationship to the one preceding it, is that every question has a point value. The first question is of medium value. If you miss a question on a topic, the next one asked will be more difficult, and of higher point value, to give you a chance at redemption. If you answer the first question correctly, the next question will be of lesser value and therefore lesser difficulty.

There is no item review in adaptive testing, and there is no going back to the preceding question(s). After you answer a question, you are done with it. You can draw a fair conclusion as to how you did by whether the next question is on a similar topic.

Performance-based testing is in its infancy at Microsoft, but it should be rolled out within the year. Again, the best preparation is to know your topic and to spend time with each question, making certain that you fully understand what is being asked before you answer. With performance-based testing, you are given a task to perform in an emulator of the product you're being tested on. Your performance is graded to see if you accomplished the task in the time and manner in which an administrator should.

Understanding the following terms and concepts will help you identify the knowledge or skill set being tested on the exam. You must understand the following terms and concepts before taking the test.

Do you need to add your own definitions or new terms? This is more than likely, because no two exam candidates will find the same list of terms equally useful. That's why there's room to add your own terms and concepts at the end of this section.

CHAPTER 9

Hotlist of
Exam-Critical Concepts

Term	Definition
Agent, SQL Server	The SQL Server service used to schedule jobs to occur at specific times or when the server isn't busy.
Alerts	System events triggered by parameters defined by a database user. Alerts can be used to notify an administrator when problems or other events occur on a SQL Server.
ANSI settings	Settings used to manage distributed transactions, locking issues, and concurrency issues on database servers.
Auditing	Used to log specific actions and events performed on a SQL Server for later analysis via the SQL Server event log.
Authentication	The act of logging in to a SQL Server database using a valid login ID.
Authentication mode, mixed	Allows both Windows NT accounts and SQL Server accounts to log in to the server.
Authentication mode, Windows NT	Allows SQL Server to map existing Windows NT accounts to SQL Server logins.
Backup, full	Backs up the entire database, including any uncommitted changes in the transaction log.
Backup, transaction log	The transaction log can be backed up separately from the database file. It provides a backup of any database changes but requires a full database backup in order to perform a restoration.
Caching	Storing frequently used information in a faster type of memory. For example, hard disk information is cached in RAM.
Central Processing Unit (CPU)	The primary calculation processor of a computer. Speed is usually measured in megahertz (Mhz).
Character set	The set of 256 characters used by SQL Server text data types.

Hotlist of Exam-Critical Concepts

Term	Definition
Code page	The set of symbols in a specific character set.
Costs	Statistics based on CPU time used to complete a SQL query or transaction.
Data and log files	When a database is created, at least two different files are created. The first is a database file (.mdf), and the second is a transaction log file (.ldf). When data is added or modified, the change statement is recorded to the transaction log and written to disk, and then the checkpoint process writes the completed transaction to the database. In the event of a failure, the transaction log is used to roll the database to a known state.
Database connection	Created when a user logs in to a SQL Server database.
Distributed Transaction Coordinator (DTC)	Manages transactions that occur across multiple SQL Servers.
Enterprise Manager	A graphical management application for administering SQL Server.
Failover support	With SQL Server 7, a virtual server can be created from two servers that have shared disk drives. If one server fails, the other server automatically picks up the processing done by the other server.
Filegroup	A named collection of files that can be used to increase performance and backup capabilities on a SQL Server computer with more than one physical disk. There are two types of filegroups: default and user-defined.
Full-Text Search Index	Allows the use of advanced queries to find forms of words in character-based datatypes.
Growing a database	With SQL Server 7, the database and log files can be configured to grow as needed automatically or can be manually increased in size. The size increment is configurable.

Term	Definition
Importing data	Several tools are provided with SQL Server 7 to import data: DTS Import and Export Wizards, DTS Package Designer, DTS Transfer Manager, bcp utility, Transact-SQL statements, backup and restore utilities, and sp_attach_db.
Index	A database object that optimizes access to frequently-queried columns in a database table.
Login	A SQL Server account that allows a user to connect to the database server.
Mapping Windows NT groups	Windows NT groups can be added to SQL Server roles or used to configure user rights directly on a database.
Network Libraries	Specify the protocols and connection methods used by clients to connect to a SQL Server.
Performance	A general term used to describe the overall ability of a system to perform useful tasks.
Performance baseline	Average values for system performance during times of regular usage.
Performance bottleneck	The slowest step in a given process.
Performance Monitor	A Windows NT tool used to view performance-related statistics.
Permissions, object	Security permissions set on specific database objects such as tables and views.
Permissions, statement	Allows for the creation of database objects such as tables and views.
Profiler, SQL Server	Monitors specific SQL Server events defined in trace files and displays the results or saves them to an export file.
Query Analyzer	A SQL Server tool that executes SQL queries and analyzes the execution of database operations.

Hotlist of Exam-Critical Concepts

Term	Definition
Query Governor	Used to impose cost limitations on queries. If a SQL query consumes more CPU resources than the limit, the transaction will not be completed.
Random Access Memory (RAM)	Physical memory installed in a computer. Usually measured in megabytes (MB).
Replication models	When setting up replication, you can configure the replication of data from a single publisher to multiple subscribers, a single subscriber receiving updates from multiple publishers, or multiple subscribers receiving data from multiple publishers. A distribution server can be configured, which receives updates from a publisher and then provides a subset of that data to subscribers.
Replication types	The three different types of replication available are snapshot, transactional, and merge.
Roles	SQL Server roles provide the same type of capability that a built-in local group or Administrator-created group offers in Windows NT. The built-in server roles provide basic SQL server capabilities. Custom server roles can be created by the SQL Server administrator if the built-in roles don't provide enough functionality.
Roles, application	Password-protected roles that can be used by an application that enforces its own security.
Roles, fixed database	Administrative capabilities can be provided at the database level using fixed database roles. These roles allow users to be grouped into a single administrative unit and given the ability to perform a task on a database, such as adding a table to a database.
Roles, fixed server	Administrative capabilities can be provided at the server level using fixed server roles. These roles provide groupings of various administrative rights, such as the ability to create a database on a server.

Term	Definition
Roles, server	Built-in roles used for managing various aspects of a SQL Server installation.
Roles, user-defined database	A SQL administrator can create roles to group users into a single administrative unit if the fixed server and database roles are not sufficient.
Scalability	The ability of a system to adapt to increasing functional demands.
Service Manager	A system tray icon that can be used to start and stop SQL Server services.
Sort order	Specified during setup, sort order determines how SQL Server will sort character-based data.
sp_configure	A SQL Server stored procedure used to view and modify server configuration parameters.
SQL Mail	Runs as a Windows NT Service. Can be used to send e-mail messages from SQL Server alerts and stored procedures.
Standby server	Provides a backup computer that can be used if the SQL Server fails. This backup server has all the database files on it, and these files are updated at regular intervals. The switch is not automatic; it must be instigated by the administrator.
Stored procedures	A database object that is a precompiled set of SQL statements that can be executed by users. Stored procedures offer increased performance when compared to executing complex queries manually.
Structured Query Language (SQL)	The syntax for executing commands on database objects. Commands include SELECT, UPDATE, INSERT, and DELETE.

Hotlist of Exam-Critical Concepts 225

Term	Definition
Subscription	An arrangement between two servers that is used to distribute updates to data. The subscriber can receive data updates that are pushed from the publisher, or the subscriber can pull updates from the publisher. The update methods are snapshot, transactional, and merge.
System administrator (SA) account	A SQL Server account that has access to perform all functions on the server.
Table	The basic database object that stores data in rows and columns.
Threads	Single units of execution used by SQL Server.
Trace Files	Used by SQL Server Profiler to define which items to monitor.
Trigger	A database object based on a SQL statement that is executed whenever a specific change is made to a database object.
Unicode	A set of 65,536 characters representing characters in most languages worldwide.
Unicode collation sequence	Specifies the sort order for Unicode data. Is used for multilanguage database support and international applications.
Upgrading to SQL 7	SQL Server 6.x can be upgraded to SQL Server 7. SQL Server 4.x can't be upgraded directly to SQL Server 7; it must be upgraded to SQL Server 6.x first. An Upgrade Wizard is available. It can upgrade all databases; transfer catalog data, objects, and user data; and retrieve replication settings, Executive settings, and most SQL Server configuration options.
View	A database object that references information from database tables. Views don't store data, but operations performed on views can make modifications to the tables that they refer to.

226 CHAPTER 8 Hotlist of Exam-Critical Concepts

Additional Terms and Concepts

Hotlist of Exam-Critical Concepts

Working through practice questions is a great way to test your knowledge of SQL Server 7. The following is a list of questions that will help you test whether you're prepared to take the exam. These questions are not presented in any particular order based on topic or difficulty. The real test will be adaptive: The questions you are asked will be based on your response to the previous one. Answers and explanations are presented after the questions. Good luck!

CHAPTER **10**

Sample Test Questions

QUESTIONS

The sample test has 45 questions, just like the actual exam, and covers each of the 6 objectives.

1. *You are installing a SQL Server for your network. The computers that will need access to the SQL database include Windows NT Workstation computers, Windows 95 computers, UNIX computers, and Apple Macintosh computers. Which login authentication mode should you select?*
   A. Windows NT authentication mode
   B. Mixed mode
   C. Secure authentication
   D. Clear-text authentication

2. *Which of the following can be changed after you install SQL Server without rerunning SQL Server 7 Setup?*
   A. Unicode collation sequence
   B. Character set
   C. Sort order
   D. Installation path
   E. None of the above

3. *SQL Mail can be used to send messages when all but which of the following occurs:*
   A. A SQL Server alert occurs.
   B. Specially formatted e-mail is received.
   C. A user-defined task is completed.
   D. A SQL Performance Monitor value meets certain criteria.

4. *Which of the following limitations occurs when Windows 95 and 98 clients use the Named Pipes network library?*
   A. The named pipe parameters must be configured manually, because the defaults won't work.
   B. Clients can connect, but the server can't send data to them.
   C. The clients can't connect to the database server.
   D. The clients can't automatically generate a list of available SQL Servers when logging in.

5. **Which of the following is not true of Full-Text Indexes?**
   A. Full-Text Indexes can decrease overall server performance.
   B. Full-Text Indexes require disk space based on the size of your databases and the columns selected.
   C. The Full-Text Search service can be installed during SQL Server Setup.
   D. SQL Server automatically maintains indexes.

6. **Which application design places the data and business rules on the server and the presentation application on the client?**
   A. Intelligent server (two-tier)
   B. Intelligent client (two-tier)
   C. *N*-tier
   D. Single master

7. **Which of the following statements is not used to modify statement permissions?**
   A. GRANT
   B. DENY
   C. REVOKE
   D. PERMIT

8. **The SQL Server Upgrade Wizard can do all but which of the following?**
   A. Import data from existing installations of SQL Server 6.x
   B. Import data from another machine running SQL Server 6.x
   C. Run automatically after the SQL Server 7 service has been installed and started
   D. Import backups made on previous versions of SQL Server

9. **The SQL Server Upgrade Wizard can automatically import data from which of the following databases?**
   A. SQL Server 6.x
   B. SQL Server 4.2
   C. Oracle 7.3x
   D. Microsoft Access

10. *Which of the following is/are not a standard type of SQL Server role?*
    A. Application roles
    B. Database roles
    C. Server roles
    D. Guest role

11. *What application design places the data on one server, business rules on another, and presentation application on the client?*
    A. Intelligent server (two-tier)
    B. Intelligent client (two-tier)
    C. *N*-tier
    D. Single master

12. *Which of the following objects can be contained by a role?*
    A. SQL Server users
    B. Windows NT users
    C. Windows NT groups
    D. Other SQL server roles
    E. All of the above

13. *The Full-Text Search service can be administered in all of the following ways* except *which one?*
    A. SQL Enterprise Manager
    B. Standard SQL statements
    C. Built-in stored procedures
    D. Control Panel's Services applet

14. *Select the best description of a job.*
    A. A job is an event that can be configured in the event of an anomaly during a task.
    B. A job can define a series of steps that will be performed on a scheduled basis.
    C. A job is an event that can be configured if an error occurs in a job.
    D. A job can define a single step that can be added to other jobs to create a task.

15. *While trying to upgrade from SQL 6.x to SQL 7, you receive a memory-related error. What is the most likely cause?*
    A. The system you're performing the upgrade on doesn't have the required amount of RAM installed.
    B. The system you're performing the upgrade on has run out of disk space.
    C. The Windows NT operating system you're running is incompatible with SQL 7.
    D. The Windows NT operating system had to grow the memory page file (pagefile.sys) during the SQL 7 upgrade.

16. *Network libraries do all of the following except what?*
    A. Specify accepted communications settings on the server
    B. Specify accepted communications settings on the client
    C. Require specific DLLs on the client and server based on enabled communication mechanisms
    D. Are used only on Windows-based clients

17. *Which of the following is not true of Windows NT Security for SQL Server?*
    A. User accounts may be stored in the Windows NT security database.
    B. Users must have a mapped login before they can access the SQL Server.
    C. A SQL Server user account and password can be used to gain access to the server.
    D. Users must have permissions to use a database before being able to access any database objects.

18. *Which of the following is not true of the System Administrator (SA) account?*
    A. Logging in as SA will allow the user to perform any function on the database.
    B. By default, the SA account has a blank password.
    C. Windows NT Administrators and Domain Administrators are automatically mapped to the SA account.
    D. The SA account can be used to grant SA access to other users.
    E. All of the above are true.

19. You have configured an alert and verified that it is firing, but the notification seems to be extremely slow. What could be the cause of the problem? Select all that apply.
    A. The network routers are the bottleneck.
    B. The Delay Between Responses is too low.
    C. The alert response is complex, requiring many operator notifications.
    D. The Delay Between Responses setting for the alert is too high.

20. Which of the following functions does a SQL Server login allow?
    A. Connection to the database server
    B. Access to a specific database
    C. Viewing data in a database object
    D. Modifying data in a database object

21. Which of the following is not true of performance optimization?
    A. Only one change should be made at a time.
    B. Measurements should be taken after each change.
    C. The goal is to eliminate all bottlenecks.
    D. Performance statistics will be largely based on hardware configuration.

22. In replication, which server receives and stores changes and then forwards the changes to a subscriber server?
    A. Publisher
    B. Distributor
    C. Subscriber
    D. None of the above

23. Which of the following most likely signifies a need for more RAM?
    A. A high number of page reads
    B. A low number of page reads
    C. A low cache hit ratio
    D. A high cache hit ratio

24. *A system administrator finds that users often execute long-running queries that often delay response times for all other users. How can she limit this?*
   A. Set a cost limit using the query governor.
   B. Increase server memory.
   C. Add an additional server CPU.
   D. Lower the number of concurrent connections allowed.

25. *Which of the following is not true of the Windows NT Performance Monitor?*
   A. The Chart view creates basic performance graphs.
   B. Performance can be measured only for the local machine.
   C. Log files can store past information for later analysis.
   D. Chart settings can be modified and saved.

26. *Which files are created when you create a database?*
   A. A primary data file, a secondary data file, and one or more transaction log files
   B. A primary data file and one or more secondary data files
   C. A secondary data file and one or more transaction log files
   D. A primary data file and one or more transaction log files

27. *An administrator suspects that a few poorly written SQL queries are reducing overall server performance. How can he best isolate the cause of the problem?*
   A. Use SQL Query Analyzer to determine the costs of specific SQL transactions.
   B. Use Performance Monitor to establish a performance baseline.
   C. Measure CPU usage using Performance Monitor.
   D. Measure CPU usage using Task Manager.

28. *When you're planning a SQL Server implementation, which of the following statements is true?*
   A. The data and log files should be placed on different physical drives to increase performance and reliability.
   B. The data and log files should be placed on the same physical drives. This will increase performance but decrease reliability.
   C. The data and log files should be placed on the same physical drives to increase performance and reliability.
   D. The data and log files should be placed on different physical drives. This will increase reliability, but performance will suffer.

29. *A user wants to schedule a long-running procedure to occur as often as possible but only whenever the server isn't busy. How can he do this?*
    A. Use the SQL Agent to schedule a job to execute after normal business hours.
    B. Create a stored procedure to optimize the query.
    C. Run the process under the SA account.
    D. Use the SQL Agent to schedule the job to occur when processor utilization falls below a certain value.

30. *Before changing advanced options on the SQL Server, which of the following commands must you execute? Select all that apply.*
    A. sp_configure 'show advanced options', 1
    B. RECONFIGURE
    C. Shutdown
    D. Restart

31. *Which of the following settings is best for the Windows NT Server service whose primary application is SQL Server?*
    A. Minimize memory used
    B. Balance
    C. Maximize throughput for file sharing
    D. Maximize throughput for network applications

32. *Which of the following are valid fixed server roles? Select all that apply.*
    A. dbcreator
    B. diskadmin
    C. public
    D. db_owner
    E. setupadmin

33. *Which of the following are valid fixed database roles? Select all that apply.*
    A. sysadmin
    B. db_securityadmin
    C. public
    D. db_ddladmin
    E. dbcreator

34. *Specify the order in which the following events occur when data in a SQL Server 7 database is changed.*
   A. The pages affected are loaded into the buffer cache.
   B. The modification is recorded in the log and written to disk.
   C. An application sends a modification.
   D. The checkpoint process writes the completed transaction to the database on the disk.

35. *Which application design places the data on the server and the presentation application and business rules on the client?*
   A. Intelligent server (two-tier)
   B. Intelligent client (two-tier)
   C. *n*-tier
   D. Single master

36. *Select the definition that best describes the Tabular Data Stream (TDS).*
   A. A transport-level protocol used for communication between a client and the SQL Server
   B. An application-level protocol used between the SQL Server and the domain controller for user authentication
   C. An application-level protocol used for communication between a client and the SQL Server
   D. A transport-level protocol used between the SQL Server and the domain controller for user authentication

37. *Your company wants to be able to make changes to corporate-wide information and distribute that information to the local SQL server for each of its 10 sites. What type of replication should be configured?*
   A. Remote distribution server
   B. Multiple publisher/multiple subscriber
   C. Multiple publisher/single subscriber
   D. Single publisher/multiple subscriber

38. **What data is copied during a full backup?**
    A. The entire database, including any uncommitted changes in the transaction log
    B. All the changes to the database, including any uncommitted changes to the transaction log
    C. The entire database, with the exception of any uncommitted changes in the transaction log
    D. All the changes to the database, with the exception of any uncommitted changes to the transaction log

39. **In replication, which server maintains the source database and then sends the published data to a distributor server?**
    A. Publisher
    B. Distributor
    C. Subscriber
    D. None of the above

40. **In replication, which server receives published data?**
    A. Publisher
    B. Distributor
    C. Subscriber
    D. None of the above

41. **Select the best description of an alert.**
    A. An alert is automatically fired if an anomaly occurs during a task.
    B. An alert defines a series of steps that will only be performed on a scheduled basis.
    C. An alert is an action taken whenever a specified event occurs.
    D. An alert defines a single step in a monitored SQL query.

42. **Auditing can be used to do all but which of the following?**
    A. Prevent unauthorized access to database objects
    B. Track system logons
    C. Notify an administrator when specific database information is queried
    D. Notify an administrator when specific database information is changed

43. *You are upgrading from SQL 6.x to SQL 7 using the Upgrade Wizard, and an error occurs. What directory would most likely contain the upgrade log files?*
   A. C:\Mssql7\Upgrade
   B. C:\Mssql7\Failure
   C. C:\Mssql67\Upgrade
   D. C:\Mssql67\Failure

44. *You need to perform a backup during normal business hours. How much of an impact will this have on the overall performance of the SQL 7 server you're backing up?*
   A. Online backups have a major impact (90 percent performance loss) on system throughput.
   B. Online backups have only a minor impact (5 percent performance loss) on system throughput.
   C. Online backups can only be performed on static transaction logs.
   D. Online backups have a moderate impact (50 percent performance loss) on system throughput.

45. *Can a SQL 6.5 publisher use a SQL 7 distributor?*
   A. Yes, but they must be the same machine.
   B. No. Only a SQL 7 publisher can use a SQL 6.5 distributor.
   C. Yes, but they must be different computers.
   D. No. The replication partners must run the same version of SQL.

ANSWERS AND EXPLANATIONS

1. **B** In an environment with non-Microsoft clients, mixed mode would be the best choice for user permissions to access the SQL Server.

2. **E** All the options require that SQL Server Setup be rerun.

3. **B** SQL Mail only processes outgoing mail; it can't respond to incoming messages. Mail can be sent when all of the other events occur.

4. **D** Named Pipes doesn't let Windows 95 and 98 users see a list of available SQL Server machines on the network.

5. **D** Full-Text Indexes must be manually updated, or you may schedule a job to routinely refresh them.

6. **A** An intelligent server (two-tier) design places the data and business rules on the same machine, with the presentation application on the client.

7. **D** PERMIT is not one of the SQL Server statement permission types.

8. **D** The Upgrade Wizard can only transfer existing databases, transaction logs, and server settings from a SQL Server 6.x installation.

9. **A** The Upgrade Wizard can only import information from SQL Server 6.x. To update older versions, you need to first upgrade to SQL Server 6.x, or manually import data and settings after setup.

10. **D** The Guest role is not a standard SQL Server role.

11. **C** The *n*-tier design places the data on one server, the business rules on another, and the presentation application on the client.

12. **E** All of the options are correct.

13. **B** The Full-Text Search service can't be modified using standard SQL statements.

14. **B** A job is like a script file containing several steps that can be scheduled to run at regular intervals.

15. **D** The most likely cause of a memory allocation error during an upgrade is the NT operating system's growing the page file to support the upgrade process. You can avoid this by increasing the size of the swap file before performing an upgrade.

16. **D** Network libraries are available for most types of clients and protocols. For example, Macintosh clients can use the AppleTalk library, and Banyan Vines users can use the StreeTalk protocol. More common protocols such as IPX/SPX and TCP/IP are also available.

17. **C** If Windows NT Security is chosen, the current user must be given logon permissions and can't enter a password.

18. **E** All of the options are true.

19. **C, D** If an alert is complex, several operator notifications will need to be sent, which could make the process seem very slow. If the Delay Between Responses is set too high, the same indication can be seen.

20. **A** A SQL Server login only allows a user to connect to the server.

21. **C** A bottleneck is a relative value, defined as the slowest step in any process, so it can never be completely eliminated.

22. **B** In replication, the publisher holds the source database and passes any updates to a distributor, which then updates the subscribers.

23. **C** A low cache hit ratio means that SQL Server must often read information from the hard disk, thus slowing performance.

24. **A** The SQL Server can be configured to prohibit any transactions that exceed a set amount of CPU time to process.

25. **B** Windows NT Performance Monitor can be used to connect to and report data from remote Windows NT machines.

26. **D** When a database is created, a primary data file and one or more transaction log files are created. A secondary data file can be created, but this doesn't happen automatically.

27. **A** The SQL Query Analyzer can give statistics based on specific transactions for evaluating resource usage.

28. **A** By placing the data and log files on different physical drives, performance is increased, because the I/O is being performed across two different data paths. Reliability is increased because the database and transaction logs are on different drives. If a disk drive fails, only one or the other is lost.

29. **D** This will ensure that the process runs whenever server load is light and doesn't assume that transactions won't be done after-hours.

30. **A, B** You must run both commands before advanced options will be available for viewing and modification.

31. **D** This setting is intended for applications that manage their own memory and is most appropriate in this scenario.

32. **A, B, E** The valid fixed server roles are dbcreator, diskadmin, and setupadmin. Public and db_owner are examples of fixed database roles.

33. **B, C, D** The valid fixed database roles are db_securityadmin, public, and db_ddladmin. Sysadmin and dbcreator are examples of fixed server roles.

34. **C, A, B, D** When an application requests data to be updated, the affected pages are loaded into memory, and the change is written to the buffer and the transaction log. Once those operations are complete, the checkpoint process writes the completed transaction to the database on the disk.

35. **B** When the presentation and the business rules are both on the client, the design is known as an intelligent client (two-tier) design.

36. **C** The TDS is the application layer protocol used to establish a connection and communicate between a SQL 7 client and server. This application protocol is encapsulated in a transport protocol, such as TCP/IP.

37. **D** In this case, the updates will be performed from one SQL server and sent to several subscriber servers. This configuration is known as a single publisher/multiple subscriber configuration.

38. **A** A full backup backs up the entire database and the transaction log, including any uncommitted changes.

39. **A** In replication, the publisher holds the source database and passes any updates to a distributor, which then updates the subscribers.

40. **C** In replication, the publisher holds the source database and passes any updates to a distributor, which then updates the subscribers. The subscribers ultimately hold the published information.

41. **C** An alert is an event that can be configured to run whenever certain administrator-defined events occur. The alert can be set to perform tasks and send a message to one or more users.

42. **A** Auditing doesn't permit or deny certain actions from being performed—it only makes a log of these actions.

43. **A** When the Upgrade Wizard is run, the upgrade's log files are written to c:\Mssql7\Upgrade in a unique folder for each instance the wizard is run under.

44. **B** Online backups are designed to be able to run on an operational SQL server with little impact on the operation of the SQL server. The actual performance loss should be around 5 percent.

45. **C** SQL 6.5 can act as a publisher with SQL 7 acting as a distributor. This function must be performed on two different machines.

In this chapter, we'll take a look at some information pertaining to real-world SQL Server installations. These concepts aren't covered on the exam, but the ideas presented here will help you as you work with SQL Server in real-world environments. Specifically, we'll cover these issues:

- Choosing a database server and evaluating SQL Server 7
- The basics of Online Analytical Processing (OLAP)
- Multitier client/server architecture and Web database publishing
- Distributed management

The goal of this chapter is not to completely explain new technologies and concepts, but to give you an idea of how you can better use SQL Server in your own environment.

CHAPTER 11

Did You Know?

Choosing a Database Server

Microsoft's SQL Server 7 represents a great leap forward for this database server platform. There are many things to consider when choosing a database server for any given environment:

- **Scalability.** How well will the database server software be able to use hardware upgrades?
- **Ease of use.** How easy is it to manage the system?
- **Development.** What special features are available to developers for creating applications?
- **Flexibility.** How configurable is the database server? Does it support Web-based information access and modification?
- **Security.** How strong is security, and how easily can security permissions be managed?
- **Reliability.** Does the application server require frequent reboots, or do applications sometimes bring down the server?

It's important to consider the needs of an environment when choosing a database platform. For example, if you will be creating a fairly simple Web-based database front-end, flexibility and ease of use will be primary concerns. On the other hand, if you will be supporting thousands of concurrent users accessing a mission-critical application, scalability, security, and reliability will be important factors.

Evaluating SQL Server

Competition for SQL Server includes products from Oracle, Sybase, Informix, Arbor, and several other database vendors. Based on previous versions, Microsoft's SQL Server has gained a reputation for being flexible and extremely easy to use. It has also provided security features that are well integrated with the Windows NT security database and excellent performance for small- to medium-sized businesses. Being a relatively new product in the enterprise marketplace, however, Microsoft hopes to make SQL Server 7 and future versions more scalable and able to handle large-scale environments. Specific improvements include support for clustering and much larger databases. Clustering allows multiple physical servers to function in configurations that allow fault tolerance and load balancing. Performance has been increased dramatically through the implementation of parallel query processing and row-level locking (which alleviates many of the locking problems associated with large database objects). More information about new features in SQL Server 7 is available from Microsoft at www.microsoft.com/sql.

Time will tell how well these new features address real goals. When choosing a database solution, it's important to evaluate your current conditions and predict future requirements. Then, fit the strengths and weaknesses of the potential solutions to your requirements.

On the other end of the spectrum, it's important not to ignore the needs of "personal" database users. Microsoft created SQL Server 7 Workstation to support end-users who require database access on their personal computers and notebooks. This may be for development reasons or to load a small portion of a company database that must be available on the road. The actual source code that creates the foundation of SQL Server 7 is the same whether you're running the personal edition or the Enterprise version of SQL Server, thus ensuring compatibility between the platforms.

WEB DATABASE PUBLISHING

Using Web-based front-ends to access and modify data is a popular technique appearing on Internet and intranet applications everywhere. Web-based front-ends have the benefit of allowing client-independent access to data. Users must only be familiar with working within a Web browser to access the information they need. Microsoft's Visual Interdev, part of the Visual Studio development suite, allows for the quick and easy creation of data-dependent Web pages. It works with Microsoft's Internet Information Server (IIS) Web platform to present dynamically generated Web pages. SQL Server 7 also supports the ability to automatically generate and update Web pages based on database information. This alleviates problems associated with creating client/server applications to view simple data. For more advanced Web-based applications, Open Database Connectivity (ODBC) drivers allow developers to easily access and modify information from various database types with minimal modifications to code.

Multitier Client/Server Architecture

In distributed environments, data is often stored in databases on remote machines. Clients run programs to access and manipulate this information. In a three-tier client/server solution, the functions are broken down as follows:

- **Presentation layer:** A user interface presents data in a form that the client can use. The Presentation layer may be a Web server or a database-dependent application that resides on the client.

- **Business Rules layer:** Data is obtained or modified according to user actions. The business rules test for appropriate user permissions, determine if a transaction is valid, and ensure that the entire transaction is either completed or rolled back.

- **Back-End Resources layer:** Ultimately, information is stored in various database servers or mainframes operated by an organization. These resources provide data that is accessed and modified by the Business Rules layer.

The overall goal is to move information from the back-end resources to the client. Figure 11.1 shows a basic three-tier client/server architecture using Microsoft products. Microsoft refers to this collectively as Windows Distributed Internet Applications Architecture, or DNA. DNA is a methodology for applications development that involves distributed processing on multiple machines. All Microsoft products—including operating systems, development tools, and applications—support DNA in some way. For more information on DNA and how various products fit into this scheme, see www.microsoft.com/dna.

The benefit of dividing these functions is that it allows for greater scalability and flexibility. For example, if the Web servers are found to be the bottleneck, you can upgrade them and/or add an additional server without affecting the back-end resources or the client machines. It's also likely that your company stores information in several different data sources. The advantage of having multiple tiers is that data access can be transparent to the client. Multitier client/server applications are becoming more and more common. Many businesses that haven't yet implemented them are evaluating this option.

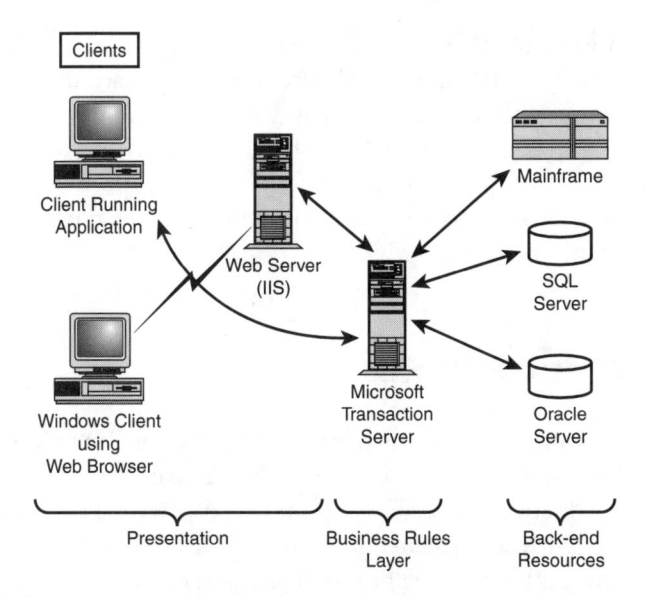

FIGURE 11.1
A typical three-tier client/server architecture using Microsoft technologies.

Distributed Management

Smaller companies often choose to have a single person responsible for all database administration. However, in larger environments, it is often necessary to distribute management tasks among several different individuals. Job functions may also be created based on task. For example, one administrator might be responsible for backing up two different databases, while another focuses on managing security accounts. The use of SQL Server roles can make distributed management easier by providing a convenient way to maintain these permissions. This also helps in auditing actions and holding users responsible for actions.

On-Line Analytical Processing (OLAP)

New in SQL Server 7 is the ability to perform On-Line Analytical Processing (OLAP). Standard database tables are two-dimensional data structures. OLAP allows the creation of complex data cubes that represent information in multiple dimensions. Data cubes can perform complex grouping functions that analyze data. Creating OLAP applications involves thinking of data in terms different from standard database access. Microsoft Office 2000 components and other products will feature the ability to deal with these data types. The goal is to make your company's data more easily accessible and useful for decision support, reporting, and real-time analysis. For more information on OLAP, see the Books Online that accompanies SQL Server 7.

Moving Forward

It is difficult to find a business of any size that doesn't rely on database technology in some way. The challenge is to make these systems as efficient and productive as possible. Often, keeping several database servers running efficiently can seem like a full-time job. Future versions of Windows and SQL Server will make managing environments of any size easier for users, managers, and IT professionals. However, it's just as important to make sure that information is easily available to those who need it and that your business is utilizing this information to its benefit. There is almost certainly a place for SQL Server 7 in most environments, and it's up to you to maximize its benefits!

INDEX

A

access
  remote data, 122
  troubleshooting, 167-169
accounts
  creating, 62
  system administrator (SA), 71, 225
  Windows NT
    choosing, 33
    mapping, 73, 75
adaptive testing, 212, 217-218
adding
  accounts, 62
  applications, 28, 30
  components to setup, 51
  counters, Performance Monitor, 131-132
  databases, 75, 77, 95, 97-99, 109
  files and filegroups, 95, 97-98
  indexes, Full-Text Search, 65-66
  logins, 72-74, 79
  logs, 95, 97-98
  mail profiles, 62
  objects, 26
  permissions, 84-85
  publications, replication, 117
  queries, 136
  roles, 81-82
  server links, 122
  stored procedures, 144
  traces, 90, 134-135
administrative tasks, automating, 118-119, 121
Advanced tab, SQL Server Agent, 146
Alert System tab, SQL Server Agent, 146
Alert view, 133
alerts
  defining, 119
  setting, 87, 147-148
  troubleshooting, 160-161
ALTER DATABASE statement, 97
ANSI settings
  configuring, 62-63
  described, 220

answering questions on
  certification exam, 210-211
answers to sample questions
  for certification exam,
  240-243
Application component, 21
application roles, 33-34,
  78, 223
applications
  BCP, 20, 41, 101
  Client Configuration, 20
  Data Transformation Services
    (DTS), 102
  designing, 28, 30
  Enterprise Manager, 144, 221
  OSQL, 21
  Performance Monitor, 20,
    129-133, 222
  Profiler, 20, 89-90, 133, 222
  Query Analyzer, 20, 135, 222
  Query Governor, 144-145,
    222-223
  Service Manager, 20
  Setup, 20
  SQL Mail, 62-63, 224
  Wolfpack, 40
architecture, clients and
  servers, 248
assigning object permissions,
  83, 85-86
auditing
  databases, 86, 90
  described, 220
authentication, 31, 123, 220
automating administrative
  tasks, 118-119, 121
availability, data, 40

B

Back-End Resources layer, 248
BACKUP DATABASE
  statement, 110
backups, 38-40, 104-113,
  157-158, 220
Balance setting, 142
baselines, performance, 222
BCP. *See* Bulk Copy Program
bottlenecks, 128, 222
Bulk Copy Program (BCP),
  20, 41, 101
BULK INSERT statement,
  101, 104
business layer, 29
Business Rules layer, 248

C

caching, 220
calculating backup and
  restoration times, 107
capacity, hardware, 34-38
captured data, viewing, 135
capturing information to
  text files, Performance
  Monitor, 133
catalogs, database and
  system, 26
Central Processing Units
  (CPU), 220
certification exam
  critical terms and concepts,
    220-225
  sample questions, 230-243
  testing tips, 206-218
changing
  database sizes, 35-36
  permissions, 84-85

security settings, Windows NT
  users, 71
values, Scale option, 132
character sets
  choosing, 52-53
  described, 220
charts, running, 130
choosing
  accounts, Windows NT, 33
  alerts, 119
  character sets, 52-53
  delimiters, 169
  jobs, 119
  object permissions, 83, 85-86
  operators, 120-121
  server roles, 32
  servers, 246
  sort order, 52
  Unicode collation
    sequence, 54
clients
  architecture, 248
  communications, 21-22
  configurations, 29-30
  configuring, 59
  connectivity, troubleshooting,
    164-167
  installing, 59
Cluster Server, 40
clustered indexes, 24
code pages, 52, 220
**COL_LENGTH column
  function, 27**
command lines
  starting, stopping, and pausing
    SQL Server, 58
  upgrading SQL Server, 60
command-line utilities
  BCP, 20, 41, 101
  OSQL, 21

commands
  CREATE DATABASE, 96-97
  sp_configure, 140-141, 143
communications
  clients and servers, 21-22
  hardware, 37-38
**components, 18, 20-22,
  42, 51**
configurations
  Internet, 30
  n-tier, 29
  network, starting, 165
  setting, 140-141
configuring
  alerts, 120
  ANSI settings, 62-63
  authentication, 123
  clients, 59
  failover servers, 40
  Full-Text Search service,
    63-66
  growth rate, databases, 98-99
  operators, 120
  questions asked about on
    certification exam, 206-207
  security, 69-90, 198-199, 207
  servers, replication, 117
  SQL Mail, 62-63
  SQL Server 7.0, 47-67,
    194-198
**Connection tab, SQL Server
  Agent, 146**
connections
  clients, troubleshooting,
    164-167
  databases, 221
**controlling rights,
  Windows NT groups, 31**
corrupt backups, 108

costs
    described, 221
    setting limits, 144-145
counters, 129-132
CPU. *See* Central Processing Units
CREATE DATABASE command, 96-97
Create Jobs Wizard, 119
creating
    accounts, 62
    applications, 28, 30
    counters, Performance Monitor, 131-132
    databases, 75, 77, 95, 97-99, 109
    files and filegroups, 95, 97-98
    indexes, Full-Text Search, 65-66
    logins, 72-74, 79
    logs, 95, 97-98
    mail profiles, 62
    objects, 26
    permissions, 84-85
    publications, replication, 117
    queries, 136
    roles, 81-82
    server links, 122
    stored procedures, 144
    traces, 90, 134-135
customizing Full-Text Search service, 64

D

data
    access, remote, 122
    availability, 40
    backing up, 38, 40
    captured, viewing, 135
    files, 221
    importing, 221
    maintaining and managing, 93-94, 97-99, 103-125, 199-201, 207
    populating indexes, 66
    pumps, 102
    types, 24
data layer, 29
Data Transformation Services (DTS), 41, 101-102, 104
Database Creators server role, 79
Database Interface component, 21
databases
    adding users, 75-77
    auditing, 86, 90
    backing up, 104-113
    catalogs, 26
    changing sizes, 35-36
    choosing servers, 246
    connections, 221
    creating, 95, 97-99
    distribution, 24
    growing, 98-99, 221
    linked, 34, 123
    loading, 99, 103-104
    master, 24, 109
    model, 24
    Msdb, 24
    northwind, 24
    Pubs, 24
    relational, 24
    replication, 113-118
    restoring, 104-113
    roles, 23, 80-82
    security, 69-90, 123
    starting, single-user mode, 58
    Tempdb, 24
    user-created, 24
    Web, publishing, 247

DATALENGTH data type
 function, 27
DB_ID name function, 27
Declare Referential Integrity
 (DRI) statement, 83
decreator server role, 23
defaults
  described, 24
  filegroups, 35
  passwords, system administrator
   (SA) account, 71
defining
  alerts and jobs, 119
  operators, 120-121
  server roles, 32
definitions of concepts for
 certification exam, 220-221,
 223-225
Delete statement, 83
deleting unused space,
 indexes, 64
delimiters, specifying, 169
Deny setting, 85
designing applications, 28, 30
diagnosing SQL Server
 problems, 155-169
differential backups, 39, 111
Disk Administrators server
 role, 79
DISK REINIT statement, 109
disk space, SQL Server
 upgrades, 155
diskadmin server role, 23
displaying
  auditing information, 86
  captured data, 135
  current settings, 140
  traces, 91
distributed management, 249
distributed queries,
 troubleshooting, 162-164

Distributed Transaction
 Coordinator (DTC), 20, 221
distribution databases, 24
Distributor component, 42
DRI. *See* Declare Referential
 Integrity statement
DTC. *See* Distributed
 Transaction Coordinator
DTS. *See* Data Transformation
 Services

E

editing
  database sizes, 35-36
  permissions, 84-85
  security settings, Windows NT
   users, 71
  values, Scale option, 132
Enterprise Manager, 144, 221
erasing unused space,
 indexes, 64
error messages
  backups, 157-158
  distributed queries, 162-164
estimating
  backup and restoration
   times, 107
  database size, 35-36
evaluating SQL Server,
 129, 246
events, finding, 88
exam for certification
  critical terms and concepts,
   220-225
  sample questions, 230-243
  testing tips, 206-218
Execute statement, 83
exiting SQL Server, 58
explanations of sample
 questions for certification
 exam, 240-241, 243

F

failing certification exams, 213
failover servers, 40
failover support, 221
features of SQL Server 7, 17, 19-24, 26-28, 30
filegroups, 35, 221
files
   creating, 95, 97-98
   data, 221
   groups
      backups, 111
      creating, 95, 97-98
   log, 221
   placing, 34
   text, capturing information to, 133
   trace, 225
finding events, 88
fixed database and server roles, 32, 78, 223
foreign languages, character sets, 52
full backups, 39, 109-110, 220
Full-Text Indexing Wizard, creating indexes, 65
Full-Text Search Index, 221
Full-Text Search service, 63-66

G

General tab, SQL Server Agent, 145
global groups, granting access, 169
glossary of concepts for certification exam, 220-225
Grant setting, 85
granting access,
   SQL Server, 169

groups
   files, 35, 221
   granting access, 169
   mapping, 32, 222
growing databases, 98-99, 221

H

hardware
   Central Processing Units (CPU), 220
   planning, 34-38
   upgrading, 148
help, 21

I

identifying
   alerts and jobs, 119
   operators, 120-121
   server roles, 32
importing data, 222
indexes, 24, 64-66, 221-222
information_schema, 27
Insert statement, 83, 100
installations, typical, 51
installing
   clients, 59
   Full-Text Search service, 63-66
   Network Libraries and protocols, 54, 56
   questions asked about on certification exam, 206
   services, 56
   SQL Server 7, 15-67, 194-198, 246-250
intelligent client configuration (2-tier), 29
Internet
   configurations, 30
   publishing databases, 247

J-K

Job System tab, SQL Server Agent, 146
jobs
  defining, 119
  scheduling, 145-146
  troubleshooting, 160-161

L

languages
  foreign, character sets, 52
  Structured Query, 224
launching
  Create Jobs Wizard, 119
  databases, single-user mode, 58
  DTS wizards, 102
  Performance Monitor chart, 130
  SQL Server, 58, 167-168
  SQL Server Profiler, 134
  stored procedures, 144
  traces, 135
libraries
  Named Pipes Net-Library, 166
  network, 54, 56, 165, 222
limiting resources, Query Governor, 144-145
linked databases, security, 34, 123
linking servers, 122
loading
  databases, 99, 103-104
  server network libraries, 165
local groups, granting access, 169
log files, 221
Log view, 133
Logical Disk counter, 131

logins, 70-75, 79, 222
logon. *See* logins
logs, 35, 95, 97-98

M

Mail, SQL, 62-63, 224
mail profiles, creating, 62
maintaining data, 93-125, 199-201, 207
management, distributed, 249
managing
  data, 93-125, 199-201, 207
  indexes, Full-Text Search, 65-66
  logins, 71-72, 75
  permissions, 83, 85-86
  replication, 113-114, 116-118
  roles, 77-79, 81-82
  security, 69-90, 198-199, 207
mapping
  accounts, 73, 75
  groups, 32, 222
master databases, 24, 109
Maximize Throughput settings, 142
measuring SQL Server performance statistics, 129
memory, 138-139, 142-143, 223
Memory counter, 131
merge replication, 44
messages, error
  backups, 157-158
  distributed queries, 162-164
metadata, 26
Microsoft, mindset in writing certification exam, 208-209
Microsoft Cluster Server, 40
Microsoft Search, 57
migrations, planning, 40-41

Minimize Memory Used
  setting, 142
mixed authentication mode,
  31, 220
models
  databases, 24
  replication, 42-43, 223
modes
  mixed authentication, 31, 220
  single-user, starting
    databases, 58
modifying
  database sizes, 35-36
  permissions, 84-85
  security settings, Windows NT
    users, 71
  values, Scale option, 132
monitoring
  performance, 128-151,
    201-202
  questions asked on exam, 207
MS DTC. *See* **Distributed
  Transaction Coordinator**
Msdb database, 24
MSSQLServer, 19
Multiple Subscriber/Multiple
  Publisher model, 43
multitier client/server
  architecture, 248

N

n-tier configuration, 29
Named Pipes Net-Library, 166
naming objects, 25-26
network libraries, 54, 56,
  165, 222
Network Library
  component, 22

Network Segment
  counter, 131
non-clustered indexes, 24
nonexistent backups, 108
northwind database, 24

O

objectives for certification
  exam, 206, 208
objects
  naming, 25-26
  permissions, 83, 85-86, 222
OLAP, 249
online help, 21
Open Data Services
  component, 22
opening
  Create Jobs Wizard, 119
  databases, single-user
    mode, 58
  DTS wizards, 102
  Performance Monitor
    chart, 130
  SQL Server, 58, 167-168
  SQL Server Profiler, 134
  stored procedures, 144
  traces, 135
operators, defining, 120-121
optimizing performance,
  128-151, 201-202, 207
options
  memory, 143
  Scale, changing values, 132
  Server Authentication, 71
  Services, starting, stopping,
    and pausing SQL Server, 58
origin of questions on
  certification exams, 214
OSQL, 21

P

pages, code, 52, 221
passwords, system administrator (SA) account default, 71
Pause state, 58
pausing SQL Server, 58
performance
  baselines and bottlenecks, 222
  monitoring and optimizing, 128, 130-151, 201-202
  questions asked about, certification exam, 207
Performance Monitor, 20, 129-133, 222
performance-based questions, 216
performance-based testing, 218
permissions, 31, 83-86, 222
Physical Disk counter, 131
placing
  files, 34
  servers, 37
planning
  backups, 106, 108-109
  installation and upgrades, SQL Server 7, 15, 17-23, 26-41, 45, 195-196
  questions asked about on certification exam, 206
  replications, 42
populating data, indexes, 66
presentation layer, 29, 248
procedures
  stored, 25, 27, 143-144, 224
  taking certification exam, 212-214
Process Administrators server role, 23, 79

profiles, mail, 62
Profiler, 20, 89-90, 133, 222
programs
  BCP, 20, 41, 101
  Client Configuration, 20
  Data Transformation Services (DTS), 102
  designing, 28, 30
  Enterprise Manager, 144, 221
  OSQL, 21
  Performance Monitor, 20, 129-133, 222
  Profiler, 20, 89-90, 133, 222
  Query Analyzer, 20, 135, 222
  Query Governor, 144-145, 222-223
  Service Manager, 20
  Setup, 20
  SQL Mail, 62-63, 224
  Wolfpack, 40
properties, setting, 145-146
protocols
  installing, 54, 56
  Tabular Data Streams (TDS), 167
psychometrics, 217
public database role, 23
Public role, 78
publications, creating, 117
Publisher component, 42
publishing Web databases, 247
Pubs database, 24

Q

queries
  creating and testing, 136
  distributed, troubleshooting, 162-164
  improving performance, 143-145

260 QUERY ANALYZER

Query Analyzer, 20, 135, 222
Query Governor, 144-145, 222-223
questions
   asked on exam, 206, 208
   origin, certification exams, 214
   performance-based, 216
   ranking, 215
   samples for certification exam, 230-241, 243
quitting SQL Server, 58

R

Random Access Memory (RAM), 223
ranking questions, 215
RDBMS, 17
recreating master databases, 109
Redirector counter, 131
relational databases, 24
remote data access, 122
remote Distributor server model, 43
removing unused space, indexes, 64
replaying traces, 135
replication
   managing, 113-114, 116-118
   merge, 44
   models, 42-43, 223
   planning, 42
   snapshot, 44
   transactional, 44
replications, troubleshooting, 159-160
Report view, 132
resolving SQL Server problems, 155-169

resources, limiting, 144-145
response times, 138
restorations, troubleshooting, 157-158
restoring databases, 104-113
retaking certification exam, 214
Revoke setting, 85
rights, 31, 83-86, 222
roles
   Application, 33-34, 78, 80, 223
   database, 80-82
   Database Creators, 79
   databases, 23
   db_, 81
   described, 22-23, 223
   Disk Administrators, 79
   Fixed Database, 78, 223
   Fixed Server, 78, 223
   managing, 77-79, 81-82
   Process Administrators, 23, 79
   Public, 78
   Security Administrators, 79
   servers, 23, 32, 78-79, 223
   Setup Administrators, 79
   System Administrators, 32, 79
   user-defined, 32, 78, 224
rowsets, 162
running
   Create Jobs Wizard, 119
   databases, single-user mode, 58
   DTS wizards, 102
   Performance Monitor chart, 130
   SQL Server, 58, 167-168
   SQL Server Profiler, 134
   stored procedures, 144
   traces, 135

S

SA. *See* system administrator account
sample questions, certification exam, 230-239
scalability, 148, 224
Scale option, changing values, 132
scheduling jobs, 145-146
schema, 24, 27
Search tool, 57
searching events, 88
security
   configuring and managing, 69-90, 198-199, 207
   linked databases, 123
   planning, 30, 32-34
Security Administrators server role, 23, 79
Select statement, 83, 100-101, 104
selecting
   accounts, Windows NT, 33
   alerts, 119
   character sets, 52-53
   delimiters, 169
   jobs, 119
   object permissions, 83, 85-86
   operators, 120-121
   server roles, 32
   servers, 246
   sort order, 52
   Unicode collation sequence, 54
Server Administrators server role, 23, 79
Server Authentication option, setting, 71
Server counter, 131

servers
   architecture, 248
   choosing, 246
   communications, 21-22
   configurations, 29-30, 117
   failover, 40, 221
   linking, 122
   network libraries, loading, 165
   placing, 37
   remote Distributor, 43
   replication, 117
   roles, 23, 32, 78-79, 224
   standby, 40, 224
Service Manager, 224
services
   Data Transformation, 41, 101-102, 104
   Distributed Transaction Coordinator (DTC), 57
   Full-Text Search, 63-66
   installing, 56
   MSSQLServer, 19
   needed when starting SQL Server, 167
   SQL Server 7, 57
   SQL Server Agent, 19, 57, 145-148
Services option, starting, stopping, and pausing SQL Server, 58
setting
   alerts, 87, 147-148
   configurations, 140-141
   cost limits, Query Governor, 144-145
   Full-Text Search service priority, 64
   memory, 138-139, 143
   properties, SQL Server Agent, 145-146
   Server Authentication option, 71

settings
  ANSI
    configuring, 62-63
    described, 220
  Balance, 142
  current, viewing, 140
  Deny, Grant, and Revoke, 85
  security, changing
    (Windows NT users), 71
  Windows NT Server
    Service, 142
Setup Administrators server role, 23, 79
setups
  adding components, 51
  unattended, 60
single publisher/subscriber models, 42
single-user mode, starting databases, 58
sizes, databases, 35-36
snapshot replication, 44
software
  BCP, 20, 41, 101
  Client Configuration, 20
  Data Transformation Services (DTS), 102
  designing, 28, 30
  Enterprise Manager, 144, 221
  OSQL, 21
  Performance Monitor, 20, 129-133, 222
  Profiler, 20, 89-90, 133, 222
  Query Analyzer, 20, 135, 222
  Query Governor, 144-145, 222-223
  Service Manager, 20
  Setup, 20
  SQL Mail, 62-63, 224
  Wolfpack, 40

sort order
  choosing, 52
  described, 224
sp_configure command, 140-141, 143
specifying
  alerts and jobs, 119
  delimiters, 169
  operators, 120-121
  server roles, 32
sp_addlinkedsrvlogin stored procedure, 123
sp_configure stored procedure, 224
sp_droplinkedsrvlogin stored procedure, 123
sp_help stored procedures, 27
SQL. *See* Structured Query Language
SQL Mail, 62-63, 224
SQL Profiler, 20, 89-90, 133, 222
SQL Query Analyzer, 20, 135, 222
SQL Server Agent, 19, 57, 145-148
SQL Server Client Configuration, 20
SQL Server Enterprise Manager, 144, 221
SQL Server Performance Monitor, 20, 129-133, 222
SQL Server Profiler, 20, 89-90, 222
SQL Server Query Analyzer, 20
SQL Server Service Manager, 20
SQL Server Setup, 20
SQL Server Upgrade Wizard, 41, 155-157

standby servers, 40, 224
Start state, 58
starting
   Create Jobs Wizard, 119
   databases, single-user mode, 58
   DTS wizards, 102
   Performance Monitor chart, 130
   SQL Server, 58, 167-168
   SQL Server Profiler, 134
   stored procedures, 144
   traces, 135
statements
   ALTER DATABASE, 97
   BACKUP DATABASE, 110
   BULK INSERT, 101, 104
   Delete, 83
   DISK REINIT, 109
   Execute, 83
   Insert, 83, 100
   permissions, 222
   Select, 83, 100-101, 104
   Update, 83
states, 58
statistics, measuring SQL Server performance, 129
STATS_DATE index function, 27
Stop state, 58
stopping SQL Server, 58
storage
   databases, estimating, 35-36
   disks, SQL Server upgrades, 155
stored procedures
   described, 25, 224
   improving query performance, 143-144
   sp_addlinkedsrvlogin, 123
   sp_configure, 224

sp_droplinkedsrvlogin, 123
sp_help, 27
Structured Query Language (SQL), 224
Subscriber component, 42
subscriptions
   described, 224
   replication, 118
support, failover, 221
switching between SQL Server versions, 61
Sylvan Prometric, 212
sysadmin role, 32
sys tables, 26-27
system administrator (SA) account, 71, 225
System Administrators server role, 23, 79
system catalogs, 26

T

tables, 25-27, 225
tabs, SQL Server Agent, 145-146
Tabular Data Streams (TDS), 21, 167
taking certification exam, 212-214
tasks, automating, 118-119, 121
TDS. *See* **Tabaular Data Streams**
Tempdb database, 24
terminating SQL Server, 58
testing
   adaptive, 212, 217-218
   critical terms and concepts, 220-225
   performance-based, 218
   queries, 136

sample questions, 230-243
tips for, 206-218
text files, capturing information to, 133
threads, 225
throughput, 138
time estimates, backup and restoration, 107
timeframe, certification exam, 209-210
tools
   BCP, 20, 41, 101
   Client Configuration, 20
   Data Transformation Services (DTS), 102
   designing, 28, 30
   Enterprise Manager, 144, 221
   OSQL, 21
   Performance Monitor, 20, 129-133, 222
   Profiler, 20, 89-90, 133, 222
   Query Analyzer, 20, 135, 222
   Query Governor, 144-145, 222-223
   Service Manager, 20
   Setup, 20
   SQL Mail, 62-63, 224
   Wolfpack, 40
trace files, 225
traces, 90-91, 134-135
transaction logs
   backups, 39, 111, 220
   size, 35
transactional replication, 44
triggers, 25, 225
troubleshooting SQL Server, 157-169, 202, 204, 207
tuning, 138-139, 141-142
typical installation, 51

U

unattended setups, 60
Unicode, 54, 225
Update statement, 83
Upgrade Wizard, 155-157
upgrades
   hardware, 148
   planning, 15, 17-23, 26-41, 45, 195-196
   SQL Server, 41, 60, 155-157, 225
   troubleshooting, 155-157
user-created databases, 24
user-defined roles, 32, 78, 81-82, 224
USER_NAME ID function, 27
utilities
   BCP, 20, 41, 101
   Client Configuration, 20
   Data Transformation Services (DTS), 102
   designing, 28, 30
   Enterprise Manager, 144, 221
   OSQL, 21
   Performance Monitor, 20, 129-133, 222
   Profiler, 20, 89-90, 133, 222
   Query Analyzer, 20, 135, 222
   Query Governor, 144-145, 222-223
   Service Manager, 20
   Setup, 20
   SQL Mail, 62-63, 224
   Wolfpack, 40

V

values, changing, 132
versions of SQL Server, switching between, 61

viewing
auditing information, 86
captured data, 135
current settings, 140
traces, 91
views
described, 25, 225
Performance Monitor, 132-133
schema, 27

W-Z

Windows NT
accounts
choosing, 33
mapping, 73, 75
authentication, 31, 220
counters, 131
groups
controlling rights, 31
mapping, 222
settings
memory, tuning, 142
security, changing, 71
wizards
Create Jobs, 119
DTS, 102
Full-Text Indexing, creating indexes, 65
Upgrade, 41, 155-157
Wolfpack, 40
World Wide Web
configurations, 30
publishing databases, 247

New Riders Titles

MCSE Fast Track: Networking Essentials
1-56205-939-4, $19.99, 9/98

MCSE Fast Track: Windows 98
0-7357-0016-8, $19.99, 12/98

MCSE Fast Track: Windows NT Server 4
1-56205-935-1, $19.99, 9/98

MCSE Fast Track: Windows NT Server 4 Enterprise
1-56205-940-8, $19.99, 9/98

MCSE Fast Track: Windows NT Workstation 4
1-56205-938-6, $19.99, 9/98

A+ Fast Track
0-7357-0028-1, $34.99, 3/99

MCSE Fast Track: TCP/IP
1-56205-937-8, $19.99, 9/98

MCSE Fast Track: Internet Information Server 4
1-56205-936-X, $19.99, 9/98

MCSD Fast Track: Solution Architectures
0-7357-0029-X, $29.99, Q3/99

MCSD Fast Track: Visual Basic 6, Exam 70-175
0-7357-0018-4, $19.99, 12/98

MCSD Fast Track: Visual Basic 6, Exam 70-176
0-7357-0019-2, $19.99, 12/98

MCSE Fast Track: SQL Server 7 Database Design
0-7357-0040-0, $29.99, 6/99

NEW RIDERS CERTIFICATION TITLES

TRAINING GUIDES

Complete, Innovative, Accurate, Thorough

Our next generation Training Guides have been developed to help you study and retain the essential knowledge that you need to pass your certification exams. We know your study time is valuable, and we have made every effort to make the most of it by presenting clear, accurate, and thorough information.

In creating this series, our goal was to raise the bar on how certification content is written, developed, and presented. From the two-color design that gives you easy access to content to the new software simulator that allows you to perform tasks in a simulated operating system environment, we are confident that you will be well-prepared for exam success.

Our New Riders Top Score Software Suite is a custom-developed set of full-functioning software applications that work in conjunction with the Training Guide by providing you with the following:

Exam Simulator tests your hands-on knowledge with over 150 fact-based and situational-based questions.
Electronic Study Cards test your knowledge with explanations that are linked to an electronic version of the Training Guide.
Electronic Flash Cards help you retain the facts in a time-tested method.
An Electronic Version of the Book provides quick searches and compact, mobile study.
Customizable Software adapts to the way you want to learn.

MCSE Training Guide: Networking Essentials, Second Edition
1-56205-919-X, $49.99, 9/98

MCSE Training Guide: Windows NT Server 4, Second Edition
1-56205-916-5, $49.99, 9/98

MCSE Training Guide: Windows NT Server 4 Enterprise, Second Edition
1-56205-917-3, $49.99, 10/98

MCSE Training Guide: Windows NT Workstation 4, Second Edition
1-56205-918-1, $49.99, 9/98

MCSE Training Guide: Windows 98
1-56205-890-8, $49.99, 1/99

MCSE Training Guide: TCP/IP, Second Edition
1-56205-920-3, $49.99, 11/98

Training Guides

MCSE Training Guide: SQL Server 7 Administration

0-7357-0003-6, $49.99, 5/99

MCSE Training Guide: SQL Server 7 Database Design

0-7357-0004-4, $49.99, 5/99

MCSD Training Guide: Solution Architectures

0-7357-0026-5, $49.99, Q3/99

MCSD Training Guide: Visual Basic 6 Exams

0-7357-0002-8, $69.99, 3/99

A+ Certification Training Guide

1-56205-896-7, $49.99, 8/98

MCSE Training Guide: Internet Information Server 4, Second Edition

0-7357-0865-7, $49.99, 5/99

TRAINING GUIDES
First Editions

Your Quality Elective Solution

MCSE Training Guide: Systems Management Server 1.2, 1-56205-748-0

MCSE Training Guide: SQL Server 6.5 Administration, 1-56205-726-X

MCSE Training Guide: SQL Server 6.5 Design and Implementation, 1-56205-830-4

MCSE Training Guide: Windows 95, 70-064 Exam, 1-56205-880-0

MCSE Training Guide: Exchange Server 5, 1-56205-824-X

MCSE Training Guide: Internet Explorer 4, 1-56205-889-4

MCSE Training Guide: Microsoft Exchange Server 5.5, 1-56205-899-1

MCSD Training Guide: Visual Basic 5, 1-56205-850-9

New Riders Certification Titles

TESTPREP SERIES

Practice, Check, Pass!

Questions. Questions. And more questions. That's what you'll find in our New Riders *TestPreps*. They're great practice books when you reach the final stage of studying for the exam. We recommend them as supplements to our *Training Guides*.

What makes these study tools unique is that the questions are the primary focus of each book. All the text in these books support and explain the answers to the questions.

Scenario-based questions challenge your experience.

Multiple-choice questions prep you for the exam.

Fact-based questions test your product knowledge.

Exam strategies assist you in test preparation.

Complete yet concise explanations of answers make for better retention.

Two practice exams prepare you for the real thing.

Fast Facts offer you everything you need to review in the testing center parking lot.

MCSE TestPrep: Networking Essentials, Second Edition

0-7357-0010-9, $19.99, 12/98

MCSE TestPrep: Windows 95, Second Edition

0-7357-0011-7, $29.99, 12/98

MCSE TestPrep: Windows NT Server 4, Second Edition

0-7357-0012-5, $19.99, 12/98

MCSE TestPrep: Windows NT Server 4 Enterprise, Second Edition

0-7357-0009-5, $19.99, 11/98

MCSE TestPrep: Windows NT Workstation 4, Second Edition

0-7357-0008-7, $19.99, 12/98

MCSE TestPrep: TCP/IP, Second Edition

0-7357-0025-7, $19.99, 12/98

**MCSE TestPrep:
Windows 98**

1-56205-922-X, $19.99, 11/98

**A+ Certification
TestPrep**

1-56205-892-4, $19.99, 12/99

**MCSD TestPrep:
Visual Basic 6
Exams**

0-7357-0032-X, $29.99, 1/99

TESTPREP SERIES
FIRST EDITIONS

MCSE TestPrep: SQL Server 6.5 Administration, 0-7897-1597-X

MCSE TestPrep: SQL Server 6.5 Design and Implementation, 1-56205-915-7

MCSE TestPrep: Windows 95 70-64 Exam, 0-7897-1609-7

MCSE TestPrep: Internet Explorer 4, 0-7897-1654-2

MCSE TestPrep: Exchange Server 5.5, 0-7897-1611-9

MCSE TestPrep: IIS 4.0, 0-7897-1610-0

How to Contact Us

IF YOU NEED THE LATEST UPDATES ON A TITLE THAT YOU'VE PURCHASED:

1) Visit our Web site at www.newriders.com.

2) Click on Product Support, and enter your book's ISBN number located on the back cover in the bottom right-hand corner.

3) There you'll find available updates for your title.

IF YOU ARE HAVING TECHNICAL PROBLEMS WITH THE BOOK OR THE CD THAT IS INCLUDED:

1) Check the book's information page on our Web site according to the instructions listed above, or

2) Email us at support@mcp.com, or

3) Fax us at (317) 817-7488 attn: Tech Support.

IF YOU HAVE COMMENTS ABOUT ANY OF OUR CERTIFICATION PRODUCTS THAT ARE NON-SUPPORT RELATED:

1) Email us at certification@mcp.com, or

2) Write to us at New Riders, 201 W. 103rd St., Indianapolis, IN 46290-1097, or

3) Fax us at (317) 581-4663.

IF YOU ARE OUTSIDE THE UNITED STATES AND NEED TO FIND A DISTRIBUTOR IN YOUR AREA:

Please contact our international department at international@mcp.com.

IF YOU WANT TO PREVIEW ANY OF OUR CERTIFICATION BOOKS FOR CLASSROOM USE:

Email us at pr@mcp.com. Your message sho include your name, title, training company or school, department, address, phone number, office days/hours, text in use, and enrollment Send these details along with your request fo desk/examination copies and/or additional information.

WE WANT TO KNOW WHAT YOU THINK

To better serve you, we would like your opinion on the content and quality of this book. Please complete this card and mail it to us or fax it to 317-581-4663.

Name _____

Address _____

City _____ State _____ Zip _____

Phone _____ Email Address _____

Occupation _____

Which certification exams have you already passed? _____
_____
_____
_____

Which certification exams do you plan to take? ___
_____
_____
_____

What influenced your purchase of this book?
❑ Recommendation ❑ Cover Design
❑ Table of Contents ❑ Index
❑ Magazine Review ❑ Advertisement
❑ Publisher's reputation ❑ Author Name

How would you rate the contents of this book?
❑ Excellent ❑ Very Good
❑ Good ❑ Fair
❑ Below Average ❑ Poor

What other types of certification products will you buy/have you bought to help you prepare for the exam?
❑ Quick reference books ❑ Testing software
❑ Study guides ❑ Other

What do you like most about this book? Check all that apply.
❑ Content ❑ Writing Style
❑ Accuracy ❑ Examples
❑ Listings ❑ Design
❑ Index ❑ Page Count
❑ Price ❑ Illustrations

What do you like least about this book? Check all that apply.
❑ Content ❑ Writing Style
❑ Accuracy ❑ Examples
❑ Listings ❑ Design
❑ Index ❑ Page Count
❑ Price ❑ Illustrations

What would be a useful follow-up book to this one for you? _____
Where did you purchase this book? _____
Can you name a similar book that you like better than this one, or one that is as good? Why? _____
_____
_____

How many New Riders books do you own? _____
What are your favorite certification or general computer book titles? _____
_____

What other titles would you like to see us develop? _____
_____

Any comments for us? _____
_____

MCSE FAST TRACK: SQL SERVER 7 ADMINISTRATION   0-7357-0041-9

Fold here and tape to mail

Place
Stamp
Here

New Riders
201 W. 103rd St.
Indianapolis, IN 46290